VELASQUEZ' 'SAFE OIL PAINTING' FOR BEGINNERS AND ART TEACHERS

Free Internet Videos
Painting without Hazardous Materials

Includes Free access to the author's DVD
"Oil painting with milk
Safety for new painters and school art cases"

by
Louis R. Velasquez
copyright 2013, Louis R. Velasquez
all rights reserved
Published in the USA

COPYRIGHT NOTICE

Title: VELASQUEZ' 'SAFE OIL PAINTING'
FOR BEGINNERS AND ART TEACHERS
Sub-Title: Free Internet Videos Painting without Hazardous Materials
Copyright by Louis R. Velasquez, 2013, all rights reserved
Published by: Createspace, Seattle WA , USA
And digitally by Kindle Publishing company, December 2013

CONTAINED HEREIN IS AN ABRIDGED EDITION OF:
TITLE: OIL PAINTING LESSONS WITH REMBRANDT AND 'CALCITE SUN OIL':
SUB-TITLE: Artist's Health and Safety without Hazardous Solvents Resins Varnishes and Driers
Copyright by Louis R. Velasquez, 2012, all rights reserved
Published by: Createspace, Seattle WA , USA

PREVIOUS PUBLISHING HISTORY
Previously published in March 2012 by CREATESPACE.COM
TITLE: SOLVENT FREE OIL PAINTING: Painting with the Old Masters' Van Eyck Secret Medium
ISBN: 9781470171759 *copyright 2012 Louis R. Velasquez, all rights reserved*

Previously published in 2008 by Wordclay.com
ISBN: 978-1-6048-1354-8 (sc) Previous LCCN: 2008939691
Title: "OIL PAINTING with 'CALCITE SUN OIL':
Safety and Permanence without Hazardous Solvents, Resins, Varnishes and Driers"
Registered as Reg. TX 6-405-667, by Louis R. Velasquez   © 2008 by Louis R. Velasquez..

Previously published in 2004 - Independently
TITLE: Calcite Sun Oil: A grinding and Painting medium for Oil Painting',
Reg. TX 6-215-210. ©2004, Louis R. Velasquez, All rights reserved.
All subsequent revised editions are copyright protected by Louis R. Velasquez
The formula for 'Calcite Sun Oil' and 'Calcite Stand Oil' and other alternate mixtures,
are Patented with the United States Government, Patent Number 7141109 , 2006.
The name, 'Calcite Sun Oil'® is a Registered Trademark with the U.S. Government, 2006.

ANTI-PIRACY NOTICE

THIS BOOK IS NOT AUTHORIZED TO BE SOLD NOR TRADED NOR
SHARED FREELY THROUGH DIGITAL TRANSMISSION VIA THE INTERNET,
VIA COMPUTERS OR BY ANY PHOTO COPY MEANS,
WITHOUT THE EXPRESSED PERMISSION
OF THE COPYRIGHT OWNER OR HIS LEGALLY AUTHORIZED AGENTS.
PIRACY IS THEFT AND A VIOLATION OF US COPYRIGHT LAWS.
VIOLATORS WILL BE PROSECUTED TO THE FULLEST EXTENT OF THE LAW.
COPYRIGHT INFRINGEMENT WILL BE REPORTED TO THE F.B.I.

PLEASE FIGHT PIRACY!
The author requests to be notified if anyone encounters any website
or organization offering a copy of this book for sale or trade or for free.
Please contact the author through the website below.
CONTACT LOUIS R. VELASQUEZ -   WWW.CALCITESUNOIL.COM

VELASQUEZ' 'SAFE OIL PAINTING' FOR BEGINNERS AND ART TEACHERS
Free Internet Videos
Painting without Hazardous Materials

Includes Free access to the author's DVD
***"Oil painting with milk
Safety for new painters and school art cases"***

INTRODUCTION

Welcome beginning artists, and teachers of school art classes.

Here you will learn how to paint with complete safety and without exposure to Hazardous solvents, resins, varnishes, driers, or other dangerous materials.
This book is divided into four parts and includes free access to a one hour long instructional DVD produced by the author.

PART 1- TEACHER TALK   page 5

This section for Art teachers provides assistance regarding a 'Disciplined Based Art Education' program. A free internet video produced by the author guides both the teachers and the students on the actual steps involved in oil painting with safe materials. Helpful information related to being a Fine Artist is also included. Teachers should also read PART 3.

PART 2 – TEACHER'S REFERENCE GUIDE   page 31

An abridged copy of my professional level art book, *"Oil Painting Lessons with Rembrandt and ' Calcite Sun Oil'* will be helpful in teaching advanced information on safe oil painting.

PART 3 – BEGINNING OIL PAINTERS WITHOUT A TEACHER. P.160

Beginning oil painters of all ages who study without a teacher will learn from the book and from a free Internet video.
The video will teach "How to oil paint", " How to draw" , " How to design a painting", plus instruction on Art History, Creativity, Originality, Painting styles, and other topics.

PART 4- MISCELLANEOUS INFORMATION: p.195

Miscellaneous information, the bibliography ,the author's biography.

PART ONE
TEACHER TALK

Welcome Teachers!
You will be teaching safe Oil Painting by use of this book together with the internet video I produced. Please view it and the instructions in PART 3.

THE BEGINNER'S VIDEO FOR THIS BOOK
The title of the beginners video is :
CSO VELASQUEZ - BEGINNERS BOOK- OIL PAINTING
To access it, go to www.youtube.com
And type the title in the search box.

OTHER VIDEOS FOR PROFESSIONAL AND ADVANCED ARTISTS
I have produced other videos for professional artists which you may find helpful. To access them go to www.youtube.com .
Type in the title of the video you wish to see.
As time passes I will produce new free videos to guide Artists with safe painting materials. Simply by typing - CSO VELASQUEZ - will locate all my videos.

CSO VELASQUEZ- AIR PUMP LINSEED OIL PART 1
CSO VELASQUEZ- AIR PUMP LINSEED OIL PART 2
CSO VELASQUEZ- DAVID HOCKNEY- Secret Knowledge
PART 1 - VAN EYCK SECRET MEDIUM - CSO VELASQUEZ
PART 2 - VAN EYCK SECRET MEDIUM - CSO VELASQUEZ
PART 3 - VAN EYCK SECRET MEDIUM- CSO VELASQUEZ

The "Discipline Based Art Education"

Since there are variations in the Art Standards adopted by different localities, please adapt my Lesson Plans to meet the needs of your students.
Many Lessons overlap and include many of the standards … but not all of the Standards are addressed in this book.

GUIDEING THE STUDENTS
In teaching young art students, I tried to keep a few important concepts always in mind. These are not in order of importance.

ONE: INDIVIDUALITY: Always focus on the needs of each student and know each student is an individual with specific needs. Each student is different and there are many reasons and causes for their differences.
TWO: SAFETY: Always keep each student safe from any and all danger, both physically and emotionally.
THREE: PRAISE: Always give each student encouragement and support to build self-esteem and confidence.
FOUR: INTERESTING AND FUN: Make the Lessons as interesting as possible while supporting the learning objectives of the lessons.
FIVE: ENCOURAGEMENT: Require students to learn to express themselves in speech and writing with ever better improvements.
SIX: SENSITIVITY: Always Evaluate the artworks and the learning process with positive reinforcement. Artists are very sincere, sensitive persons who treasure their creations. Do a demonstration for the student because artists learn by watching. Let them ask the questions. Be careful with criticisms.

THE "VISUAL ART EDUCATIONAL STANDARDS"

STANDARD ONE: DESIGN: Also called 'Artistic Perception", or , "Aesthetic Formal Design', it teaches knowledge, understanding and use of 7 Elements of Design and 7 Principles of Design. A section in this book addresses the issues of Design.

STANDARD TWO: ART MAKING: Also called 'Creative Expression', it requires students to make artworks in a variety of media. This book will focus on only on teaching Oil Painting , Drawing, and Designing. It will teach two methods of oil painting, Milk Oil Paint and Traditional Oil Paint.

STANDARD THREE: ART HISTORY: Also called 'Art Historical and Cultural Context', it will introduce students to Masters of Artworks and their Masterpieces. A section in this book and the video presents an overview of several Master Oil Painters from Western civilization, from the 1300's to modern times.

STANDARD FOUR: EVALUATION: .[This standard is not addressed in this book] Also known as 'Aesthetic Valuing', it teaches students how to express their personal views and opinions about artworks they see, in speech and writing, with use of the terms learned in the Elements and Principles of Design.

STANDARD FIVE: CONNECTIONS: [This standard is not addressed in this book] Also known as " Connections, Relations, Applications", this standard places art in the context of daily life. It introduces students to opportunities in higher education Art studies, employment, and use of art in daily lives. This standard requires a specific book of instruction .

EXAMPLE OF A LESSON PLAN

TEACHER: _____
DATE: _____
GRADE: _____
CONTENT SUBJECT: VISUAL ART: _____

LESSON PLAN
PROJECT TITLE: _____
TIME REQUIRED : _____

LEARNING OBJECTIVE _____[What the students will learn and be able to do]
Examples: Pronounce and spell … Differentiate between … Make or produce … Written and verbal Quizzes

TEACHING METHODS: [choose by circling] Video; Photos; Handouts; Direct verbal instruction; Original art; Demonstration; One on one assistance; Group work; Field trip; Written and Verbal Quizzes

STUDENTS LEARNING METHODS: [choose by circling] Observe … Listen to … Read about … Write about …; Verbal or written responses to questions about the art project
STUDENT ASSESSMENT: Daily verbal quizzes and reviews; Written reports on Project completion; Group discussions of finished artworks; Exhibition of Artworks

[continued]

TEACHER MARKS WHICH STANDARDS WERE ADDRESSED
[Applicable to the particular lesson or project]

ONE: ___ ARTISTIC PERCEPTION [FORMAL DESIGN}:
Learning the Elements and Principles of Visual Design.
Demonstrating their knowledge by using them in practice, speech and writing.

TWO: ___ CREATIVE EXPRESSION [MAKING ART PROJECTS]:
Creating Art works and learning art making skills in a variety of media or techniques.

THREE: ___ ART HISTORICAL and CULTURAL CONTEXT:
Learning the role of visual arts in human history and cultures.

FOUR: ___ AESTHETIC VALUING [ASSESSMENT and CRITIQUES]
Responding to artworks, by analyzing and making personal judgments about artworks in accord with the Formal Elements and Principles of Design.

FIVE: ___ CONNECTIONS, RELATIONSHIPS, APPLICATIONS:
Understanding Art in the real world of higher education, employment, value to daily living.

THE FIVE STEP TEACHING PLAN

ONE: THE ANTICIPATORY SET: Verbal review of the current project with real life objects or examples of related photo or video examples of master artists or masterpieces as a foundation to stimulate student interest and creativity. Rules and expectations are discussed.

TWO: INSTRUCTION BY THE TEACHER: A verbal and visual presentation of procedures for the project and showing examples of the project by past students and real life objects related to the project.
OPTIONAL: Teacher demonstrates the project hands-on.
OPTIONAL: Brief discussion or Quiz of the previous day's hands-on work.

THREE: GUIDED PRACTICE : Students begin the hands-on project and the teacher circulates the room with personal assistance and guidance for all students.

FOUR: REVIEW and CLOSURE: The project ends for the day with cleanup and a brief review of the project requirements by the teacher to discuss issues and answer questions.

FIVE: INDEPENDENT PRACTICE [OPTIONAL]: Teacher assigns home study or research in preparation for daily quizzes or final written reports .

LESSON PLAN COMMENTS

The LESSON PLAN FORMAT presented for a 'Discipline based visual art education program" is flexible. The plan can be altered to fit local education requirements and regulations.

Many good books on teaching oil painting are available and successful teachers read many to guide them. The various books repeat the same list of required materials, such as brushes, easels and paint colors. The author believes all university trained Art teachers are aware of which brushes, easels and tube oil paints exist. Therefore, this book will not repeat those lists of materials.

HAZARDOUS solvents and painting mediums containing dangerous ingredients are taught in current books teaching oil painting. Some of the ingredients are toxic and/or carcinogenic or harmful to student health in subtle ways.
With this book, for the first time in modern Oil Painting classes, traditional oil paint as used by some of the greatest Masters, can be taught with complete safety, without using hazardous solvents, resins, varnishes or driers.

THE ART OF BEING AN ARTIST

NOTE: The following pages of PART ONE will be reprinted in PART THREE. This is for the benefit of beginners studying without a teacher.

In the following pages, I will try to explain what, or why are the Aesthetic reasons for being an "Artist". This book is mainly a guide for "making" a painting. It involves the materials and how they are used in order for them to be long lasting and archival. It is true that Artists put so much effort into making their work, they want the finished art to be around for many years, so it may be appreciated. Yet, young artists need to be guided as to the "why" of creating artworks.

CRAFTSMANSHIP is a term that describes the " making" of objects for human use. Objects such as a chair or table are important and serve a function. For thousands of years, humans made functional objects by hand. This hand-made quality is the keystone to " craftsmanship" .

Today, because of the Industrial Revolution of electricity and machinery, businesses began the mass production of functional objects. Yet, still today, hand-made objects are valued and appreciated for their hand made beauty.

Paintings too, like a chair are hand crafted functional objects. But something SPECIAL, exists in paintings. This quality of something very special is recognized in paintings, music, poetry and other areas and is called "ART".
I recall learning that "ART" is the result of " INSPIRED CRAFTSMANSHIP".

Please note: *In order to be fair, the ancient word " craftsmanship" has always excluded the word " woman", and it should include it. Women artists have always been as gifted as men artists. I have heard the term " Craftpersonship" used . Perhaps it should be used always.*

INSPIRED CRAFTWORK !
THE REASON FOR MAKING PAINTINGS.

Art is created by humans because of a need to express their personal ideas about the world they live in, and the need to express their personal sense of beauty. Here below are several topics that I, as an artist, have always thought about and tried to better understand. They are the REASONS for making paintings.

AESTHETICS [pronounced Esthetics](THE CONCEPT OF BEAUTY)
On the cover of this book is a collection of small paintings of my daughter Sandra. They are placed next to each other in a frame. Each painting measures 7 inches by 5 inches. Each painting is in the style of a different historical era. They represent European based styles from the 15th century through the 20th century.

I painted these to demonstrate how an artist might choose a different style to paint the picture of the young girl. Every person who looks at this series of paintings has a favorite. No one agrees as to which one is best. In fact, it is IMPOSSIBLE to say which one is best, because we all have different opinions about what " beauty" is.

Throughout history, persons have attempted to define "beauty". Some persons, who believe they are "experts", have made rules, expecting others to follow them. Creative artists have always ignored these rules. Creative artists make their own rules about what is beautiful or not. Creative artists follow their instincts and intuition.

In paintings, we can see Aesthetics in the style of the paintings.
My book will not give an opinion on what style of painting is best.
We are fortunate to live in the modern era, where we have access to libraries, museums, and the Internet. We live in the "information age" and we can use the resources to our advantage to create interesting artworks.

THE ART OF PAINTING

My book is about the TECHNICAL part of paintings.
This means ... it is about the materials we use, and the manner we use them.
As you learn the lessons in this book and video, I will ask you to follow my instructions as best you can. This means, I need you to follow the STYLE
That I use in teaching the lesson. You do not need to copy the style exactly.

Once you learn the materials we use and how we apply them, you can create your own paintings in your own styles. You will love the creativity of exploring the ideas learned in this book and videos, as you develop new styles as you paint your own pictures.

The small paintings of my daughter on the cover, show a historical development of painting in Europe. It is very important that you understand that the European Oil Painting history is a very small part of the Art history of the world.

Generally, European oil painting dates from the 1300's through the present. This is a period of 700 years. Art from Africa is over 100, 000 years, and Art from the American continents is over 17,000 years old. Australia's Aboriginal Art is well over 100,000 years old. Some cave paintings in Europe are 50,000 years old, but they are not oil paintings.

If you study the Art of the entire World, you will expand your consciousness. You can use the art images and reasons for having been made, from all parts and all eras of the World, in creating your own personal NEW visions of the world.

BEAUTY IS IN THE EYE OF THE ... ?

It has been said: " Beauty is in the eye of the beholder."
This means the person viewing the art can decide on whether or not the artwork is " beautiful" , " relevant" , " meaningful" , or " important".

I strongly differ with that view because the "beholder" is passing judgment on the creative efforts of another person's individual aesthetic , or, cultural views. I believe it is best not to pass judgment.
Instead, the "beholder" could ask questions about the artwork. By doing so, the beholder's personal biases are set aside, and one can learn something new.

I prefer to say: " Beauty is in the heart and mind of the artist." It is the artist, in fact, who is doing all the creative work. If we ask questions, instead of passing biased judgments, we can learn new things.

MISSION STATEMENTS WRITTEN BY ARTISTS
Prior to the modern era of technology, few master artists ever spoke about their views on aesthetics. Only one letter written by Rembrandt exists, in which he tries to explain what his goal was in painting one particular painting. Rembrandt lived in the 1600's. Vincent Van Gogh lived in the 1800's and wrote hundreds of letters about what he was trying to accomplish with his paintings.

Today, artists are expected to write a "mission statement" , which is usually a brief paragraph explaining their objectives in painting. Since artists are always evolving, the mission statement changes accordingly.

TECHNICAL MATTERS OF IMPORTANCE

THE OIL WE WILL USE IN OUR LESSONS
Beginners will use a low cost linseed oil that can be used immediately. The oil is available in every art supply store.

If Teachers choose to, they can prepare the SUPERIOR OIL of the Old Masters. This oil has to be processed at home. When using the AIR PUMP, it takes 25 days to produce the oil.

Teachers can also choose to use the AIR PUMP on a small bottle of Alkali Refined Linseed Oil. This takes only 15 days to produce a faster drying linseed oil.
DO NOT use the Air Pump on the thick Stand Linseed Oil.
Use it only on the THIN linseed oil.

A BRIEF HISTORY OF ARTISTS OIL
Artists have used different kinds oils for oil painting. The oils artists most commonly used are Linseed oil, walnut oil, and poppy seed oil. We will use only linseed oil because it has been the main oil used by the master painters.

Linseed oil and some other vegetable oils are classified as "DRYING OILS ". They dry hard by exposure to the air. Many other vegetable oils are called "non-drying " oils. One is olive oil and it never dries. Butter is a non- drying fat obtained from milk.

Linseed oil has been used since antiquity, but our modern use of linseed oil for oil painting began in the 1100's. Still, it was not popular because it dried very, very slowly. This slow drying oil, frustrated artists and persons who wanted to buy paintings. So, instead of using oil paints, artists painted with **tempera paints** because they dry within minutes. The most popular **Tempera** was made from eggs. It is called Egg Tempera paint. Another popular **Tempera** was Milk Tempera which is called Casein. In 2011 I created a NEW Oil Paint. It is called "MILK OIL PAINT" and is fully explained in the video.

In the 1300s, artists learned a few important things about linseed oil.
They learned that if the linseed oil was exposed to constant air and constant heat, it would begin to thicken like honey. This thickened linseed oil became a faster drying oil for oil painting. Soon the Tempera paints became obsolete, and all major artists were painting with oil paints. Egg tempera painting was revived in the 1800's and today many fine artists use it.

In the 1800's Manufacturers learned how to mass produce linseed oil. They process it with caustic chemicals. It is the oil used by most artists today.
It is called Alkali Refined Linseed Oil.

THE 21ST CENTURY EXTRAORDINARY 'AIR PUMP OIL'

The lessons in this book will use the common linseed oil sold at any art supply store. I made the choice to use this oil because it is best for beginning students who have no real need for the Superior Oil of the Old Masters at their stage of learning. Later, they can use the knowledge in this book to process their own Superior Oil.

Today we can use our electrical technology to create an oil that dries even faster than the oil used by the great Old Masters. We can use a low cost aquarium air pump to pump air constantly through the oil. It takes between ten and fifteen days for the oil to be ready for use.

This electrical technology lets us create a fine oil that dries very fast. This allows us to eliminate all toxic and hazardous metal driers that were once added to oil paint in order to make it dry faster. Now, we can eliminate the hazardous materials and we can paint more safely.

TEACHERS AND BEGINNERS AND AIR PUMP OIL
Teachers and Beginners without a teacher, may wish to use the new AIR PUMP OIL. A video series I produced is free to watch on the Internet.
Please go to the website- www.youtube.com;
Then type these words in the search box: CSO VELASQUEZ AIR PUMP OIL
Please pay special attention to the details on how to use the Air Pump.
You may also go to my website : www.calcitesunoil.com

IMPORTANT POINTS ON THE AIR PUMP OIL
The weather is very important for processing your " AIR PUMP OIL" .
If it is done outside, the weather must be DRY with low HUMIDITY.
If it is done inside , the room must be DRY with low HUMIDITY.

If the weather is HOT and MUGGY outside, like it sometimes is in Florida, the air pump will pump MOISTURE from the air, into the oil. This then will Produce a Very slow drying oil. If the air outside is muggy and humid, use the air pump inside in a dry warm room.

If the weather is DAMP and RAINY outside, like it is in Oregon or Washington, the air pump will blow moisture from the air into the oil and the oil will be slow drying. If the air outside is wet and humid, use the air pump inside in a dry warm room.

MATTERS OF CREATIVITY
THE OLD MASTERS' DRAWINGS
The Old Masters used drawings as a way to PLAN a painting.
If a painting was ordered, the painting was first designed. This would let the artist and the customer know what the final painting would look like.

You can think of the drawing as a BLUEPRINT for the painting.
It was much like how an architect will draw blueprints for designing a house.
Once the blue print plans were finished, any competent builder could follow the blue print, and could build the house.

The Old Masters were painters who had to earn a living.
They were able to draw a design and finish the painting by themselves, but sometimes they had too many customers. Then they would just draw the design. Once the drawing was perfectly designed, they hired competent assistants to finish the painting from the finished drawing. If they decided to, they could have the assistant make lots of copies of the same painting.

Sometimes, the Master artist was not pleased with the painting made by the assistants. In today's business world, this is called "quality control".
The Master would then make corrections by adding and changing parts of the painting. The Master would then ... sign his name on the painting.
In previous centuries, this was an accepted tradition.

Today, this is not the normal procedure for artists.
Yet, some modern artists are following exactly that procedure . Salvador Dali is an example of a modern Master who has hired assistants to help finish his paintings.

HOW AND WHY ARTISTS MAKE DRAWINGS
Artists draw in various ways ... for specific reasons.

SOME COPY NATURE
Artists sometimes copy something they can see in front of them. This
COPY drawing has an important purpose. It is how an artist learns what something really looks like. If every motorist tried to draw a stop sign, they would learn exactly what it looks like.

SOME DO NOT COPY NATURE
Artists sometimes do not want to copy something exactly as it looks.
They wish to change how it looks as they DESIGN a painting. They might draw the neck of a person longer, or the face might be made thinner. They might draw the feet really large the way a cartoonist might draw.

SOME TRACE PHOTOGRAPHS
Some artists do not draw well, but they have very creative ideas.
So, they TRACE photographs. Grandma Moses was a famous artist who died at the age of 101. She did not begin to paint until she was 80 years old. She did not draw well, so, she would cut photographs out of magazines. Then she would arrange them on the canvas. Then she would tape them down and would use a TRANSFER PAPER to TRACE the photos onto the canvas.

SOME ARTISTS PROJECT PHOTOGRAPHS
Today some, but not all, modern artists use projectors in a dark room. They project photographs onto the canvas and they trace the images. This is not a modern idea. In the 1400's, artists found out how to use mirrors and glass lenses to make crude projections. They would trace the images and by this method they made paintings that look like photographs...400 years before photography was invented.

MY PERSONAL EXPERIENCE WITH TRACING
I do not enjoy tracing. I once painted a picture of a snow goose.
I took a photograph of a dead goose that had been treated by a taxidermist.
It looked very life like. I bought a projector and traced every line of that goose onto the support. It was so boring, that I never traced another photo.

MY PERSONAL WAY OF DRAWING
I love the emotional and physical passion of drawing ! I love swinging my hand and fingers as I see the lines unfold an image as I CREATE something new.

When I draw I follow a certain thought. I say to myself , " vague design -outline define." This means that I depend on myself to be very loose as I begin. I draw with light thin lines in the beginning. The more sketchy it is the more important it is to my CREATIVE IMAGINATION. I begin to see objects and images in the numerous sketchy lines and shadows.

Once I am finished with the sketchy drawing, I then slow down and I carefully draw outlines right over the sketchy lines. All this time, I keep my mind open to new images that I can see in the drawing. I change things as my heart desires.

INTUITION is a very important component of drawing and painting. You must learn to trust yourself, meaning your ideas, thoughts, and feelings.

A MODERN REVELATION FOR ARTISTS
DAVID HOCKNEY exposed the SECRETS OF THE OLD MASTERS

The Old Masters from Northern Europe , in the 1400's painted some of the best preserved oil paintings in history. Their oil paintings have a "jewel like " appearance because of the great beauty of their sparkling colors. Their paintings are full of extraordinarily fine naturalistic details. Many portraits they painted, look exactly like photographs.

In the late 20th century, Mr. Hockney published a book titled "Secret Knowledge". I recommend that every art student read his valuable and important book.
Mr. Hockney proved conclusively that many of Europe's most famous Old Master artists PROJECTED and TRACED the images. By tracing, they were able to paint pictures that look like photographs. He demonstrated how by using mirrors and glass lenses they could PROJECT the images onto the canvas or wood panel.

Mr. Hockney also showed that many great Masters did NOT trace.
Many Old Masters, like many Modern Masters today, can paint and draw very realistically without projecting and tracing images. Neither Michelangelo nor Rubens traced, and their paintings look realistic, but they do not look like photographs.

Many art students draw poorly, but they are very creative. These students can learn how to trace and can then create fine paintings that are very beautiful.

THE MODERN DIRECT PAINTING METHOD OF VINCENT VAN GOGH

The method of Oil Painting taught in the book and Video is the Layered Method. This explains the procedure for the Direct Method of Oil Painting.

Before beginning to paint a picture some artists draw the outline before they paint. Others do not draw before they paint. They prefer to draw and paint at the same time, with the paint.

Vincent Van Gogh would set up his easel in front of the SUBJECT .
He preferred painting directly on the white canvas. He would use bright blue oil paint and with a small brush, he would draw an OUTLINE of the subject .

By outlining the subject he was actually DESIGNING the COMPOSITION of the painting. The subject could have been a LANDSCAPE ... or a PORTRAIT ... or a STILL LIFE.

Once he made the bright blue outline, he then would FILL IN the spaces and areas with his oil paints while the blue outline was still wet. This method allowed Van Gogh to complete a painting very rapidly.

THE DIRECT PAINTING METHOD
[also called ' Alla Prima"]

To paint with this direct method you simply LEAVE OUT THE MONOTONE.
You can still begin with MILK OIL PAINT if you wish, and you can complete the entire painting with only the MILK OIL PAINT.
Or you can complete the painting with the TRADITIONAL OIL PAINT.

You can paint the entire painting with just MILK OIL PAINT
OR, You can paint the entire painting with TRADITIONAL OIL PAINT
OR, you can begin with MILK OIL PAINT and finish with TRADITIONAL OIL PAINTS

IMPORTANT POINTS TO REMEMBER
1. ONCE YOU begin using the TRADITIONAL OIL PAINTS, you CANNOT paint Milk Oil Paints on top of the Traditional Oil Paints.
2. The Direst method of painting is done in one layer.
3. The Direct method of painting does not use a monotone.
4. After the painting dries, a correction layer can be applied.

INSTRUCTIONS
FOR THE DIRECT OIL PAINTING METHOD

STEP ONE : PREPARATION
Begin by obtaining the photograph of the subject you will paint
Seal the support you will paint on so it is non-absorbent
-Follow the instructions in PART THREE
Draw and ink the portrait on the support. Freehand or trace
-Follow the instructions in PART THREE
Prepare the emulsion
-Follow the instructions in PART THREE
Condition the paint with the emulsion, on the grinding table
-Follow the instructions in PART THREE

For this method you can buy extra colors
Read the labels and do not buy hazardous colors. Ask the store manager for assistance. Read the labels!
   Bright Primary colors : Red Yellow Blue
   Bright Secondary colors : Purple, Green, Orange
   Bright brown : Sienna brown
   Black : Mars black
  White : Titanium Dioxide white (use only this white)

STEP TWO : PAINT WITH ANY AND ALL COLORS
You can make a bright color dull, by mixing a bit of brown sienna
Add a bit of black to darken a color
Add a bit of white to lighten a color
Begin to apply paint thinly.
You can add thicker paint as you go

Paint the medium toned colors first [it helps]
Paint the darks
Paint the lights
Blend as you paint

Mix colors to create exciting unexpected colors
Scrape off the paint of any areas you do not like

STEP THREE: CORRECT THE COLORS
Add a bit of black to darken a color
Add a bit of white to lighten a color
Paint the paint thicker or thinner
Blend as you paint
Scrape off the paint of any areas you do not like

STEP FOUR: MAKE CORRECTIONS
After the painting dries, corrections can be applied .
Before applying the corrections, apply an "Oil out ".

THE ADVANTAGES
OF THE DIRECT PAINTING METHOD
1. The completed painting has a fresh sketchy quality
2. The painting is quickly finished , sometimes in just a few hours
3. The creative responses of the artist are immediately painted

The Direct Painting method is not primarily concerned with painting in a photo-realistic style.
The Direct Painting method is more concerned with FORM EXPRESSION .
When the artist is not concerned with painting photographically, the artist can have more freedom of expressing the 7 FORMAL ELEMENTS .

THE LANGUAGE OF PAINTING
is FORM and CONTENT

The word FORM, in painting means two things.
One meaning is the 3D FORM:
An example is this. The Form of a water pitcher is a three dimensional object.
Another meaning is the DESIGN FORM: One can say "the Form of a seashell is very intricate and very complicated with all its colors, and textures."

FORM

The word **FORM** when used in discussing paintings and in creating them, refers to the FORMAL aspects of DESIGN.
DESIGN is a word that can be described as ARRANGEMENT, or STRUCTURE and also COMPOSITION or FOUNDATION.
Generally they refer to the organization of the painting. How things are arranged or placed on the canvas.

FORM, as organizing things in the painting, uses several different words. Humans made these words up so they could intelligently say what they thought of these things when they talked with others about them.

FORM is expressed by the FORMAL considerations of a painting. These are the 7 ELEMENTS OF DESIGN and the 7 PRINCIPLES OF DESIGN.

INTUITIVE DESIGN [FORM]

One can Design and paint by INTUITION alone without ever learning the words created by academics. As proof, I showed them many famous and precious examples of African paintings, some being thousands of years old, made by persons who had no art schools or art colleges nor even a written language.

CONTENT: What does a painting "mean"?

"CONTENT" can be just as complicated to understand as the word "FORM".
Content in a painting has to do with what the painting is about.

Paintings are silent and normally do not have signs.
Today in most museums persons can rent an AUDIO TOUR to explain what the paintings mean. Without that, a person looking at a painting is left on their own to interpret for themselves what the painting MEANS, or is all about.

CONTENT is different from the SUBJECT in the painting.
A painting of a boy and a dog is the subject.
A picture of a boy and a dog, where the boy was walking
away and the dog was tied to a chain and the dog begins to cry.
This is the content, this is its meaning.

Pictures of an arrangement of colors and lines, demonstrates how hard it is to know what the subject or the content is.
The pictures make sense when it is explained that they are close up views of things seen through a microscope.
These highly magnified close ups of natural objects can be a piece of wood, another a butterfly wing, or a sidewalk.

These lessons demonstrate that the CONTENT of a painting could be anything that gave it a certain meaning. Many times a painting has a different meaning to different people.

WRITING ABOUT CONTENT AND FORM
SOME ARTISTS DO WRITE ABOUT THEIR WORK
Artists create paintings, and their paintings represent their personal ideas and their meanings. Some artists write about what that MEANING is by writing about what they are trying to "SAY" through their paintings.

This is helpful, because if they don't write down why they made the painting and what they were thinking about, some "Art expert", will come along and will write down their own opinion about what the artist was trying to say.

SOMEARTISTS DO NOT WRITE ABOUT THEIR WORK
Few of the greatest painters wrote down what they were trying to express in their paintings. Most were just trying to earn a living by painting pictures for money. To them it was a job, like any other job people have.

Today in many art classes, teachers will discuss the MEANING OF CONTENT in student paintings. This is because people enjoy discussing thoughts and hearing opinions. This communication joins people together for intellectual discussions.

It is important to remember that all comments about the meaning of artworks, unless expressed by the artist, are PURELY SUBJECTIVE , meaning, they are simply opinions that cannot be proven or disproven.

HOW TO MAKE AN EMULSION
BY USING EGG INSTEAD OF MILK

The video and book instructions teach you how to make an Emulsion of milk and oil. An artist can also choose to make an emulsion of egg white and oil. It takes more time and effort. It is a good project to learn. Then, in future oil painting, you can choose either emulsion to' CONDITION'. the tube oil paint colors as the video demonstrates.

INSTRUCTIONS
REQUIRED: TWO EGGS, A BOWEL , A SPOON and a GLASS JAR
Break both eggs carefully. Carefully separate the white from the yolk. Discard the yolk. WE WILL NOT USE THE YOLK. If any yolk gets into the bowl, carefully remove it. Place the egg whites in a bowl. Use a metal spoon. Do not use an electric blender nor a plastic spoon. Beat the egg white until it froths . Periodically use the spoon to remove the froth and place the froth in a clean jar. Continue to beat the egg white in the bowl. Periodically remove the froth as before. Continue this until all the egg white has been frothed and removed. Let the froth stand still for about 30 minutes so it will distill. Periodically break through the froth to allow air. When finished, the pale yellow liquid is called GLAIR.

MIX THE GLAIR AND THE THICK OIL
Use a teaspoon. Place two spoonfuls of the glair in a small jar. Place three spoonfuls of the thickened linseed oil into the same jar. Take your time. Make sure all the sticky oil gets off the spoon each time. Add a couple of pennies or small stones into the jar. Cap the jar tight. Shake this well, vigorously . Count from 50 to 100 to insure the mixture is correctly made.

The completed emulsion will be a very opaque white color. The egg emulsion will last only a few days before it begins to decompose. Place the capped jar in a cool place with the lid tightly on. Once you see a tan or brownish color, or detect a bad odor, discard the entire jar and contents. Some artists keep it in the refrigerator but it will gain water though condensation.

YOU MUST HAVE A GRINDING TABLE

This is a low cost, glazed floor tile. Do not get a pure white nor a solid black because they are hard to see the colors well. Any mid tone color is ok. The size can be about 12 inches by 12 inches, or preferably larger.

CONDITIONING THE OIL PAINT

Squeeze out a small daub of each oil paint color onto the grinding table.
If you see a lot of oil come out when you squeeze the paint from the tube, then, you must put the paint daub on a paper towel. This will blot out that excess oil. It only takes about 15 seconds. Once done, use the palette knife to transfer the paint to the grinding table

Now, Place two drops of the emulsion next to each daub of paint.
Use a palette knife to mix the two together. You need to GRIND the two together. The difference between MIXING and GRINDING is in the pressure you apply. Mixing requires no pressure but grinding does.
First, just mix the two together. Now, you must grind the two together very well using pressure. It only takes seconds.

We mix the emulsion with the tube oil paint for several reasons.
1. It accelerates the drying of the paint
2. It makes the paint more glossy with rich color depth
3. It increases the flow for easier application and blending
4. It stops the paint from dripping

We mix the emulsion with the tube oil paint for several reasons.
1. It accelerates the drying of the paint
2. It makes the paint more glossy with rich color depth
3. It increases the flow for easier application and blending
4. It stops the paint from dripping

THIS CONCLUDES PART ONE FOR TEACHERS

PART TWO:
THE ABRIDGED EDITION BOOK FOR TEACHERS

I published my **final** edition of my professional level book on Oil Painting in December 2012.

The title is: ***OIL PAINTING LESSONS WITH REMBRANDT AND "CALCITE SUN OIL": Artists Health and Safety without Hazardous Solvents, Resins, Varnishes and Driers.***

The complete book is 285 pages long.
This abridged Edition is only the first 133 pages. The complete book has Eleven Parts. Only Part one is included here in this book.
The complete book covers all the topics I have researched, tested and written about. Please see the TABLE OF CONTENTS.

Art teachers can use this Abridged Edition as a resource guide to teaching Oil Painting without any Hazardous materials on an advanced level.
Please note that the page numbers are changed from the complete Edition.

[ABRIDGED EDITION]
OIL PAINTING LESSONS WITH REMBRANDT AND "CALCITE SUN OIL":
Artists Health and Safety without Hazardous Solvents, Resins, Varnishes and Driers.

[The page numbers have been altered from the Complete Edition]

TABLE OF CONTENTS

INTRODUCTORY CHAPTER Page 36 GLOSSARY P.40
THE CSO OIL PAINTING METHOD is summarized and simplified for instant use

P. 53 PART ONE - OIL PAINTING

P. 53 Chapter One - 21st century advancements

P. 59 Chapter Two - The Rebirth of the Old Masters' Oil

P. 62 Chapter Three - Cleansing the Oil of Mucilage

P. 73 Chapter Four - Thickening the Oil

P. 81 Chapter Five – Chalk and Oil Mixtures

P. 88 Chapter Six – Emulsions, the Wonder Medium

P. 98 Chapter Seven- The Oil Out

P. 106 Chapter Eight – The Van Eyck Secret Medium

P. 111 Chapter Nine – Tube Oil Paints and Hand Ground Paints

P. 117 Chapter Ten – Oil Painting Methods

P. 126 Chapter Eleven – The Five Step Oil Painting Method

P. 131 Chapter Twelve – Alternate Chalk Oil Mixtures and the Resin Effect

P. 136 Chapter Thirteen – Studio Practice

p. 136 Materials List- the essentials of the equipment you will need

p. 139 Burnt Plate Oil - an extremely slow drying oil. It is made for Lithography, not Painting

p. 142 Drying Times of Paints - demonstrating the importance of UNREFINED linseed oil

p. 143 Acrylic Paints vs. Oil Paints – discussion of the modern and the old media

p. 143 Isolating the Support - discusses the importance of this preparatory step

p. 147 Care of the Palette, Hands, Excess Paint - valuable studio information

p. 148 Never Wash Brushes Again - saving hours of tedious unnecessary work
p. 149 Final Permanent Layer - the difference between temporary and permanent protection
P. 150 Fixative - a safe procedure to prevent drawings from smudging
p. 151 Practical Ways to Paint a Picture – a summary of simple procedures.
p. 153 Umber oil and Half-White – accelerating the drying of the under painting
p. 154 Example of painting with Aguado – explanation of a procedure
p. 157 Example of painting procedure – example of a painting procedure
p. 158 Preparing the support – the foundation of a painting

P. PART TWO: OIL PAINTING

Additional Oil Painting Information

Issues concerning the oil

Francisco Pacheco's method of cleansing oil

How Linseed oil dries

Concerns of Linseed oil

Differences between oils

Alkali refined oil

Sun thick oil

Color of oil

Dehydrator Oil

Hot plate oil for winter

House painting oil

Frederic Taubes - an American Master painter

Cleansing oil and Fat on Lean

Hazardous materials

Non Absorbent grounds

Safe Fixatives

Additives to oil paint

How paint dries

Chalk warning

PART THREE : LESSONS FROM THE OLD MASTERS
PART FOUR : CSO-EGG TEMPERA
PART FIVE : CSO-CASEIN TEMPERA
PART SIX : COMPARING TEMPERAS
PART SEVEN : MILK OIL PAINT
PART EIGHT : JACQUES MAROGER'S FAILURE
PART NINE : MISCELLANEOUS
PART TEN : TESTIMONIALS
PART ELEVEN : CONCLUSION

DEDICATION
Mr. Frederic Taubes
(1900-1981)
www.frederictaubes.com

I respectfully dedicate this book to the memory of Mr. Frederic Taubes (1900-1981), an important American artist and educator, who I consider to be my teacher. Without his early guidance, I would have fallen by the wayside. I am happy to have met him in person twice. I herein share the details of that first meeting:

When I was about 15, I had written a few letters to Mr. Taubes, who lived in New York. I found out he would be teaching a summer painting session, 45 miles from my home in California, and per our letters, he invited me to visit him for a critique. On the day of the visit, I walked up to Mr. Taubes with an arm full of oil paintings. After greeting me, he flipped through the stack, all within one minute, not even taking one out of the stack to look at it. I felt sad, and I said, "Mr. Taubes, would you like me to hold them out for you, so you can see them, one at a time?"

He responded, "Young man, if you give me a bowl of soup, I only need to taste it to know if it is good, I don't have to eat the whole bowl!" He then took each painting, one by one, and slowly looked at each one. I saw a smile come over his face. He then asked me, "Are you related to 'Old Man' Velazquez?"

… I wish I could visit with him today.

ACKNOWLEDGMENTS

I wish to acknowledge the support, encouragement, and knowledge I have received from many unnamed persons, each of whom contributed to my growth as a painter. My formulation of Calcite Sun Oil as a grinding oil, and development of these extraordinary Emulsions, is the result of my lifelong curiosity, studies and experiments. I could never have accomplished any of this without the publications of the three very important scholars and educators named here.
To each of them, I say, "Thank you!"

Ms. Carmen Garrido-Perez
Author of 'Velazquez: Tecnica y Evolucion' (1992), and many books and articles.
Head of the Conservation Department, the Prado Museum, Madrid, Spain

I am especially greatly indebted to Ms. Carmen Garrido-Perez for sharing her work, she has been THE MOST IMPORTANT CATALYST for my studies and experiments with Calcium Carbonate as a paint additive. Ms. Garrido-Perez' extensive research into the magnificently preserved paintings of Spain's great 17th century painter, Diego Velazquez, provided the final bit of information I needed to connect the knowledge on materials and application methods of the Old Masters.

Professor Dr. Ernst Van De Wetering
Head of the Rembrandt Research Project
Author of many books and articles on the subject of Rembrandt

Mr. Van De Wetering deserves his international reputation for his work with the Rembrandt Research Project. Rembrandt's paintings astound all who see them, when seen in the original as reproductions cannot relay the magic one senses when in their actual presence. Much of the magic is contained in the extraordinary mastery of his paint application and the sensuous appearance of the colors, brushstrokes and textures of his paint. Many have called him an Alchemist because of the uniqueness of his paint quality.

Mr. Van De Wetering's recent book, "Rembrandt: The Painter at Work", summarizes the results of his lifelong studies of Rembrandt's work. Filled with much information, answering questions and raising numerous new questions, the book is an excellent source for Rembrandt scholars. I too have studied it intently, seeking answers to my questions, my curiosity becoming more stimulated with each new fact or each new question. His book describes Rembrandt's important use of Emulsions and Calcium Carbonate.

His comments on scientific studies, and on the nature of thixotropic qualities seen in Rembrandt's work, only stimulated my need to know more. I thank Mr. Van De Wetering for his tireless dedication, and the sharing of his knowledge of the materials and methods of application, of one of the world's true wonders,
the paintings of Rembrandt Harmenzoon Van Rijn. In a list of the leading painters of his time, it was written how highly he was regarded. " *Rembrandt, the miracle of our age*" – Gabriel Bucelinus, 1664

A MARVELOUS MOMENT WITH Prof. Dr. ERNST VAN DE WETERING, HEAD OF THE REMBRANDT RESEARCH PROJECT
On October 27th, 2010, I attended Prof. Dr. Van De Wetering's lecture at the Getty Museum in Los Angeles, California..
After the lecture, I approached him as he stood surrounded by Getty scientists, and I said, "May I shake your hand, my name is Louis Velasquez." He instantly smiled broadly and he said....**"Ohhh ... the man of the Binding Medium!!"**
We shook hands briskly, exchanged greetings and a few words. Then he was escorted away. I am proud to share this
information with you. Demonstrating his awareness of ...CALCITE SUN OIL, a Grinding and Binding Medium for oil painting.

Mr. Frederic Taubes (1900-1981)
Renowned American Artist and Educator
Author of over 20 books on Oil Painting

My early interest in paintings by the Old Masters led me to paint in oils. The books and magazine articles authored by Mr. Frederic Taubes taught me the methods and materials of oil painting as he understood them. A reputable American artist himself, he wrote about the materials and methods of the Old Masters with great insight and with boundless admiration for their Masterpieces. I was lucky to have met him in person when I was 15, a day I took my paintings for him to critique. His critique is retold in the dedication page of this book.

Mr. Taubes' theorized the painting medium of the Old Masters was comprised of the hard resin Copal, mixed with linseed oil through heating. Experiments and studies made throughout his long life were the basis for his beliefs, as were scientific results of his day, and his consultations with experts in their fields. Yet, some writers on art materials disagreed with Mr. Taubes on the use of Copal by the Old Masters, claiming the dark hard resins of copal and amber would eventually darken the paint.

Regardless of the critics, I used only Mr. Taubes' Copal products throughout my early and middle life, as I painted in oils. As Mr. Taubes claimed, the Copal resin improved the manipulation of the paint in several ways, to include; easier blending, depth of color, glossy surface, clarity and adherence, and a variety of techniques were made possible whether thin or impasto paint were used. His claim that the Copal resin increases the permanence of the painting, will only be proved by time. It is too early to tell, as my earliest oil paintings with his Copal products date only from 1957.

Though Mr. Taubes encouraged artists to make their own paints by hand-grinding pigments with oil, I was happy using oil paints available in tubes, and I never ventured to try it - until the year 2003. Years after Mr. Taubes' death in 1981, his products were no longer on the market. However the continued demand for his products created imitators, who produced "Taubes-like" products claiming use of hard resins mixed with oils.

Once the authentic Taubes products were not available, I began a search for a painting medium, offering the same benefits and qualities as Taubes' products. I settled for various mixtures of Stand Linseed oil and turpentine. My experiments with additions of soft resin to my painting medium, like the widely popular and much used Dammar resin, validated Mr. Taubes' strict admonishment: SOFT resins, such as Dammar, added to the painting medium, create an impermanent and weak paint film always susceptible to easy removal, no matter how old the film of paint.

I experimented with the supposed classic painting medium mixture, of 1 part Stand oil and 1 part turpentine, to mix with my tube oil paints. I learned much later that Stand Oil sold today is a 19th century invention, and has drying deficiencies. I soon learned the 'classic' medium also limited certain manipulations of oil paints. It was only much later I learned just how limiting it was, and why.
I am greatly indebted to Mr. Frederic Taubes for his studious dedication to the methods and materials of oil painting and the Old Masters. For inspiring me ... this book has been dedicated to his memory.

See Frederic Taubes' wonderful imaginative paintings at www.frederictaubes.com

INTRODUCTORY CHAPTER

QUICK GUIDE TO 'CSO-OIL PAINTING'
This INTRODUCTORY CHAPTER serves a valuable purpose.
It is a CONDENSED SUMMARY of basic information an artist needs to immediately begin to paint with the CSO/ EMULSIONS method. The book contains detailed information.

OIL PAINTING MATERIALS
The extraordinarily preserved 600 year old oil paintings of the Van Eyck's, and the paintings of Rembrandt, Velazquez, Rubens Van Eyck and others, attest to the superior quality of their materials. Modern science has identified those materials. The CSO method uses three archival ingredients available to the Old Masters; Their Superior Flax oil, Egg Glair, and Calcium Carbonate Chalk. They are commonplace and simple, yet so profound if mixed and used correctly. In my tests these form a technical superiority over todays Resin-Solvent-Drier methods. This book will teach you how to prepare and use them with the very same methods the great Masters used.

'CALCITE SUN OIL' [CSO]
CSO is a Revolutionary New GRINDING OIL BINDER for oil paints based on the Old Masters' ancient knowledge. It is designed for mixing with modern TUBE OIL PAINTS or to HAND GRIND one's own oil paints from dry pigment powders as the Old Masters did.

THE TEN BENEFITS of 'CALCITE SUN OIL' and the EMULSIONS
DRYING is accelerated without driers
ADHESION, without drips and beading
BLENDING is facilitated
TRANSLUCENCY is increased
BODY of Impasto or Glazes
COLOR DEPTH and LUSTER is increased
MICRO-FINE LINES and DETAILS are allowed
THIXOTROPIC quality is promoted
SUEDE EFFECT of Tube Oil Paints is eliminated
WRINKLING of impasto is eliminated

IMPORTANT NOTICE ON THE OIL YOU CAN CHOOSE TO USE
The superior oil of the Old Masters is not on the market yet. I predict that one day it will be. Meanwhile please review your oil choices.

OIL CHOICE NUMBER ONE: BUY A SLOWER DRYING SUBSTITUTE OIL
If you don't have any time to spare and wish to begin oil painting, artists can use the slower drying "Alkali Refined STAND Linseed oil" which is available in every Art store nationwide. With this low priced substitute THICK linseed oil, the artist can easily prepare the slower drying 'CAL-STAND OIL' , described in my book. By using the Art Store Linseed Stand Oil to make 'Cal-Stand Oil', the artist gives up the FAST DRYING quality of the superior oil of the Old Masters, and will have to wait longer for paint layers to dry. This may not be a problem for most beginners as they usually do not paint every day as do Professional artists. PLEASE also see choice number three below, because with a bit of time, one can produce at home for very little cost, a superior substitute THICKENED oil by use of the AIR PUMP METHOD.

OIL CHOICE NUMBER TWO: USE THE 'AIR PUMP OIL METHOD: This new method shortens the time required in making your own THICKENED Linseed/Flax Oil. It can be thickened within 15 days from beginning to end. I did not invent this new method but I have tested it and I approve of it. The procedure is described fully in the book. Beginners can use the 'air pump method' to THICKEN the low cost Alkali Refined THIN OIL bought at the Art store and make their own THICKENED OIL that will be far superior to the current Art Store STAND oil which is nothing more than decomposed BOILED OIL.
The AIR PUMP OIL will soon make the Art Store thickened "STANDLINSEED OIL" obsolete

OIL CHOICE NUMBER THREE: PREPARE YOUR OWN "SUPERIOR OIL OF THE OLD MASTERS "
To prepare the Old Masters' traditional 'Superior Linseed/Flax Oil, it requires some space, time, and a few items. One buys cold-pressed FLAX oil from a health food store [read the details in the book for warnings to watch for] and it is cleansed for ten days, then sun thickened. It takes between 30 and 60 days of adequate summer heat to Sun Thicken the CLEANSED unrefined Flax oil. Some artists are at a disadvantage because they have short summers with limited heat. For them and others, the new "AIR PUMP OIL" method can also be used to accelerate the thickening of the superior oil of the Old Masters.

SOURCE FOR PURCHASING CHALK AND OIL
The Calcium Carbonate powder and LINSEED/FLAX oil can be ordered Online.
I recommend only **'Calcium Carbonate Chalk from Champagne, France'.** It is available online at KREMER PIGMENTE. Currently it is item # 58000 , listed under fillers , carbonates. Google KREMER for the most updated location near you. They have offices worldwide with the main office in Germany and one in New York City. I use North American Flax oil sold by Barleans, but one must read the label and not buy flax oil for pets nor with highest lignans added. I also recommend the high grade 'Linseed' oil from Kremers, currently item # 73020. Read the MSDS [Material Safety Data Sheet] and you will note it is cold pressed from UNROASTED seeds. I WARN readers that as years pass, companies change hands and new owners will change their products. Readers must be careful in buying the Chalk and the Oil in future years. Read all the labels and write and ask questions. The final responsibility is yours. *BEWARE of some art stores selling "FRENCH CHALK" ... it is NOT the same as Calcium Carbonate Chalk from Champagne, France.*

THE CSO-EMULSIONS METHOD SIMPLIFIED

CSO USES ONLY 3 MATERIALS BESIDES YOUR TUBE OIL PAINTS. THESE ARE:
1. THE SUPERIOR OIL OF THE OLD MASTERS - Easy to process, but you can use a substitute oil.
2. CHALK CALCIUM CARBONATE- very low cost and inexpensive.
3. GLAIR - frothed and distilled egg white.

THESE THREE INGREDIENTS MAKE TWO MIXTURES THAT ARE USED TOGETHER
1. MIXING THE OIL AND THE CHALK- IN CORRECT RATIOS - MAKES THE "CSO"
2. MIXING THE OIL AND GLAIR - IN CORRECT RATIOS- MAKES THE "VISCOUS EMULSION"

THE TWO MIXTURES ABOVE ARE MADE AND USED IN THIS MANNER
1. MIX THE CSO 50/50 WITH TUBE PAINTS - Hand grinding dry pigments is an option - but not necessary. Use the THIN oil when Hand Grinding oil and dry pigments, then mix the CSO with it. An option to creater the fastest drying oil paint is to grind the CSO with dry pigments and thin the viscous CSO oil paint with the 'VE' Viscous Emulsion.
2. USE THE ' VISCOUS EMULSION' FOR MANY PURPOSES - It is an Oil Out, a thinner, a stiffener to make impasto, and a final varnish that is a non-removable protective film. The Emulsion is the 'wonder medium' of the Van Eycks, but the application method is just as important.

BEFORE PAINTING YOU MUST USE AN "OIL OUT" TO LUBRICATE THE SURFACE
[UNLESS YOU WISH A DRY BRUSH EFFECT].
IT IS CRUCIAL THAT IT BE APPLIED CORRECTLY. IT IS VERY EASY TO APPLY.
THE 'OIL OUT' EMULSION MUST BE APPLIED BY HAND ONLY - NEVER WITH A BRUSH.
This unique application method is the 2nd part of the Van Eyck secret medium - it explains why the simple procedure was lost and became a lost method and secret.

THE CSO/ EMULSIONS METHOD IS REALLY THAT SIMPLE. OF COURSE IT IS ALSO VERY COMPLEX, WITH MANY NUANCES. THESE ARE EXPLAINED IN THE BOOK.
Please continue with the INTRODUCTORY CHAPTER to understand the basics of the CSO-EMULSUIONS method .

GLOSSARY

THE SUPERIOR OIL OF THE OLD MASTERS: A raw unrefined cold pressed food grade Flax oil that is cleansed of its mucilage by a safe method. Once the mucilage is removed the oil is allowed to remain <u>thin</u> or it is <u>thickened</u>. Keep oil in both conditions because they each serve an important role in oil painting. This oil is called by many different names in this book. NOTE: There are NO 'LIN" seeds in nature. Linseed oil is pressed from FLAX SEEDS. The reasons for the different names is explained in the text.

SUN THICKENED LINSEED FLAX OIL: The traditional Old Master method, was to thicken their oil in direct hot summer sun. *[Beware of brand name inferior Sun Thickened Linseed oil sold in Art stores – it is Alkali Refined oil and slow drying, and it is not the same quality as the oil used by the Old Masters].*

HEAT THICKENED LINSEED FLAX OIL: The Old Masters in cold climates used heat from fire to thicken their oil. It was heated in open containers exposed to oxygen as it thickened.

THICK OIL: Oil that has purposefully been thickened [polymerized]. It is viscous and sticky. The oil can be thickened in the sun or by artificial heat.

AIR PUMP OIL: A modern method to thicken the oil by use of a low cost aquarium Air Pump. It is the fastest drying oil and a thin layer dries in under 14 hours when mixed with chalk [into CSO] and then mixed with tube oil paints. If mixed with chalk [to make CSO] and then mixed with dry pigment powders and Hand Grinding, a thin layer can dry in under 5 hours. NOTE: Different pigments dry at different rates.

POLYMERIZED: This means the oil is viscous and has been thickened. Polymerization of the oil is caused by exposure to oxygen, time and heat. This oil if exposed to oxygen during its thickening, it is a faster drying oil. If not exposed to oxygen during the thickening, it is a slow drying oil.

NON-POLYMERIZED: This means the oil is loose and thin and has not been thickened by any means. It is thin and limpid and slow drying. Keep this oil in an airtight bottle to stop it from thickening. This oil is yellow in color before sunlight exposure. Place the clear glass container in a sunny window to bleach the color out.

THIN OIL: Oil that has NOT been thickened [not polymerized]. It is very limpid, bright yellow to pale yellow in color, and is a slow drying oil. Keep the cap tight on the jar to stop the oil from thickening.

NON-SUN OIL: Oil that has not been exposed to the sun. Oil can be bleached by sun exposure.

CO-POLY OIL: The term stands for 'combination polymerization', and is an oil made by mixing portions of thin and thick oil in order to gain some painterly advantage to slow down the drying of thickened oil.

STAND OIL: The traditional thickened oil of the Old Masters. It gets its name because it was allowed to 'stand' in the sun's heat for 15 to 60 days depending on the desired viscosity.

ALKALI REFINED LINSEED "STAND" OIL: A thickened modern industrial BOILED oil refined by use of alkali caustic Lye chemicals such as sodium hydroxide. Mass produced since the 19th century. This oil is BOILED without oxygen exposure to cause the oil to thicken. The high heat boiling causes decomposition and the oil to have a shortened life span. Modern STAND OIL is not the 'stand' oil of the Old Masters.
The modern industrial Stand oil is oil that has been BOILED. This oil will soon become obsolete by the new 'Air Pump Oil' method described in this book.

REFINED LINSEED OIL: A thin 'alkali refined linseed oil' modern industrial linseed oil refined by use of caustic alkali chemicals that harm the oil.

LINOXYN [alternate spelling is LINOXINE]: When a film or layer of linseed flax oil and or oil paint hardens, through the OXIDATION process, it is called LINOXYN. Sir Arthur Church in his book, " The chemistry of paints and painting', identified one of the several different glycerides that is in linseed/flax oil as being non-oxidizing, meaning it never gets fully hard. He says this glyceride, called OLEIN, is what keeps the linoxyn pliable and flexible over the hundreds of years of oxidation of the oil thereby preventing cracking of the oil paint. Although the oil hardens in a few days, it takes several hundred years for linseed/flax oil to completely oxidize.

OXIDATION [alternate spelling, OXIDIZATION]: Linseed flax oil hardens through oxidation, not though evaporation.

CALCITE SUN OIL: My modern re-creation of Rembrandt's mixture of Calcium Carbonate Chalk and the Superior oil of the Old Masters in a carefully measured ratio.

CSO: Abbreviation for Calcite Sun Oil.

CSO OIL PAINT: Any oil paint – tube oil paint or hand ground oil paint- that has been mixed and ground well with CSO in varying amounts, but normally a 50/50 ratio.

CALCIUM CARBONATE: An ancient limestone substance millions of years old. It has many forms, such as Chalk, Calcite, Aragonite, Marble. Since it is from the cretaceous period it is also called creta or kreta.

CSO-EMULSION: A mixture of oil and egg glair. CSO has developed three Emulsion mixtures for use with the CSO method of Oil Painting. The Viscous Emulsion [VE], the Non-Viscous Emulsion [NVE] , and Espeso.

GLAIR: The white of the egg that is frothed and distilled. It contains NO egg oil. It is 85% water and 15% albumen, a very sticky substance that makes it valuable as a paint binder.

OIL OUT: This term stands for "OIL rubbed in and oil wiped OUT". This procedure is crucial to oil painting and serves many functions. The text will explain these important functions.

OIL OUT MEDIUMS: CSO has developed 4 unique mediums to be used as an ' OIL OUT" medium. Three are Emulsion mixtures of Egg Glair and Oil. They are: The Viscous Emulsion [VE], the Non-Viscous Emulsion [NVE] , and Espeso . The fourth is called AGUADO and is not an Emulsion. The Emulsions MUST be applied by hand but the Aguado can be applied with a brush.

THIXOTROPY: Allows painting WET PAINT - ON TOP OF -WET PAINT - without disrupting the lower layer of wet paint. Some writers say thixotropy depends on the size of the pigment particles, but it is false. Thixotropy is solely dependent on the ingredients of the liquid medium mixed with the oil paint.

QUICK GUIDE - PAINTING WITH CSO

There are many, many, many ways to paint a painting. Therefore, I offer this as ONE WAY that will help. BUT, I stress that all creative artists must be free to experiment and to develop a method that suits their goals best. The CSO/EMULSIONS method is proven to be safe and permanent and extraordinary in every respect of technical procedures. All I ask is that you please follow my instructions exactly as I have made them. Then, once you master it—then—go ahead and change things to suit you. By doing this, you will gain very important INTIMATE KNOWLEDGE of these extraordinary materials and procedures, their possibilities and their limitations. This will help you gain the mastery you desire.

FIRST- You must paint on a non-absorbent support. This technical principal is firm. If you paint on an absorbent support, it will absorb the oil from your paint and in time that dry paint will powder and crack. There is no value to having the support "slightly absorbent'. Oil painters need a FULLY NON-ABSORBENT support to paint on. Seal the raw wood or canvas with animal skin glue. Preferably use traditional Rabbit skin or Hide glue. Apply two liberal coats and let the first coat dry well before applying the second coat.

SECOND – Begin by applying two LIBERAL coats of hot hide glue to the canvas, and one coat on the reverse. Rub the glue in well. Make certain the cloth is completely saturated with the glue. Let these dry. THEN apply one thin SOUPY coat of traditional gesso made of a mixture of: hide glue and calcium carbonate powder. This mixture should be soupy with more glue than chalk. This gesso can be pure white or it can be toned with dry pigment powders. When using flexible canvas as the support, DO NOT apply the gesso with a brush as it forms a brittle continuous film. Use a broad scraping tool to fill the weave of the canvas. When applied to a rigid wood panel, one can use a brush to apply the gesso. Scientific examinations by the Prado Museum show Velazquez' late paintings – on canvas- received a thin gesso primer as I describe. The Getty scientists in Los Angeles California, show Titian also used this priming on an extraordinarily well preserved very large oil painting on canvas in their collection: Adonis and Venus.

THIRD - When the gesso is dry, USE A BRUSH and apply one thin coat of hide glue or a liberal coat of non-fat milk, and let dry hard to seal the gesso. ALL types of gesso are very absorbent. If not fully sealed, the absorbent gesso will absorb oil out of the oil paint, leaving the oil paint under bound. Under bound oil paint dries matte, lacks color depth, and is fragile. QUESTION: Can one paint on acrylic primed canvas. ANSWER : Yes. But recall that ALL TYPES OF GESSO are absorbent. Seal the acrylic gesso with two coats of NON-FAT milk [*or with thinned down acrylic varnish either matte or gloss*]. Do not use whole milk nor low fat milk as the butter fat will not dry. Let the milk coats dry well for several hours or overnight. Time required depends on your weather conditions and ventilation.

FOURTH - Choose good quality tube oil paints, or grind your own paint. If an excess of oil oozes out when you uncap the tube, blot most of the oil out on a paper towel before adding the CSO. Hand Ground paint dries the fastest and is preferable for under painting. Use THIN oil to hand grind dry pigments, then mix with CSO.

FIFTH - Make the 'Calcite Sun Oil'. Neither 'Calcite Sun Oil' nor the required FAST drying Superior oil of the Old Masters are yet on the market. Follow the instructions in the book on preparing the oil and the CSO. The recipe is one spoon of sun oil and three compacted spoons of chalk. DO NOT ADD MORE OIL than called for in this recipe. Trust me. They will mix by constant movement of the palette knife. GRIND well together until fully mixed. It takes only a couple of minutes.
NOTE: For those who do not have the Fast drying oil, they can use a slow drying SUBSTITUTE mixture called 'Cal-Stand Oil', easily made with Alkali Refined Stand Linseed Oil. Please know this oil is slow drying and delays the painting process for several days. Please review the procedure for making 'Cal-Stand Oil' in the book.
NOTE: Please view the DVD on CSO-OIL PAINTING. It contains a 12 minute demonstration on how to make CSO with important issues to avoid.

SIXTH - Mix the tube oil paint with 'Calcite Sun Oil'.
[OPTION: Make your own oil paint by grinding oil with dry powder pigments into a thick paste. But use THIN NON SUN THICKENED oil to grind your hand made oil paint].
Grind together each color of tube oil paint [or hand ground paint] with an equal amount of 'CSO', about 50/50. You do not need to measure exactly - just make an estimate. Some colors require a bit less or more of CSO. Experience will guide you. Grind well the CSO and the paint together in circular motions, by applying pressure with a flexible straight edged palette knife. The grinding takes 5 to 10 seconds for each color.
NOTE: You can make oil paint become a lighter value of dark/light by adding a bit more CSO.
NOTE: If you use too much CSO with the paint—you must add a drop or two of the 'VISCOUS EMULSION" to prevent wrinkling of the oil paint.
NOTE: one or two very small drops of the 'viscous emulsion' will NOT impede the paint flow, BUT adding several more drops will make the oil paint stiffer. This is excellent for creating high impasto textures. Read the section on creating Rembrandt's thick white impasto paint.

SEVENTH - Make the VISCOUS EMULSION from sun thickened oil and egg white GLAIR (frothed and distilled egg white is called Glair). It takes approximately five minutes to make the Glair and less than a minute to make the Emulsion. Mix 3 spoons of the thickened oil and 2 spoons of the Glair in a jar. Add a couple of pennies. Cap and shake vigorously for one or two minutes. The emulsion has many uses. [1] It can be used to THIN the paint. [2] It can be used to THICKEN the paint [3] It can be used to create an "OIL OUT". An 'oil out' is a lubricant that improves the handling of the oil paint application. [It can be used as a final varnish. Please follow the book's instructions on the making the Glair and on the correct RATIO for making the Emulsions, as well as for the CRUCIAL APPLICATION method of the Emulsion ' OIL OUT'. Please view the DVD on CSO-OIL PAINTING for a better understanding.

EIGHTH - Thin the Oil Paint, or make thick Impasto paint if needed . CSO mixed with tube paint rarely needs thinning. If it does, add one drop of emulsion and grind together with the palette knife, (never use a brush to mix the two). Grind one drop at a time until you get the fluidity you want. Do not dip your brush into the Emulsion and swish it into the paint as a method of thinning paint. That is an unsound habit that weakens the oil paint. To create thick impasto paint, add several drops of the 'viscous emulsion' and grind well with a palette knife. This was Rembrandt's secret on how he created his thick, non-wrinkling, impasto oil paint. You will see how quickly the oil paint will become rigid and stiff and it will not wrinkle when dry. Follow the easy instructions in the book's section: 'Rembrandt's White Oil Paint'.

NINETH - Apply the Emulsion 'Oil Out' by HAND until you feel resistance.
The term ,"OIL OUT" means: "OIL rubbed in and oil wiped OUT".
Please follow the instructions in the book EXACTLY as written. It is crucial to apply the Emulsion correctly. You MUST use your bare hand, NEVER USE A BRUSH. Apply the Emulsion over the surface of the canvas as thinly as possible. GENTLY remove any excess with a dry paper towel or rag. Do this gently and also dry your hands. Then, rub the Emulsion with a moderate pressure in small circular motions with the bare hand, in hand sized areas, UNTIL YOU FEEL A DRAG or a resistance to the rubbing.

The RUBBING creates FRICTION. The friction creates HEAT. The heat EVAPORATES the slight amount of moisture in the egg. You will note that the Emulsion is a milky white color, but as you rub it thinner and thinner, you will see it instantly FLASH into a TRANSPARENT FILM. The Emulsion becomes crystal clear like a sheet of glass. It is important to create an ULTRA-THIN FILM of Emulsion. This thin wet layer of emulsion is called an "Oil Out" because this term describes the actions and the goal in order to achieve an ultra-thin DAMP film on which to paint upon.

Some English speaking artists use the erroneous terms of "cushion' or 'couch' to describe an 'OIL OUT'.
IN ENGLISH, the word 'cushion ' is a pillow.
IN ENGLISH, the word ' couch' is a sofa.
IN FRENCH, the word **'couche'** means a thin film of oil or paint [pronounced ' koo-shay'].

TENTH - Paint onto the DAMP/WET Emulsion film. There is no need to rush as the oil out will remain workable for 12 hours. Always paint onto the DAMP/WET Emulsion using your CSO-OIL PAINT made by mixing a 50/50 mixture of CSO and tube oil paints. When finished, let it dry at least until it is 'tacky dry' before applying another layer. 'Tacky dry' means that the paint has become set and if you rub it with a new layer of emulsion 'oil out', it will not smear. This tacky dry condition takes a different amount of time depending on many factors. Normally this is under 30 hours. Once the paint is 'tacky dry', apply another application of the 'oil out' and begin to paint on top of it while it is damp.

NOTE: If you desire a fuzzy paint layer, do not 'oil out', or, do as Velazquez did at times. Velazquez' work shows fine blending and at times we see a very fine fuzzy dry brush effect. You can duplicate this by allowing the 'oil out' to 'set' for about 6 to 12 hours, then paint onto that damp 'set' sticky film.

ELEVENTH - Paint any number of additional layers. To paint again, repeat the 'oil out' on the dry or "tacky dry" areas you want to paint over. Additional layers can be done as many times as desired. 'Oil Out' any dry spots as you work on the painting. You do not have to wait for the paint to dry 'hard' before applying a new paint layer. It is OK to 'oil out' a 'tacky dry' layer and paint on it. You do not have to 'oil out' the entire painting if all you want to do is correct a small area. Before painting, you must 'oil out', unless you specifically desire a fuzzy dry-brush effect.

NOTE: IF you see that the ' oil out' medium is not sticking well - meaning, that you see it group into droplets - simply dip your finger into a bit of dry chalk and rub it into the ' oil out' emulsion as you are applying it. You will note that the white chalk becomes transparent and not noticeable and will have good adhesion.

NOTE: Once the painting is completed. Allow it to become tacky dry then do this. Apply with your bare hand, an ultra thin layer of the VISCOUS EMULSION all over the entire painting. WIPE off all excess and finish with hand rubbing. This FINAL LAYER is a permanent part of the oil painting and is not removable and it dries with a SILKY SHEEN. Six months later, if you wish a HIGH GLOSS , you can apply a coat of removable dammar varnish, but it is not needed.

TWELFTH - 'FAT ON LEAN' is not required
With CSO OIL PAINTING, there is no need to follow the principal of "FAT ON LEAN".
That principal is ONLY used when SOLVENTS or VARNISHES are mixed into the oil paint.
With CSO, when painting in layers, follow this simple guide:
"Paint FAST drying colors and thin layers of paint in the under layers.
Paint SLOW drying paint colors and thicker paint in the top layers.
THICK paint takes longer to dry. It is best to paint thinly in the lower layer.
Do not apply FAST drying oil paint mixtures on lower layer impasto that has NOT dried hard. When you work on a GRISAILLE or a MUTED COLOR under painting stage, add some BURNT or RAW UMBER to the white oil paint and grind it well together. Umber will accelerate the drying of the white paint.
IMPORTANT NOTICE: Modern white tube oil paint is frequently made with a very slow drying POPPY OIL and this will cause technical problems if the under painting is not dried well.

THE THREE MOST COMMON ERRORS WHEN USING CSO

FIRST ERROR: NOT THINNING THE PAINT CORRECTLY.
Modern painters have habits that are hard to break. They were taught to have a clip-on container attached to the hand palette. Then, to dip their brush into a painting medium liquid, and to swirl it with the paint on the hand palette.
You MUST break this habit. The Old Masters did not thin their paint in that manner. The Old Masters NEVER used these palette cups. Instead, they insured 100% control of their paint, by thinning or thickening the paint on the Grinding Table. A low cost glazed floor tile about 18" X 18" makes a good grinding table. Do not buy a black one nor a white one because these two colors make it difficult to accurately see the colors. Any neutral mid tone color will allow you to see color accurately. Brushes are ineffective 'grinders' because they soak up' liquids like a sponge and thin the paint unequally.

The correct tool for thinning paint is a palette knife. To thin the paint correctly, add ONLY one drop of the Emulsion to the CSO OIL PAINT and grind it well on the Grinding Table. If needed, add one more drop and grind it well together again. Once the desired consistency is achieved, transfer the paint to the hand palette for use.

NOTE: To thin CSO paint made by mixing CSO and Tube paint, use the "VISCOUS EMULSION".
NOTE: To thin the Hand Ground paint made of CSO and dry pigment powder, use the 'NON-VISCOUS' Emulsion.
NOTE: CSO OIL PAINT should not be liquefied. If you desire a thinner paint, thin it with the 'Non-Viscous Emulsion", not with the "Viscous Emulsion".

SECOND ERROR: NOT APPLYING THE EMULSION 'OIL OUT' CORRECTLY.
The Emulsion 'Oil Out' MUST be applied only with the bare hand - NEVER with a brush. In my opinion this application method is the lost secret of the Van Eyck Secret Medium. My experiments allow me to believe the Van Eyck's used ratio mixtures of glair and oil, followed by this very unique application method to achieve their unique effects.

A brush application can never get the layer thin enough, and more importantly, the Emulsion 'Oil Out' must be RUBBED into the surface by hand - **not with a rag because a rag has texture that will lift the paint** – rub with moderate pressure until you feel a drag. A brush cannot apply this ultra-thin film correctly. The Rubbing is crucial. The Emulsion is a true wonder medium, but it will fail if it is not RUBBED in thoroughly. YOU MUST RUB for several minutes until you feel a DRAG or a RESISTANCE to the rubbing. This tension is NOT as noticeable when using canvas, because the weave of the canvas holds the Emulsion like small reservoirs. On wood panels, the tension is felt quickly.

RUBBING causes FRICTION which causes HEAT, which causes the moisture in the egg to EVAPORATE. Once evaporated, the remaining Albumen in the egg will become very sticky and insures the adhesion of the oil to the surface and prevents the viscous oil from dripping or spreading. IF you are rubbing and feel no tension after a few minutes, you have too much Emulsion on the surface. Use a dry rag and GENTLY wipe [DON'T RUB] off all excess from the surface ... and also DRY your hand. Then re-rub the Emulsion with your bare hand. DO NOT RUB WITH A CLOTH or TOWEL.. The aim is to apply the thinnest possible film. Once applied correctly you will paint into the ultra-thin DAMP EMULSION FILM. The Emulsion is a remarkable "Wonder medium" if used correctly and you will be able to paint micro-fine details and fine hair lines like DURER and VAN EYCK.

THIRD ERROR: USING the SUPERIOR SUN THICKENED OIL INCORRECTLY
The UNREFINED cold pressed Sun Thickened oil is a wonderful product. The Old Masters knew of its strength and pliability, and of its fast drying property. They also knew of its GREAT DISADVANTAGE that it will drip and spread uncontrollably. DO NOT make the mistake thinking you can thin your paint with this oil by using it in pure form. IF you try to use this oil in pure form, as a paint thinner, it will cause bleeding, detail distortion and dripping. The Old Masters discovered that addition of a little egg GLAIR [not the egg yolk] in the form of an Emulsion, would STOP the oil from sagging, and to become FIRM so it will stay in place.
Therefore, use this superior oil only for two things.
Mix it with Calcium Carbonate powder to make CSO.
Mix it with Glair to make the 'Viscous Emulsion'.

QUIZ
Take this quiz before you read the book and then again after wards. We learn new things by testing ourselves. This quiz will help you better understand the CSO Method.

Q1. WHY IS AN EMULSION PREFERRED OVER A MIXTURE OF OIL AND RESIN?
A1. When a resin is mixed with oil, they co-mingle. They each dry at a different rate. The Oil will take centuries to 'dry' [oil does not dry by evaporation, it must cure/oxidize], and the resin hardens as soon as any solvent is evaporated. The oil remains pliable and the resin becomes increasingly brittle over a short period of time. The oil if properly cleansed and exposed to sun light remains non yellow while the resin becomes very yellow as it dries over short periods of time. The best example and proof of this is Rembrandt's painting, 'The shooting company of captain Frans Banning Cocq", painted in 1642. When Sir Joshua Reynolds [1723-1793] saw it, he wrote that it was yellowed and so dark, it must be a ' night' scene, so it was called "The Night Watch". The name stuck. Then modern conservation cleansing removed the numerous resin varnish layers. Once completed, Rembrandts true colors were seen. The whites are pure white. The yellows and grays and reds are true. Though it is still called 'The Night Watch', it is clearly an AFTERNOON scene, not a NIGHT scene.

Q2. WHY DOES MY FLAX-LINSEED OIL LOOK YELLOW IN THE JAR?
A1. When the oil is in a jar, the oil is being seen in concentration. If one drop is placed on a pure white glazed plate or tile, and rubbed in thinly, as in painting, the oil is fully transparent and non-yellow. The UV rays of sunlight, direct and indirect, will continue bleaching the oil.

Q3. WHICH IS BEST FOR MAKING 'CSO', CALCIUM CARBONATE CHALK OR CALCIUM SULPHATE?
A3. Calcium Carbonate comes in many varieties. Examples are: Chalk, Calcite, Aragonite, Marble and Mother Nature is not too careful of the purities of these. There are some pure samples in Nature, such as the Chalk from Champagne France. Calcium Sulfate is called Gypsum and in the Italian Renaissance era, before and later, artists used it for making Gesso. This was a mixture of Hide Glue and the Gypsum. When either the Carbonate or the Sulphate are mixed with Hide Glue, the resulting mixture is opaque and solid white. When either is mixed with oil, the resulting mixture is transparent when thin or translucent when thicker [up to a point]. The artists used whichever one was available. In Italy, the Sulphate was more commonly available. In the North of Europe, Holland, etc., the most commonly available was the Carbonate. You can choose the one you like.

Q4. WHAT DID REMBRANDT USE TO MAKE HIS 'CSO'.
A4. Rembrandt did not use the term 'CSO' to describe his chalk oil mixture. 'CSO' is a modern name I created to identify and to be able to academically discuss an oil and Calcium Carbonate mixture. Rembrandt used only Calcium Carbonate Chalk mixed with his oil as an additive to his oil paint. Velazquez used either the Chalk, or the Calcite in making his paint additive mixtures. When the Chalk is mixed with the oil, the CSO is a light beige color and the mixture is very smooth and soft. When the Calcite is mixed with oil the CSO is a brighter white but it is grainy in texture. Artists should experiment with the various powders. At the Kremer store on the internet, they are called "fillers'.

Q5. MUST ONE ALWAYS MEASURE THE RATIO OF CHALK AND OIL WHEN MAKING CSO?
A5. NO. In fact, there are many subtle ratio mixtures of CSO. An artist should experiment to gain intimate knowledge of the materials. However, the ratio I give of 3 parts compressed Chalk [versus a loose amount] and one part oil, results in a generally optimum mixture. My formula is a guide. Artists will note that there are Variables that will impact the result. Using a THIN oil versus a THICK oil will give different results. Also, a THICK oil can vary greatly in and of itself. The Master painters chose and had preference for oil of different viscosities. Rembrandt [his late work] and Rubens chose a viscous thick oil . Velazquez and Van Dyck chose a more fluid oil. Pacheco, Velazquez' teacher wrote that the oil he thickened was ready after 15 days in the hot summer of Seville. I live in San Diego California and the summer heat is temperate. I need 40 to 60 days of summer sun.
The new 'AIR PUMP OIL', even in San Diego, only needs 10 to 15 days of air pump oxygen exposure to make a moderately viscous oil that will dry within 14 hours if used in making the CSO and mixed with tube oil paints. This same oil if made into CSO and mixed with dry pigments will dry in about 5 hours, if used in thin paint layers. In conclusion: Each of us is different and we must experiment to determine our choices.

Q6. HOW MANY 'OIL OUT' MEDIUMS ARE THERE?
A6. CSO has created four. Three are an Emulsion and one is not an Emulsion. They are named and described in the book. Each gives a different result and artists should experiment with each to learn what they will and will not do.

I also wrote that there can be others one can create and use, such as one that is a mixture of garlic juice and oil. This is called ' Alioli', and is in fact a mixture used in cooking in France and Spain. In their recipe, olive oil is used and olive oil is no-drying. Once I saw this mixture, I thought artists can possibly create an oil out medium with use of drying flax/linseed oil and garlic juice. It is recorded some Old Masters rubbed raw garlic on their oil paintings to help prevent the next oil paint layer from beading up and for better adhesion of the new layer. As of this date, I have not finished testing my version of the 'Alioli' mixture. One important point to make is this: Do not use pure oil as the 'oil out' medium. Oil by itself, will spread and drip, especially a polymerized oil. The Emulsion 'Oil out' mixture of the egg glair with oil, stops the new layer of oil paint from spreading or dripping, as does also an addition of chalk which acts as a stabilizer.

Q7. WHAT IS THE SECRET MEDIUM OF THE VAN EYCK BROTHERS?
A7. No one knows because the Van Eycks did not leave a book with instructions. However intelligent artists with a logical approach can use observation and testing to make a valid opinion. I believe the SECRET MEDIUM of the Van Eycks is two things that work together. The first part is a simple Emulsion, like the ' Viscous Emulsion' I created. The second part is a crucial application method and use of that Emulsion. These are described in my book and demonstrated in live film in my DVD on Oil Painting and on the DVD on the Van Eyck Secret Medium.

Q8. SHOULD EGG YOLK OR WHOLE EGG BE USED IN MAKING EMULSIONS FOR OIL PAINTING?
A8. My tests convincingly tell me that neither the yolk alone nor the whole egg scrambled should be used with oil painting. The main reason is that the Yolk has a great amount of slow drying egg oil and it will cure hard and become brittle within a year. The proof that it will cure brittle is the Egg Tempera paint uses either only the yolk or the whole egg AND must never be painted on flexible supports, and only on hard rigid supports. Also, the Egg yolk tempera paint must never be painted thickly or the paint will crack. Flax/Linseed oil will not dry [cure-oxidize] brittle and remains flexible for hundreds of years. This DIFFERENCE of curing time, between egg yolk oil and vegetable Flax/ Linseed oil, is the main scientific chemistry reason not to mix the two oils. The other more easily understood reason is that in oil painting, with flax/ linseed oil as the binder, one does NOT NEED ANYMORE OIL.

Q9. WHY IS THE EGG WHITE THE PREFERRED PART OF THE EGG TO USE IN MAKING AN EGG-OIL EMULSION?

A9. Simply because the egg white has NO EGG OIL. The egg white has a varied consistency and must first be beaten vigorously until it froths. Then the froth is allowed to distill into an evenly balanced liquid. The resulting liquid is called GLAIR. This ancient word simply means 'clear' and refers to the clear of the egg. BY ITSELF, glair is brittle, but when mixed with oil it enters INTO the oil on a molecular level. This is called an Emulsion. Once inside the oil molecule, it will not separate from the oil. Glair is transparent, colorless, limpid not viscous, and fast curing. It does not impede nor impact the oil except in one very important benefit to oil painters. The Glair will cause the thick viscous linseed/ flax oil to stop flowing and thereby stop dripping down the painting. This is its greatest benefit in that by carefully adding it, one can control the flow. By adding a greater amount of glair, the oil paint will completely freeze up and become non-flowing. This allows an artist to create high impasto that will not wrinkle. This was Rembrandt's great secret mixture. His thick viscous oil paint has absolutely no wrinkles. The main ingredient of the Glair is very sticky and is called Albumen. Glair must first be mixed with oil to create an Emulsion before it can be effectively mixed with oil paint.

Q.10. WHAT IS MUCILAGE IN OIL AND WHY MUST IT BE REMOVED?

A.10. First, there are no "LIN" seeds in nature. People ask, " then where does LINSEED oil come from?" The oil known as Linseed oil is pressed from dry ripe FLAX SEEDS. These seeds are tiny and the shell is hard. It takes great pressure to press the oil. In the old days, artists used screw presses. Today hydraulic presses are used. Either one pulverizes the shells and the oil that is released contains minute husk particulate from the seed husks. The fresh pressed oil also contains the mucilage. Mucilage is held in full suspension in the oil and no amount of time left standing will remove the mucilage. The heavy seed husk particulate will drop over time but much of the husk particulate will not. Mechanical filtration will remove most of the particulate but it will not remove the mucilage. Mucilage is invisible to the unaided human eye. When a method is used to group up the mucilage it is snowy white in color, and grouped together it resembles a very fine powder. This mucilage will ferment, and decompose over time. It then gets darker and finally becomes the color of dark brown. If the mucilage is not removed, any oil paint made with this unclean oil will darken over time. The darkening changes the oil paint colors and is irreversible. A good example of decomposition and darkening is seen in a banana. When fresh, the outside peeling is a bright beautiful yellow. But, with each passing day, it soon gets dark spots then finally turning completely dark brown black. Once it is dark, it is irreversible.

Q.11. WHAT FACTORS DETERMINE THE DRYING OF OIL PAINT?
A.11. Artists can control the drying of their paint, making it slower or faster drying,
PIGMENT: Some colors dry faster than others. Umber is a very fast drying color.
THICKNESS: Thick paint layers dry slower than thin paint layers.
VENTILATION: Ventilation that is moving makes oil paint dry faster than stagnant air.
HUMIDITY: Dry air dries faster than humid moist air.
TEMPERATURE: Hot air dries faster than cold air.
OIL CHOICE: Polymerized oil dries faster than non-polymerized oil. Mixing Polymerized oil and non-polymerized oils in various ratios will alter the drying. Normally, Flax oil dries faster than poppy or walnut oils.
INERT ADDITIVES: Adding substances such as chalk or powdered glass causes oil paint to dry faster.
METALLIC DRIERS, RESINS AND SOLVENTS: These hazardous, toxic, carcinogenic materials are not used in the CSO method of oil painting because they are hazardous and damage the oil paint. Driers darken oil paint and cause brittle paint. Solvents cause a break of binder from pigment powder. Resins turn yellow. These conditions are not desirable.

TEACHING AND LEARNING PAINTING

To learn FINE ART painting you must have a good teacher who will teach the TECHNICAL part of painting. My book does not teach the AESTHETICS of painting. I leave this up to you to see original paintings, read the biographies of great Master painters, talk with your friends and things that will IMPACT YOU and lift your passion for EXPRESSING YOUR THOUGHTS AND IDEAS. The mission of my book is to teach safe and permanent methods of painting.

I wish I could teach every artist this remarkable method of CSO / EMULSIONS in person. BUT, obviously, I cannot do that. I found that a book is a good teacher for some artists and not good for others. This is because many artists do not want to read. They just want to be SHOWN HOW TO DO SOMETHING. Like, HOW TO make the emulsion, or how to apply it ... etc.

You will note that my book has no photos nor drawings or diagrams. My website has numerous color photos that will help artists understand the various topics discussed. I also post all UPDATES on my website. And I invite artists to write to me with questions. I respond to all E-mail inquiries with answers to all questions.

I have made 5 DVD'S that will be very helpful for artists to learn how to master the CSO / EMULSIONS method of Oil Painting. I have always said that the method is so SIMPLE and EASY. It IS very simple but yes, the foundation of the CSO/ EMULSIONS method is VERY profound, and no other book, university professor or private painting teacher, or videos are teaching it. I recommend students view the DVDS first then read the book for a more detailed fuller understanding of the method. Here are the FIVE DVD'S I have produced. They are available online. Check my website for offers.

NOTE: ALL MY DVDS are on NTSC FORMAT. I understand all modern computers and DVD players will play both the PAL and the NTSC.

DVD: "OIL PAINTING WITH CALCITE SUN OIL" NTSC, COLOR, 85 MIN, ENGLISH, -R DISC. A DVD FOR TODAY'S ADVANCED AND PROFESSIONAL PAINTERS WHO PAINT IN MODERN STYLES, OR OLD MASTER STYLES. Learn the Methods and Materials used by REMBRANDT, RUBENS, VELAZQUEZ, VAN EYCK and other great Old Masters. The live action teaches how to prepare your own SUPERIOR OIL used by the Old Masters, plus preparation and use of the Emulsions, plus much more.

DVD: " TEMPERA PAINTING WITH CSO-EGG TEMPERA - R DISC, NTSC, COLOR, ENGLISH, 56 MINUTES. THE FIRST IMPROVEMENT IN EGG TEMPERA IN 600 YEARS since CENNINO CENNINI WROTE HIS BOOK IN THE EARLY 1400'S . NOW ARTISTS CAN PAINT WITH FULL IMPASTO IN A MORE DIRECT MANNER WHILE ALSO PAINTING THINLY AS IN THE RENNAISSANCE METHOD.

DVD: "THE NEW MILK OIL PAINT AND THE VAN EYCK SECRET MEDIUM"
THE ADVANCED VERSION OF MILK OIL PAINT FOR ADVANCED PAINTERS
-R DISC, NTSC, COLOR, ENGLISH, 90 MINUTES .
The new " MILK OIL PAINT" medium, and the details of the Secret Medium of the VAN EYCKS.
CONTENTS: 1. Milk Oil Paint 2. CSO-CASEIN TEMPERA PAINT 3. UNDERPAINTING WITH CASEIN TEMPERA 4. VAN EYCK SECRET MEDIUM 5. DETAILED TECHNICAL INFORMATION 6. ADDITIONAL TECHNICAL INFORMATION

DVD : 'OIL PAINTING WITH MILK: Safety for new painters and School Art Classes"
BEGINNERS VERSION OF MILK OIL PAINT --R DISC, NTSC, COLOR, ENGLISH, 64 MINUTES
THIN WASHES DRY IN 5 MINUTES. IMPASTO DRIES IN 1 HOUR. Use alone, or as a FAST DRYING UNDER PAINT LAYER FOR TRADITIONAL OIL PAINTS. MILK OIL PAINT is a new 21st century oil paint, it is not a Tempera paint .Learn how to mix the "MILK GEL" with normal tube oil paints. This new discovery replaces expensive water-miscible oil paints and their various thinners! MILK is pure CASEIN and milk nothing new to painting. Milk is an ancient paint binder used since humans first opened their minds and eyes to the beauty of ART creation. HOWEVER , I have developed a remarkable NEW OIL PAINT FORMULATION, a new METHOD and PROCEDURE for easily using MILK with OIL PAINTS. Do not confuse MILK OIL PAINT with CASEIN TEMPERA PAINT. Now, NEW PAINTERS, SCHOOL ART STUDENTS and ART TEACHERS can create wonderful oil paintings in a SAFE environment without use of hazardous or toxic materials.

DVD: OIL PAINTING RUBENS [warning; this DVD contains hazardous materials]
 -R DISC, ENGLISH, NTSC, 85 MINUTES. **WARNING:** *My site, Books and DVDS focus on SAFETY FOR ARTISTS. However, Rubens' paintings are so important that I felt obligated to study his methods and materials in depth. THE RUBENS DVD CONTAINS USE OF HAZARDOUS MATERIALS and demonstrates RUBENS' use of HAZARDOUS MATERIALS.THIS DVD is not for children nor amateurs. It is STRICTLY an academic research project to preserve RUBENS' knowledge for advanced artists who are interested in better understanding his methods and materials. The DVD has live demonstration on FOUR recipes using PINE TREE TAR RESIN - , two are NON HAZARDOUS and TWO ARE HAZARDOUS. In addition, instruction on the CASEIN TEMPERA medium of painting is included.*

PART ONE: OIL PAINTING

The subject of Oil Painting was divided into two parts.
PART ONE has the information to proceed with understanding the CSO/EMULSIONS methods.
PART TWO has miscellaneous research and developments the artist will find to be helpful.

CHAPTER ONE
TWO IMPORTANT 21ST CENTURY ADVANCEMENTS
THE REBIRTH OF THE OLD MASTERS' SUPERIOR OIL
THE 'CALCITE SUN OIL / EMULSIONS METHOD

THE MOST IMPORTANT aspect of the oil painting medium is in removing the mucilage from the unrefined FLAX SEED oil. This realization came to me early as I developed the 'Calcite Sun Oil'/ Emulsions, method of oil painting. The Old Masters' Superior oil is the foundation and backbone of the greatest oil paintings of history. Today's Artists cannot match the permanence nor the beauty of the 'paint quality' of the Old Masters with the industrial alkali refined linseed oil sold in art stores.

'Superior Linseed/Flax Oil', is a term I created out of necessity to distinguish it from the modern industrial linseed oils, such as Alkali Refined Linseed Oil, Alkali Refined Stand Linseed Oil, and others made of chemically REFINED oils. Artists should be aware of the oil labeled as 'sun thickened linseed oil', sold in brand name art stores. These misleading oils are NOT equal to the Superior oil used by the Old Masters. Read the very small fine print on the back label. It will say it is Alkali Refined Linseed Oil. This oil is a very slow drying oil as are other industrial linseed oils that have been treated by caustic chemicals. The term, "STAND LINSEED OIL" is a clever marketing misnomer that fools the unwary artists. Today's STAND LINSEED OIL should be labeled for what it is – BOILED OIL- because is nothing more than oil that has been BOILED far past the safe heating temperature of 230 degrees Celsius. Linseed/ Flax oil begins decomposing once heated past 230 degrees Celsius. This means the oil's normal lifespan of the known and proven age of over 600 years, is shortened and prematurely aged.

'Calcite Sun Oil'[CSO] , is a new and revolutionary **Grinding Oil Paint Binder** for Oil Painting based on modern scientific studies of ancient knowledge. Scientific studies established the use of Calcium Carbonate in the excellently preserved 380 year old paintings of the 17Th century masters, Velazquez and Rembrandt, Rubens and the Van Eycks. The CSO method makes possible for today's painters to recapture and duplicate the marvelous effects we admire in the Old Masters' paintings. We can do this safely and easily.

In 1988, the National Gallery of London published their results showing calcium carbonate in Rembrandt's paint as well as Protein Emulsion mixtures in the oil paint. Later studies by the eminent Rembrandt scholar, Ernst Van De Wetering, and other studies also show use of Calcium carbonate and Emulsions in the paintings of Rembrandt and the Van Eyck brothers.

In 1992, the Prado Museum in Madrid, Spain, published the results of their scientific studies of the paintings by Diego Velazquez. The study, overseen by Ms. Carmen Garrido-Perez, the Director of the Prado's Conservation Department, showed Velazquez added large quantities of calcium carbonate **to all his colors, not just the white**, as well as finding he added protein emulsions into his paint. Studies by other scientist show Peter Paul Rubens added calcium carbonate powder and protein emulsions to his paint. Later you will read WHY these master artists added both of these ingredients to their oil paint and when you yourself use them you will experience a beauty and control of the oil paint medium as never before.

Beginning in the year 2000, the knowledge uncovered by the scientists, led me to experiment and to formulate 'Calcite Sun Oil'. Its abbreviated name is CSO and it is a mixture of a superior Linseed/Flax Oil mixed in a specific ratio proportion with Calcium Carbonate Chalk into a viscous substance. This mixture dries into a hard and permanent cement bound by the pliability of the oxidized flax oil binder with the powdered limestone powder.
CSO is outstanding for those artists choosing to make their own paint with dry pigments, and ideal for artists who use modern tube oil paints. My testing and experiments resulted in specific methods of application, allowing today's painters to achieve the effects of the Old Masters' paint quality. Equally important, 'Calcite Sun Oil', offers the contemporary oil painter complete safety and permanence, without use of any hazardous solvents, resins, varnishes or driers.

The CSO method of oil painting, rests solidly on the superior oil of the Old Masters, which is defined as: *UNREFINED, cold pressed, linseed/flax oil that has been safely cleansed of its mucilage, then slowly sun thickened in the hot summer sun until its natural moisture has been evaporated, where the oil is bleached pale, with a requisite degree of viscosity*. **This is the oil used by the Old Masters, and is the foundation of the preservation of their 500 year old paintings.** Later you will read of a new 21st century advancement where we can create a superior oil equal to that of the Old Masters by means unavailable to them. This is the "AIR PUMP OIL'.

THE REBIRTH OF THE OLD MASTERS' OIL
THE TRADITIONAL SUPERIOR OIL OF THE OLD MASTERS
Their oil disappeared in the 19th century with the onset of the Industrial revolution, and its chemical cleansing of Linseed oil. One of my main goals is to raise awareness of the true facts about the Old Masters' oil and to distinguish it from 'modern" industrially produced alkali refined Linseed Oil, used in oil painting since the 19TH century.

THE 19TH AND 20TH CENTURY'S MISTAKEN ART "EXPERTS"
The 19th century ushered in advancements in Science and Technology. Still many Artists, Scientists and Authors of the 19th and 20th centuries made wrong guesses about the materials used by the Old Masters. Ancient manuscripts were studied but incomplete information, or outdated words, or errors in translations led many astray.

A brief list of famous art "experts" includes the names of; Eastlake, Laurie, Doerner, Maroger, Taubes, Mayer, and many others. Some of these were painters, others were not. Each of these persons wrote books giving their opinions of the materials used by the Old Masters. Frequently, these "experts" vehemently disagreed with each other. Science has proven many of the views of these men regarding materials of the Old Masters to be completely wrong.

Some authors of the 20th century stated Rembrandt mixed resins with his paint. Modern Science has shown Rembrandt did not mix resins with his paint. Jacques Maroger stated Rembrandt used great amounts of wax to make his thick paint impasto. Science has shown no use of wax, but found great amounts of Calcium Carbonate powder was mixed with Rembrandt's paint to increase its body as well as a protein additive. This book contains a lengthy study of Maroger's formulas and explains why he failed. Mayer's erroneous use of soft resins can easily be proven to be hazardous to the painting's archival permanence.

Taubes wrote that true cold pressed linseed oil was unavailable in the USA at mid-20th century, thus, indicating why he never used it nor knew of its great value. Taubes scoffed at the suggestion that Rembrandt added Calcium Carbonate to make his thick impasto paint. Modern Science shows Rembrandt added Calcium Carbonate as well as a protein additive to his paint to make his thick impasto paint.

These authors also made numerous faulty Emulsion recipes, adding solvents and resins, and water to the oil, in trying to compensate for the deficiencies caused by the alkali refined oil. This caused their recipes to fail, and continued the ignorance of the important knowledge and benefits of properly made Emulsions.

My criticism of the dedicated work of these authors – excepting the failed mixtures of Jacques Maroger – **should not detract from the many important observations they wrote about. The real problem they had was faulty incomplete science. I am indebted to the many fine studies by these men.**

The 19th century industrially produced Linseed oil is still the main oil in use today by artists. Linseed Oil and Flax Oil are BOTH pressed from the same FLAX SEEDS. There are no 'Lin-seeds' in nature but the word 'linon' meant 'flax' in ancient Greece. Modern industry produces two distinct variations of this oil named differently because of how the oil is processed. Oil processed with caustic chemicals is not safe for human dietary ingestion, therefore it received the industrial name of ' LINSEED OIL". Modern laws require truthful labeling of materials sold to the public, therefore we have one oil labeled 'LINSEED OIL' and one labeled 'FLAX OIL'. Flax oil is safe for humans to drink for health reasons. More importantly, the oil with the label 'Linseed Oil', and the oil labeled 'Flax Oil', have very different handling and drying properties which are extremely important to oil painting.

The oil with the 'Linseed oil' label is processed for numerous uses in the industrial market while the oil with the 'Flax oil' label is processed differently and used for human health consumption. Besides being used for waterproofing wood and other Industrial uses, the 'Linseed oil' is used in the manufacturing of Artist's oil paints, oil painting mediums and is always labeled LINSEED OIL. The most important deficiency of modern 'Linseed oil' is its slow drying. To solve this deficiency, artists add undesirable and hazardous Solvents, Resins, Varnishes and Driers to their oil paint. These ingredients negatively impact the health of the artist, as well as lowering the archival permanence of the painting. It also impacts the manipulation of the paint upon application.

Industrial 'Linseed oil' labels state the oil is Alkali REFINED, meaning the oil has been cleansed with caustic lye chemicals such as sodium hydroxide, and exposed at times to heat over 500 degrees Fahrenheit. Even with food grade FLAX OIL, the labels state the oil is 'Cold Pressed' even though this is not true, as the pressing by the hydraulic machinery heats the oil up to 110 degrees Fahrenheit. 110 degrees Fahrenheit is a safe temperature, as the oil does not begin decomposition until it is heated past 230 degrees Celsius. Some labels of art store 'Linseed Oil' say the oil is COLD PRESSED, BUT DO NOT state the oil is UNREFINED, because it has received some form of solvent chemical refinement.

THE OLD MASTERS' SUPERIOR OIL IS AVAILABLE TODAY
The oil the Old Masters used was crude raw UNREFINED oil cold pressed from FLAX seeds. Through oral tradition and centuries of observation, they recognized the irreversible browning of the paint caused by the decomposition and fermentation of the mucilage. Old treatises give numerous and various methods to cleanse the oil of the mucilage and the seed husk particulate caused by the pressing. Wikipedia says that mucilage is a 'polar glycoprotein' and a 'exopolysaccharide' and that flaxseeds are a rich source of it.

The Old Masters' superior FLAX OIL is not sold in Art supply stores as ' Linseed Oil is. But, it is sold today as FLAX OIL at health food stores. Unrefined FLAX OIL is the oil closest to that used by the Old Masters with one possible exception which is explained later. Unfortunately, though FLAX oil is abundantly available, it is not in a ready-to-use condition and it must be processed at home. The cleansing process is simple but certain equipment and materials are needed and approximately 8 to 10 days are required to remove the mucilage. Sun Thickening requires an additional 30 to 60 days of summer heat and direct sun rays, depending on one's geographical location. The new AIR PUMP METHOD described below cuts the thickening process to 15 days.

IMPORTANT NOTE: In 2012 I learned of a new method to thicken the oil within 15 days. This is known as the "AIR PUMP METHOD". In conjunction with that, in 2012 I developed a new method to remove the mucilage from the oil in one day. It also will be described in full, later. The label on FLAX OIL will state it is UNREFINED. It is crucial for unrefined oils to be cleansed of its mucilage before ever being sun thickened.

IMPORTANT CAUTION: Artists must read the label of the FLAX SEED oil very carefully. One must not use Flaxseed oil that has had any antioxidant additives such as Vitamin E, C, or Tocopherols, Polypherols, Rosemary, or anything that is added to keep the oil from oxidizing. Manufacturers add anti-oxidants to preserve the sweet taste of the oil. Oil that is exposed to oxygen begins to become acidic and this gives the oil a sour taste. Persons who drink the oil demand a sweet taste and if it tastes sour they call it ' rancid' or ' spoiled'. However, artists demand that the oil be allowed to oxidize naturally, and want it to become acidic over time. This is how the oil cures by becoming 'hard', or 'dry . This can only happen by exposing the oil to oxygen. Read the fine print on the labels.

Artists must also beware not to buy any flaxseed oil processed for pets, normally used as a laxative for dogs and horses. It has antioxidants such as Rosemary added. Also, do not buy flaxseed oil labeled ' Highest Lignans" this oil has had additives that make the oil a dark brown-black color.

THE 'CALCITE SUN OIL/ EMULSIONS METHOD'

Since I was age 13, and for almost 50 years, I followed the leadership of previous "experts". Like others, I painted with oil paints using their formulas of Solvents, Resins, Varnishes and Driers, and like all others, I used the only linseed oil available to me from the art store: ALKALI REFINED LINSEED OIL.

After years of frustration in using their materials, I began to seek answers. Several years ago, I determined the underlying problem with the materials and formulas of ALL these previous 'experts', was their use and dependency of modern Industry produced ALKALI REFINED LINSEED OIL.

In the 1930's, Maroger flatly stated that modern alkali refined 'Stand Linseed Oil' was equivalent to the oil used by the Van Eycks. His infamous failures proved him wrong. Taubes wrote that modern alkali refined Stand Linseed Oil was superior to the Old Masters' Sun Thickened Linseed Oil. Taubes was faced with unique issues. He himself wrote in the 1950's that unrefined flax oil was not even available to the public. And secondly, he needed the low cost industrial oil to be able to produce his line of paint mediums named after himself known as 'Taubes' copal resin painting mediums. Neither of these persons wrote about the very important properties of UNREFINED FLAX OIL, nor even of methods on how to cleanse the oil of the mucilage. Their ignorance of the facts is shown by their omission in their numerous published books.

The problems I encountered with the then current materials and application processes of Taubes, Mayer, Maroger, Doerner, Eastlake, and many others led to my development of the **'Calcite Sun Oil/ Emulsions' method of Oil Painting**. This ancient method is new and revolutionary for today's artists, and it is so very simple. It uses only three simple ingredients. 1. The superior flax oil cleansed and sun thickened. 2. Egg white Glair. 3. Calcium Carbonate powder which is powdered limestone. It is all so simple but it rests on a very profound academic foundation, based on the knowledge and wisdom of the greatest of the Old Masters. What I did was learn through my personal testing and studies, HOW TO MIX AND USE, these three ingredients, and this book and my DVDS will teach you this ancient knowledge.

The success of the CSO method rests squarely on the superior oil of the Old Masters which I have named, the **'Superior Linseed/Flax Oil of the Old Masters'** in order to avoid confusing it with industrial oil. I cannot overstate the importance of this 'Superior Linseed/Flax Oil'. Its superior properties make it possible for today's oil painters to discard and eliminate ALL hazardous and toxic Solvents, Resins, Varnishes, and Driers from Oil Painting, while increasing the permanence of the artwork and facilitating the handling of the paint. The results are truly extraordinary.

SAFETY WARNING

Safety is important to all of us. My claim of Safety and Permanence does not include the artist's choices of dry pigment powders, or tube oil paints, many of which are toxic. See the book in the bibliography by Monona Rossol. It is an excellent guide for safe choices of pigments and tube oil paints. Always read the labels.

CSO, FOR USE WITH MODERN TUBE OIL PAINTS

Oil Paints bought in tubes are available in many colors. They are convenient but if they are used right from the tube with no additives, they have many deficient properties. 'Calcite Sun Oil' is a revolutionary Grinding Oil, that is IDEAL for the contemporary painter using tube oil paints. 'Calcite Sun Oil' eliminates all the deficiencies of tube oil paint, especially the distorting and disturbing "suede effect" common to use of modern tube oil paints. This unsightly 'suede effect' is caused by the additives placed in modern tube oil paints such as aluminum stearate.

The Sun thickened Superior oil used in making the 'CSO', changes the lack of viscosity of the tube paint, to a high degree of enamel-like viscosity, while the calcium carbonate creates **a firm non-collapsing body** with sensuous textures , while providing ten important benefits. When mixed with tube paint, it creates the beneficial "resin effect" which is explained in this book. The increased viscosity allows easy application and brushing with thinning generally not required. Fluid brushstrokes preserve brush markings and blending becomes effortless, while allowing the retention of firm textures. There is no sagging nor dripping of paint. Extraordinarily fine micro-lines, with sharp clear edges like those in paintings of Durer and other Old Masters are made possible.

HAND GRINDING PAINT LIKE THE OLD MASTERS

Some ask the question, "Why make paint when I can buy it?" This book will answer the question and I believe it will encourage others to grind their own. Dry pigment powders must first be ground into a thick paste with cleansed, thin oil that has not yet been thickened. "Calcite Sun Oil", is then added to this paste in approximately equal amounts or less. This mixture creates a thick, viscous, enamel-like paint that can be thinned with the 'viscous emulsion". The dry pigment powders must not be ground with thick oil because the highly viscous oil reacts much differently than that of thin non thickened oil.

When CSO is mixed with either modern tube oil paints, or when CSO is mixed with Hand ground paints, we can: "Achieve the Old Masters' Paint Quality with complete Safety and Permanence".

CHAPTER TWO
THE REBIRTH OF THE OLD MASTERS' OIL

DEFINITION OF THE OIL USED BY THE OLD MASTERS
My book was first published in 2004 and is the first to publish the accurate definition of the oil used by the Old Masters, which is: UNREFINED FLAX OIL that has been cold pressed, safely cleansed without caustic lye chemicals, and slowly sun thickened to a requisite viscosity. This oil is called "THE SUPERIOR OIL OF THE OLD MASTERS".

At times in this book, I may call it: THE OLD MASTERS' OIL, or THE OLD MASTERS' SUPERIOR OIL, or, SUN OIL, SUNNED OIL, or SUN THICKENED OIL, or 'THICK OIL", or FLAX/LINSEED OIL , or, LINSEED/FLAX OIL , or simply the 'OIL'. For purposes of this book, these various names refer to the SUPERIOR OIL OF THE OLD MASTERS defined above.

I DO NOT USE THESE VARIOUS TERMS WHEN I AM REFERRING TO MODERN INDUSTRIAL LINSEED OIL that has been cleansed by CAUSTIC LYE, or BOILED to make it thick.

The highest levels of contemporary academic authors have failed to accurately define the oil used by the Old Masters for several reasons.
ONE, they are not practicing oil painters therefore they do not understand how the oil medium functions as a painting is in progress.
TWO, they have not made the actual experiments to determine the properties of the oil.
THREE, the modern academics have erroneously accepted and trusted the market place advertising of modern Industrial Linseed oil as being either equal to or superior to the oil of the Old Masters. My experiments prove them to be wrong as do the 500 year old paintings of the Van Eycks.

IT IS AN IRREFUTABLE FACT: The Old Masters did not have modern ALKALI REFINED LINSEED OIL, which is a modern invention, and was not available to the Old Masters. Their 500 year old paintings attest to the permanence of their safely cleansed UNREFINED flax oil. The Old Masters' oil clearly has superior properties that are crucial to the painting process and to the permanence of the painting.

THE OLD MASTERS' OIL AND OIL PAINT [1300's through to the 1700's]

The Old Masters used the same basic materials for oil painting, but each one mixed and applied them in their own personal unique methods. Certainly some Old Masters had studio secrets as science has shown the use of adding protein substances to the oil paint was unknown until late in the 20th century.

The two most basic materials in Oil Painting are: (1) the oil, and (2) the dry pigment powder.
Several oils have been used throughout history, but the most widely used has been Linseed/Flax Oil. The greatest Masters have used it, and many of their paintings survive with excellent color retention and clarity. They removed the mucilage by several methods. They then bleached and thickened their oil by sun exposure in summer to make a fast drying oil that dried harder than non-sun oil. This process causes the linseed/Flax oil to become water-clear. Removal from the sun causes the linseed/Flax oil to change to a pale yellow color, but the color remains noticeably much lighter than the dark orange-yellow color of non-sun oil and is completely colorless when used thinly. My controlled tests prove that Linseed/Flax oil will NOT return to its original natural darker orange-yellow color after removal from the sun. Even when kept in total darkness for over a year, it remains a much more pale color.

Additionally it is important to note that when seen in concentration in a jar, the linseed flax oil appears to be a pale yellow- but when a drop of the oil is spread and rubbed very thinly on a surface, the oil is completely colorless. Historically, some artists preferred to use Poppy oil for the light colors because in its natural state Poppy oil is very pale. The disadvantage is that Poppy oil is very slow drying. Others preferred to use Walnut oil but modern conservation scholars as well as the DeMayerne Manuscript of the 17th century, state that walnut oil when once darkened on drying, cannot be bleached by exposure to sunlight. Exposing an old painting to sunlight will bleach out any yellowish ting of the Linseed/Flax Oil as Peter Paul Rubens wrote in the 17th century. This was confirmed by Mr. Harry Levison in the early 20th century through controlled testing.

CHALLENGES THE OLD MASTERS' FACED WITH THEIR TWO OILS
POLYMERIZED OIL and NON-POLYMERIZED OIL

The Old Masters made their BASIC Oil Paint by grinding oil with dry pigment powder. It is easy to do and takes only minutes. The choice of the oil determines the properties of the paint. The Old Masters' used oils having two different conditions of polymerization [viscosity, thickening].

(1) NON-POLYMERIZED OIL: Cleansed, unrefined, cold pressed, linseed/Flax oil which is also called THIN OIL. It is thin like water, and non-viscous, and had not been heated nor not exposed to the sun. This oil is not sticky and is an extremely slow drying oil.
(2) POLYMERIZED OIL: The same oil as above but purposely thickened to become very viscous, which is also called THICK OIL because it is thick and very sticky like honey. This oil dries faster.

There were two basic methods to Polymerize the oil.
The fast method was to heat the oil over a fire at a very low temperature for several hours, causing the oil to thicken. Excessive heat such as heating the oil at high temperatures above 230 Celsius decomposes the oil, shortening its life span. It causes the oil to become thickened but the oil dramatically becomes a dark brown yellow color permanently. Lacking modern thermometers, but following centuries of oral tradition, the Old Masters placed a goose quill in the oil as it was being heated. IF it burnt and became black, the fire was too hot and it was lowered. Modern science shows the goose quill to burn black at 200 degrees Celsius.
The slow method was to expose the oil to the sun and air for approximately 20 to 60 days. The sun method allowed the oil to do the thickening process naturally. The oil thickened gradually and slowly as it bleached water white clear, and its inherent moisture became evaporated. To keep the oil drying evenly, the artist stirred the oil at least once or twice a day.
NOTE: Read later about the NEW 'AIR PUMP OIL" that takes only 15 days to thicken the oil.

ADVANTAGES AND DISADVANTAGES
OF THICK POLYMERIZED OIL and THIN NON-POLYMERIZED OIL
The oil paint made from these two oils had advantages and disadvantages.
The Old Masters knew the differences and properties of each and used them to their advantage.

(1) Paint made with NON-POLYMERIZED oil dried extremely slowly, taking 6 to 12 days, even under the best of conditions. This slow drying condition is not conducive to creative work, or to the demands of commerce. It also dried matte without luster, had poor color depth, the dry oil skin was relatively fragile, and blending was difficult. Its only advantage was that it did not sag when it was applied to the canvas or panel, and it retained a firm stand-up texture.

(2) Paint made with POLYMERIZED oil had many advantages. It dried exceptionally fast, within 30 hours, depending on the factors that affect the drying of all paint. In addition, this paint dried with a tough glossy skin, had deep color luster, and blending was exceptionally easy. This oil also had major disadvantages: when this paint was applied to a vertical surface, the paint sagged, dripped, lost all texture, lost fine details, and caused distortions, as well as wrinkling badly if it was excessively thick or liquid.

LINSEED OIL PROBLEMS and SOLUTIONS
Seeing that the advantages of paint made with viscous Polymerized oil were important, but the deficiencies were disastrous, the early oil painters sought solutions. What could be mixed with their drying oil to eliminate the deficiencies?

Therein BEGAN the development of oil painting, as painters everywhere tried to find the solution. By the excellent preservation and extraordinary effects of the 15th century Flemish paintings, we know painters such as the Van Eyck brothers, did successfully develop a workable medium. However, they did not record their EXACT knowledge and it has been lost to history. Therein lies the confusion and disagreements we have inherited from so many experiments, by so many theorists and 'experts', over the past five centuries.

THE VAN EYCK MEDIUM QUESTION REMAINS
EXACTLY what MATERIALS and MEDIUM MIXTURES and what APPLICATION METHODS did the Van Eyck brothers actually use, to paint their exceptionally preserved and extraordinarily executed paintings? We will never know because they did not leave us a book with the information, or if it exists it has not yet been found. A later chapter has the results of my experiments with this subject, and how Egg glair-Oil Emulsions play an extremely important part in the exciting new mastery of oil paint enabled by 'Calcite Sun Oil' and the "wonder medium" of Emulsions.

Today's experts, like the many illustrious and some infamous 'experts' of past generations, continue to disagree on many important points. Our modern scientific equipment is helping unravel the secrets, but much more work is needed as conclusions are debatable. I admit that I do not have all the answers, but I am proud of the advancements I have managed to successfully complete.

CHAPTER THREE
CLEANSING THE OIL
REMOVING THE MUCILAGE

THE MOST IMPORTANT ISSUE OF THE OIL PAINTING MEDIUM IS TO REMOVE THE MUCILAGE FROM THE CRUDE, RAW, UNREFINED FLAXSEED OIL. This chapter is dedicated to raising the awareness of artists, and for those truly concerned with archival permanence of their paintings, by helping them understand this most crucial and extremely important aspect of Oil Painting. Nothing is more important than the removal of all Mucilage and crushed seed shell Particulate from the oil. When using Linseed/ Flax oil, the question about 'yellowing' is not important because daylight bleaches any yellowing from the paint film. What is critically important, is that IF the MUCILAGE is NOT removed from the oil, the oil paint made with it will become dark BROWN over time. This browning is a permanent irreversible condition and it will NEVER bleach. Over much time, the once bright beautiful colors will lose their brilliancy and become permanently darker in tonal value.

IMPORTANCE OF THE CLEANSING OF THE OIL
Mucilage-free linseed/flax oil is the foundation of the oil painting medium. It can be compared to building a house on stone vs. sand. One can have the finest ground pigments, but if the oil is inferior, this will alter and ruin the brilliancy of hue, value and chromatic brilliance over the years, as the oil darkens to amber yellow brown. MUCILAGE must be removed from the oil.

In the 17th century, Francisco Pacheco did not know the word 'Mucilage' to describe what is now commonly known to be an integral part of the oil. Empirical knowledge taught the Old Masters that mucilage is the cause of the darkening of the oil paint made with unclean oil This 'browning' causes colors to lose their brightness of hue, brightness/ chroma and lighting value over time, as the film of oil oxidizes. Science informs us the oil oxidizes over hundreds of years, during which time the oil film will absorb and release oxygen continuously, oxygen that contains moisture in varying amounts. This oxygen and moisture causes the mucilage to ferment, decompose, and darken.

I RECOMMEND TWO METHODS TO REMOVE MUCILAGE

The 'CSO-PSYLLIUM HUSK- ALCOHOL' method I developed several years ago is the easiest and most effective method of removing the mucilage from the unrefined flaxseed oil. It takes 8 to 10 days to remove the mucilage.

The 'CSO-GEL' method I recently developed is also very effective and will remove the mucilage in one day. This method requires a bit more effort.

The "PsylliumHusk-Alcohol" method is based on Francisco Pacheco's method in which Lavender flower buds are used. Unfortunately, Pacheco's method with lavendar flower buds leaves a LAVENDER SPIKE SOLVENT in the oil and is to be avoided by persons wishing to avoid contact with solvents. In contrast, the 'CSO-Psyllium husk-Alcohol' and 'CSO-GEL' methods are completely safe and have no solvent residue.

THE FINEST METHOD FOR REMOVING THE MUCILAGE
IS THE ' PSYLLIUM HUSK-ALCOHOL' METHOD

NOTE: USE 80 PROOF LIQUOR or 101 PROOF LIQUOR, BUT NOT STRONGER

NOTE: FLUID OUNCES and VOLUME OUNCES ARE THE SAME.

NOTE: DO NOT MEASURE THE DRY HUSK BY DRY WEIGHT.

The husk is sold POWDERED or WHOLE HUSK. Both grades are equally usable.

The measurements are used as a guide and need not be exact. You do not need a science laboratory to make the measurements. To make things easier, instead of measuring ounces or milliliters, use the easy measurement of "PARTS". Use any type container whether it is a teaspoon a tablespoon or a cup. This will make measuring easier.

IMPORTANT UPDATE NOTE: RECIPE CHANGES

When I first created the ' Psyllium Husk-Alcohol ' method that I based on Pacheco's measurements and materials I had no knowledge how strong his liquor was. *His ratios were 16 ounces of oil, 3 ounces of liquor and 2 ounces of Lavender flower buds.* It was much time before I finally learned what Pacheco's alcoholic strength was. My original recipe in my books and DVDS is the use of 16 ounces of oil, 3 to 4 ounces of 80 proof liquor and 2 ounces of dry husk. **This original recipe has worked well over the years.**
Tests clearly show that 6 ounces of liquor works better than 3 or 4 ounces liquor.
One can continue to use my original recipe in my past writings and DVD information. However, I RECOMMEND use the new updated RECIPE for the ' Psyllium Husk- Alcohol' method.

NEW UPDATED RECIPE: THE PSYLLIUM HUSK-ALCOHOL METHOD
MEASUREMENT IN PARTS: 16 parts oil – 6 parts liquor – 2 parts husk

MEASUREMENT IN OUNCES
16 fluid ounces of unrefined flax oil
6 fluid ounces of 80 proof alcoholic liquor such as Brandy or Vodka, Gin, Whiskey
2 ounces, by volume, of Psyllium Husk Powder
NOTE: dry volume is same as fluid measurement. DO NOT weigh the dry husk.
NOTE: The dry husk and liquor are mixed first- stir well, wait 3 minutes then add the oil.

MEASUREMENT IN MILLILITERS: milliliters, fluid ounces and volume are the same
480 Mil of oil -liquid
180 Mil of liquor - liquid
60 Mil of husk – volume
NOTE: dry volume is same as fluid measurement. DO NOT weigh the dry husk.

CLARIFICATION UPDATE NOTE ON THE NEW RECIPE:
PACHECO'S LIQUOR WAS 166 PROOF = 83% Ethanol and 17% water.
166 Proof Liquor 3 ounces = **2.49 ounces of Ethanol** and .51 ounces of water.

MY MODERN LIQUOR IS 80 PROOF = 40% Ethanol liquor and 60% water.
80 Proof liquor 6 ounces = **2.40 ounces Ethanol** and 3.60 ounces of water

MY ALTERNATE MODERN LIQUOR IS 101 PROOF = 50.5 Ethanol and 49.5 of water
101 Proof liquor 5 ounces= **2.53 ounces Ethanol** and 2.47 ounces water

IMPORTANT NOTE: First mix the liquor with the husk and stir for a couple of minutes to allow the husk to absorb the water and to prevent oil absorption. Then add the oil and shake well together for a minute and repeat the shaking a few more times over the next few hours, or overnight. Then place it in a wide container and allow to stand still for ten days in the sun or a dry room. After the ten day period, filter the oil. To retrieve ALL OIL, place the mass of husk in a wire colander and place this over a jar to allow oil from the husk to slowly drip. Let it drip overnight. **Of the 16 ounces oil, the total OIL LOSS is one ounce**.

IMPORTANT NOTE: LOW COST WEAK LIQUOR [you get what you pay for]
My friend Jordi from Reus, Spain is a fine painter and is very cautious in measurements. He advised me of his own experiments with the alcohol he used. He said that cheap liquor did not give the same results as more expensive liquor. If you question the ethanol content in your 80 proof liquor I recommend you add a bit more liquor and possibly a tiny bit more husk. I have not verified that some low cost brands contain less Ethanol, but I would not be surprised.

IMPORTANT HEALTH WARNING:
ALL UNDERAGE PERSONS MUST BE ACCOMPANIED BY AN ADULT WHEN USING LIQUOR ALCOHOLIC LIQUIDS. All liquors above 101 proof [equivalent to 50.5 ethanol] are flammable. Do not use liquor with a higher proof of 101. Do not use Denatured alcohol as it is 200 proof and is extremely dangerous to human health and highly flamable. The Psyllium husk-Alcohol method needs the percentage of water found in the 80 proof liquor in order to be effective. If you do use a liquor of 101 proof or higher, you must wear protective goggles, and this must be done outdoors with adequate ventilation. If you smoke you must have fire suppression equipment nearby. Do not stare into the oil and liquor mixture without use of protective goggles as the hazardous fumes can damage your eyes. Liquor is a mixture of WATER and ETHANOL held in perfect suspension but it can be dangerous when mixed with oil and heated.

INSTRUCTIONS

FIRST: It is very important to FIRST mix the husk and the alcoholic liquor so they mix well for a couple of minutes. Note that the husk will not absorb the liquid ETHANOL content of the liquor. The husk only absorbs the water portion. So you will still see liquid [ethanol] in the mix. DO NOT discard the ethanol as it is important. The husk will absorb the water content of the liquor and it will puff up and expand. This is good. This is important because the husk will expand and becomes a bit sticky, and will hold the mucilage that is separated by the ethanol. Stir the husk and liquor together for about 3 minutes so there are no pockets of dry husk. If the husk appears dry, add another bit of liquor. Slightly more liquor will not harm the effectiveness of the mixture. Better to use more liquor than not enough.

IF you make a mistake and first mix the dry husk with the oil, it will cause a delay because the husk will absorb the oil. This is not an insurmountable problem but it will take nature more time to have the husk expel the oil as it slowly absorbs the water.

SECOND: Once the husk and alcohol are mixed well, THEN add it to the oil and mix this thoroughly. This can be done either by vigorous shaking by hand the tightly capped jar, or an electric blender can be used. I do not use a blender as it is just one more thing to clean. The blender makes the mixing effortless and fast. Five minutes of the blender at **a very low speed** is sufficient. DO NOT USE HIGH SPEEDS because high speeds create excessive amounts of air to enter the oil and this whipping delays the separation of mucilage from the oil. Shaking the mixture several times for a few minutes each time, over the next several hours has shown to have positive effects.

If you mixed all the ingredients together and were unable to continue, place a tight cap on the jar. As long as the cap is on tight, you can allow the oil mixture to stand for days or weeks or months before proceeding to the next step. If you allow the mixture to stand in the jar for extended periods of time, such as several days, the husk will drop to the bottom of the jar and it may form a hard tight ball. If this happens, you need to break the ball up with a stick and re-shake the mixture before moving onto the next step.

THIRD: Pour the mixture into an easily crushed but firm aluminum WIDE baking container so the oil mixture is approximately 2 inches in height. I use one that is about 9X10 inches in size. Place the container outdoors in the sun and do not move it for the entire period. I no longer cover it with a sheet of glass during the day. Bugs, dirt and leaves get into the oil but it easily filters out. However at night, you must cover the container to prevent any moisture from entering the oil. I place a piece of wood plywood because I learned that a glass sheet will condense moisture under the glass. Within two days of hot summer heat, the oil will become transparent as the husk drops but it is not enough time for all the mucilage to drop. An important observation I learned is that this must be allowed to remain completely still for between 8 and 10 days. Allow for more days in cool weather. Keep the oil level under 2 inches. If the oil level is higher than 2 inches, it takes a longer period of time. A flexible easily crushable aluminum container will allow easier control of the oil as we begin the next steps.

FOURTH: DO NOT STIR NOR MOVE THE OIL FOR 8 TO 10 DAYS. Allow the oil to STAND STILL. Do not let moisture enter the oil. Stronger liquor in the new recipe may shorten the stand period.

FIFTH: After the 10 day standing period passes, pour the oil into a large funnel having a cotton ball placed into the narrow portion of the funnel. This low cost filter is very effective. Insert a small ball of natural - not synthetic - cotton ball into the narrow part of a large funnel like the type used in pouring oil into a car. Do not compact the cotton ball so tight that the oil will not pass. Do this filtering at mid-day when the oil is warm. Place the funnel over a clean large jar. The oil will slowly filter – sometimes a drop at a time. It can take several hours. If you decide to, you may do a second filtering of the oil. A second filtering of the oil with a new clean cotton ball may help, but the choice is yours. I only filter my oil once. While this step is underway, place a wire colander on top of the funnel, and place the moist husk into it. Allow the good oil to drip out slowly from the wet husk for several hours or overnight. DO NOT squeeze the cotton ball in hopes of getting more oil.

SIXTH: Once filtered, this is the cleansed oil. It will be bright yellow and transparent in cool or hot temperatures. Un-cleansed unrefined raw flax oil containing mucilage becomes cloudy and hazy in late evening cool temperatures but it becomes fully transparent in hot temperatures of the day. DO NOT be fooled by this clarity of the un-cleansed flax oil when seen in hot weather. The 10 days of standing still under the sun helped bleach the oil a bit, but the oil is still yellow in color, AND IT STILL CONTAINS ITS NATURAL MOISTURE. You can do the ten day cleansing period indoors, but the advantage of standing the oil outdoors in the hot summer direct sun is the oil begins the thickening and bleaching and the moisture content begins to evaporate. The yellow color is harmless because the damaging mucilage has been removed. The sun's Ultra Violet light bleaches the oil.
UPDATE NOTE: The new AIR PUMP METHOD also evaporates the moisture in the oil.

SEVENTH: Please see the section on Sun Thickening. The cleansed oil is now ready to be Sun thickened and sun bleached. In about two weeks of sun exposure, the oil begins to become bleached and over the next 30 to 60 days, it will become water clear. The heat of the sun will evaporate the oil's natural moisture. **UPDATE NOTE: The NEW 'Air Pump Method' will thicken the oil as well as evaporate the inherent moisture. WARNING on the air pump oil: Do not use it for more than 15 days 24/7.**

NOTE: Artists always ask, "When is the oil ready?" The answer is this: Because we all live in different geographical areas that vary in weather conditions, the oil is ready when you decide it is. Once the oil is bleached, remove a teaspoon of the oil at various intervals, such as 10 days, 15 days, 20 and so on. Take out some oil and grind with Calcium Carbonate chalk into CSO and mix it 50/50 with some tube oil paints. Check its drying and handling. The longer the oil is allowed to sun thicken, the faster drying and thicker it will become. Make notes. Some artists prefer a limpid oil, others prefer a thicker oil.

NOTE: Once the oil is removed from the sun and placed in storage jars, it will become a very pale straw color. It will not revert back to the bright yellow orange color of the raw oil. The sun thickened bleached oil will appear yellowish in a jar. Be aware that you are seeing the oil in CONCENTRATED form. Place a drop on a pure white dinner plate and rub it in thinly. You will see that your oil is completely colorless and fully transparent.

NOTE: Storage of the oil is important. Fill the jar and tighten the cap, then loosen the cap a ¼ turn to allow for expansion. Place the clear glass jar in a window that receives some sunlight. DO NOT store your sun oil in plastic containers and not in dark containers. The oil needs sunlight.

*****

MY SECOND RECOMMENDATION FOR REMOVING THE MUCILAGE
THE 'CSO GEL METHOD'

In February, 2012, an idea came to me and after many tests I created a new method to remove the mucilage from the oil in ONE DAY. Some have asked if it is better than the Psyllium Husk-Alcohol method. I cannot say it is better but it will save time, yet, the procedure is more difficult.
I named this method, 'THE CSO-GEL METHOD'.

'THE CSO-GEL METHOD'
INSTRUCTIONS
The recipe has two parts. NOTE: This recipe is for a small amount of oil.

Part One
5 parts oil
2 parts liquor

Part Two
1 part Glair: frothed and distilled Egg white.
½ part husk

EXAMPLE [in USA ounces]
Part One uses 5 fluid ounces oil, and 1 fluid ounce 80 proof Liquor.
Part Two uses 1 fluid ounce Glair and ½ volume ounce of husk.

1. PLACE the Liquor in a large heat resistance glass jar. Use ONLY 80 proof liquor such as Rum, Gin, or Vodka. **Do not use liquor of 101 proof or above due to fire hazard.**
2. ADD the oil, cap the jar and shake both well together. Let stand still. The level of the oil and liquor should not be more than half the jar's size.
3. PLACE the GLAIR, egg white in a small cup
4. ADD the husk to the egg white and mix it well.
5. IMMEDIATELY combine the contents of both jars and vigorously shake well together for a few minutes.
6. UNCAP the jar and place the jar in a metal pot with cold water. Use a large metal pot, the water level should equal the oil level in the jar.
7. To prevent any noisy rattle, place a table spoon of dry rice in the water under the jar.
8. DO THIS OUTSIDE: USE an electric griddle or any flameless heat source to cook the mixture. Bring the water to a boil then lower the heat so the water is boiling mildly and not splashing. The water will boil, but the oil does not boil. The oil will percolate as moisture is evaporated from the contents mixed with the oil. Cook for about one hour. Stir the mixture periodically. The hot oil will become transparent. The husk egg mixture will get gelatinous and sticky.

9. WEAR EYE GOGGLES as you cook the mixture to prevent hot vapors from irritating the eyes. These vapors can be hazardous to the eyes. UNDER no circumstances use any of liquor that is flammable such as 101 proof or above. Do not use Denatured alcohol it is extremely hazardous to the eyes and extremely combustible.
10. DO THIS OUTSIDE. Cook in an area having plenty of fresh ventilation to blow the fumes away. Take care that water does not splash into the oil.
11. USE AN OVEN MITTEN. REMOVE the jar from the hot water and let it cool to room temperature. As it cools, the oil becomes cloudy.
12. Once at room temperature, CHILL the oil in the refrigerator for 20 minutes. The oil becomes more cloudy
13. FILTER the cold cloudy oil through a funnel with a thick COTTON BALL filter. This cloudy oil will drain fully transparent. It will drain very slowly, one drop at a time. All filters get easily clogged. Use a new cotton ball filter if the draining stops. . Use a second funnel with a clean filter and pour the remaining oil into it. If desired, do a second filtering of the transparent oil through a fresh cotton ball placed firmly in a funnel.
14. TO TEST the cleanliness of the oil, place 2 ounces in a small 8 ounce jar filled with 4 ounces of distilled water. The oil will float on the water. DO NOT STIR NOR SHAKE the water with the oil. Simply pour in the oil and let it stand still for several days with the jar uncapped. After several days, the oil should remain fully transparent without formation of any white colored matter on the water. If some minute dust appears floating on the water, one can filter the oil again or ignore it.

*****

THE OLD MASTERS' TRADITIONAL METHOD OF CLEANSING THE OIL
The following paragraphs are for artists and researchers interested in learning more about the oil. There is some repetition of instructions and facts from earlier paragraphs. Note that this book was written over a 12 year period with constant testing, updating and research. I believe it is important to include even obsolete instructions and facts as they will help future researches avoid repetition of my obsolete tests.

The Old Masters knew it was important to remove the particulate and mucilage from the Unrefined oil, and cleansed it by various organic means. Artists today can do the same with easy methods I have developed or modified. Mother Nature plays a big role in the outcome of the cleansing of any batch of oil. Geographic and environmental factors impact the quality of the oil, and the results in cleansing.

The flax seeds are quite small, similar to the size of sesame seeds. Extracting the oil by modern methods requires heavy machinery to pulverize the seeds. The resulting oil is contaminated by microscopic sized particulate comprised of invisible fibers from the seed husk, debris, and the natural mucilage of the seed. Much of this particulate is invisible and held in suspension in the oil with the mucilage which is also invisible.

GRAVITY

The oldest method is letting the oil 'stand'. Gravity will cause the larger particulate to settle and the oil will APPEAR to be clear. **Gravity by itself will not remove the mucilage nor the very fine particulate** because much microscopic sized particulate material remains in suspension in the oil. Gravity by itself will not remove either the mucilage nor the very fine particulate, no matter how long one allows it to stand. Old manuscripts cite the need to let oil stand for years. This is unacceptable and unnecessary, as the Old Masters themselves found out, and devised methods to remove the material.

MODERN BOOKS WITH METHODS OF CLEANSING THE OIL

A.P. Laurie's book, "The Painter's Methods and Materials", Dover Publications, New York, 1967, has withstood the test of time, and is still available. A.P. Laurie was a scientist with a special interest in Artist's materials and historical manuscripts.

Mr. Laurie cites ancient manuscripts on the subject of how drying oils were cleansed. He begins with a 5th century account by Aetius, and mentions the 8th century Lucca Manuscript, then mentions Theophilus in the 11th century, Eraclius in the 13th century, and Cennino Cennini in the 14th century, concluding that linseed, poppy and walnut oils were processed and used since ancient times. He relates that the extracted oil, by however means it is extracted, is NOT pure, that it contains impurities and other foreign matter. He states that fresh extracted oil dries very slowly and artists made the oil dry faster by processing it in a variety of forms; boiling, exposure to sun. Mr. Laurie states that the bleaching of oils by sun exposure was known in the time of Dioscorides, and that boiling oil with litharge was known in the time of Galen, in the years A.D., 103-193.

Mr. Laurie states that the method of 'water washing" by shaking the oil with water came much later in history. This was a much more recent development that dates to Padre Gesuato of 1557 and even more recently in the De Mayerne manuscript of 1620. Previous methods excluded the water.

My own tests show that "WATER WASHING" is an ineffective and time consuming method for removing the mucilage, whether it is simply water or water mixed with sand and or salt .

*****

THE IRREVERSIBLE DAMAGE CAUSED BY MUCILAGE

Since the Industrial Revolution of the 19th century, raw materials of all kinds are now processed for the market as efficiently and quickly as possible. Artist's 'linseed' oil is produced on a very large scale for a world-wide market. Gone are the days of the Van Eycks and Rembrandt when the flax seeds were pressed with a hand manipulated screw press to extract the oil.

Even today's human grade cold pressed FLAX oil extracted by machinery warms up the oil because of the friction of the high pressure hydraulic machinery. I was assured by a USA manufacturer of flax oil that the temperature of the oil only reaches 110 degrees Fahrenheit. I am aware of only one company that claims to use no electrical machinery in pressing the LINSEED oil, and that is the Old Holland company of The Netherlands. They claim to use only windmill power as was done in 17th century Holland.

Most linseed oil today is labeled as Alkali Refined Linseed Oil because it is treated with a caustic chemical called Sodium Hydroxide in their Alkali Refinement process. This has removed important molecular components of the oil and caused it to become a very slow drying oil. Knowing this, I have sought out pure cold pressed UNREFINED, Unfiltered Flax oil. But, it requires cleansing with safe non caustic materials, not with caustic chemicals, and not by shaking with pure water, sand or salt.

I have improved upon some existing methods and have developed new methods to help artists cleanse their unrefined oil of its mucilage and particulate. These methods are the result of many experiments, as I was seeking answers to this very important question. I cannot overstate how crucial it is to safely cleanse the UNREFINED OIL of as much of the mucilage and particulate as possible.

The Old Masters knew of the danger the mucilage caused. They tried everything under the sun to solve this problem. They tested many procedures and ingredients that would cause the mucilage to separate from the oil for removal. This was not an easy problem to solve because the MUCILAGE is an integral part of the oil. The Old Masters in their numerous mixtures did find that ONE COMMON ingredient, alcoholic liquor was an effective ingredient.

Mucilage is microscopic in size and INVISIBLE to the unaided human eye. Under certain light conditions [a flashlight in a dark room] the existence of the matter can be seen suspended in the oil as tiny lights. Mucilage appears to my observation, to be partially aqueous [water] and oleaginous [oil] and apparently has the same weight density as the oil as they are in complete suspension.

Mucilage is a complex mixture, designed to protect the seed so it may germinate in times of stress when water is lacking. Though it is invisible when dispersed in suspension in the oil, when it is caused to be gathered together [flocculated] , it is an opaque, pure white fuzzy material. Any slight agitation will cause it to reintegrate itself with the oil. These conditions and its relation with the oil, makes it difficult to remove.

FLOCCULATION and FINEING and REFINEMENT
Flocculation, is a modern scientific term, referring to the grouping and binding together of a substance in a substance, caused by use of some added specific ingredient. In this case it refers to the binding together of the particulate, mucilage and debris in the oil so it may be separated and removed from the clear oil. Fineing, and Refinement are terms used to describe how a liquid is treated or processed to make it clear and transparent. Sellers want this because Consumers want their foods to appear cosmetically clean and wholesome.

CHAPTER FOUR
THICKENING THE OIL

BEFORE BEGINNING THIS CHAPTER
There is an extraordinary new method of thickening the oil. This method uses a low cost aquarium AIR PUMP, to pump cold air through the oil continuously for up to 15 days and nights. THIS oil is called "AIR PUMP OIL" and it will revolutionize the oil that Fine Artists use.
It is the FIRST IMPORTANT ADVANCEMENT in the manufacture of artist's thickened linseed / flax oil in over 200 years and creates an oil equal to that of the Old Masters' TRUE STAND OIL. It will make the current BOILED 'FALSE-STAND' LINSEED OIL obsolete. You will read more about this AIR PUMP OIL in this book. The process is so simple it can be done at home with minimal effort.

THE OLD MASTERS' THICKENED OIL: When oil thickens it becomes POLYMERIZED. THE REASONS the Old Masters thickened their oil was because thickened [polymerized] oil dried faster, it flowed better, and dried with a harder more protective film.

The Old Masters' TRADITIONAL oil was thickened by one of two procedures. The first procedure was faster and used by painters living in snow cold regions of Northern Europe. They used fire heating but were careful not to use high heat. They learned over centuries of oral tradition that BOILED OR HIGH HEATED oil became brown and lost its pliability and had a shortened lifespan. They learned to heat their oil over several hours or days, and the oil was thickened by exposure to gentle fire heat and oxygen exposure. This oil was not bleached and was bright yellow. This bright yellow color was not a hindrance because flax linseed oil eventually bleaches with normal sunlight exposure. In concentration it looks yellow, but when thinly applied it is colorless once the UV sun rays bleach out <u>the fugitive yellow color</u>.

The finest Old Master oil was processed in southern Europe where hot summers simultaneously bleached the oil water clear and thickened it over a period of 20 to 60 days, depending on the time of year.

NOT ALL the oil was thickened by the Old Masters for use in painting. The Old Masters used two oils. One was allowed to remain THIN. This thin oil was used to grind the dry pigments together to make paint that would dry slow and not dry out quickly. They did not have our collapsible tubes. They covered their paint to prevent contact with oxygen. Some placed the fresh paint in animal intestines as we might do with a rubber balloon.

A THIRD OIL used by the Old Masters is called a 'CO-POLY" oil. This mixture of THIN and THICKENED oil , means ' COMBINATION-POLYMERIZATION'. It was a thickened fast drying oil mixed with a THIN slow drying oil. By changing the ratios of each oil the Masters chose how fast their oil paint would dry and it would impact how the oil paint handled.

BRIEF HISTORICAL VIEW OF SUN THICKENED LINSEED/FLAX OIL

CENNINO CENNINI: In the 1400's Cennino Cennini, author of the Renaissance manuscript, *"Il Libro Dell Arte"*, claimed the best oil for oil painting was Sun Thickened Linseed Oil. Although linseed/flaxseed oil had been used for thousands of years before Cennini, it was his book that brought attention to the superiority of Sun Thickened Linseed oil for oil painting.

Exactly what Cennino said, meant, or wrote has always been uncertain to us. Interpreting older words, translating true meanings into other languages, and allowing for incomplete recipes, as well as misunderstandings, has always plagued subsequent scholars. Some scholars translated Cennino's words to say we should put the Linseed oil in a pot and to allow it to sit in the sun until it is 'half gone'. This is easily seen to be a mistranslation.

Laurie questioned the accuracy of that translation, saying Cennino's words had been mistranslated. The TRUE meaning was that the oil should be allowed to sit in the sun until the yellow color was 'gone'. Meaning bleached pale in color, not 'gone' as in 'evaporated', especially because the oil does not evaporate it just hardens. Any artist experienced in thickening oil would agree with Laurie, and the oil must have been stirred regularly because wasting precious oil by letting it skin over and dry hard is unthinkable, especially after the work of pressing and cleansing it.

Cennino's writings say nothing about stirring the oil, which is important and necessary so the top layer of the oil will not skin hard and become useless. Besides once skinned, the top layer becomes sealed and oxygen is prevented from entering the lower recesses and it will not thicken. Perhaps Cennino, believed he need not include an explanation <u>of the obvious</u>. The book was written for working ARTISTS, not academic THEORISTS.

De MAYERNE: The De Mayerne Manuscript of the 17th century is frequently cited by scholars who seek answers to methods and materials of Oil Painting of some Old Masters. Though of great historical importance, this 17th century hand written treatise/manuscript is a disorganized, incomplete, frequently imprecise, compilation of notes, compiled over many years. A major problem with the manuscript is that it has been translated from French to German and now to English, and contains ancient words in Italian. Persons familiar with the problems inherent in language translations will understand that much mistranslation occurs in translations, and that much confusion and meaning can be lost in translations from one language to another. I have personally witnessed these errors in translation, in our courts of law.

The author, Theodore De Mayerne, was a respected medical doctor with an interest in painting and it appears he had first-hand contacts with some famous painters of the time, most notably, Rubens and Van Dyck. The manuscript includes De Mayerne's <u>own personal hypotheses and ideas</u> for future experiments in painting media, and includes much useless information on subjects other than painting.

Many contemporary scholars believe that if some material or procedure was not written down, it was not known or did not exist. Proof to the contrary are facts recently come to light. Scientific studies by Professor Van De Wetering and Ms. Garrido-Perez clearly show the historical record is missing valuable information on materials, medium, and procedures used by two of the greatest of Old Masters, Rembrandt and Velazquez.

Mr. Van De Wetering cites the use of Calcium Carbonate by Rembrandt, and the use of an egg-oil emulsion in his paintings. Ms.Garrido-Perez has proven Velazquez used large quantities of Calcium Carbonate as well as use of emulsions mixed with his oil paint. Modern studies on Rubens' paintings when compared to DeMayerne's writings prove with definite certainty that DeMayerne **did not** accurately know what materials Rubens mixed into his paint. Modern science discloses his ignorance.

RUBENS: The DeMayerne manuscript strongly indicates Peter Paul Rubens used Sun Thickened Flax Oil. This proof is arrived at by noting that DeMayerne quotes Rubens as saying that to bleach a yellowed painting, one must simply place it in direct sunlight, and it will bleach. DeMayerne himself had experienced and written that Walnut oil will not bleach once it is dried and yellowed. Modern scientists corroborate this observation. Today, 400 years later, Rubens' paintings are some of the very best preserved in Art history, due in no doubt on the Sun Thickened Flax oil he used.

Some 'expert author artists' of today continue to ignorantly criticized Sun Thickened Linseed Oil. However it must be known that these criticisms are actually truthful criticisms of modern alkali REFINED Linseed oil that is the base oil used in making modern **boiled** Sun Thickened Oil. This poverty stricken industrial BOILED OIL is the TRUE cause of the deficiencies they write about. Industrial Sun Thickened ALKALI REFINED linseed oil, is a modern product having major defects, and does NOT have the superior qualities of the UNREFINED Cold Pressed Sun Thickened Flax Oil used by the Old Masters. Later you will read about Francisco Pacheco who was Velazquez' teacher, and his own 17th century method of cleansing and sun thickening his oil. His oil has proven to be fully archival.

REMBRANDT: One of the greatest of artists was Rembrandt Van Rijn (1606-1669). His middle and later period paintings demonstrate a complete mastery of the oil paint medium. He was the first to use the palette knife in applying thick layers of paint on his paintings. Frederic Taubes, an important American artist, art educator, and author of over 20 art books on the methods and materials of the old and modern master painters, correctly states that Rembrandt's oil paint was viscous and made with highly viscous polymerized linseed oil paint. Scientific tests prove it was linseed/Flax oil, and the thick viscous paint has NO wrinkles. The question was : 'HOW DID REMBRANDT DO THIS SO THE THICK OIL WOULD NOT WRINKLE NOR DRIP DOWN? Rembrandt's secret is the addition of some chalk and an egg-oil Emulsion to his paint, and it is explained in this book.

VELAZQUEZ: Also in the 1600's, one of the world's greatest painters, Diego Velazquez lived and painted his masterpieces in Spain. His paintings (those not mistreated or mishandled by others), survive today in an exceptional state of preservation and an exceptional freshness preserving his fluid, magnificent virtuosity of application of his clear colors. Velazquez' principal oil was Sun Thickened Flax Oil, with large amounts of Calcium Carbonate and a protein additive mixed with the paint. Within a 6 month period of 1628 and 1629, Rubens visited the King of Spain on a diplomatic mission. During this stay Rubens had frequent contact with Velazquez, who was the Spanish King's favorite painter. One can only guess what the two great painters discussed regarding their choices of materials and their application methods of painting. Unfortunately, neither left posterity a book explaining how they painted or the materials they used. My thoughts are that they believed the simple information was so common-place, there was no need to record it in a book. The one recorded bit of advice Rubens gave the young 29 year old was to switch from dark brown grounds to a pale colored gray or light colored ground. This, as Rubens explained would add life and brilliance to the colors- and as Velazquez aged, his thicker paint eventually evolved and became almost the thinness of watercolors. Velazquez used impressionistic techniques 200 years before the French Impressionist movement of 1870.

FRANCISCO PACHECO was Velazquez' teacher for 6 years. Velazquez entered his studio at age 13. Pacheco's book published in 1649 gives his method of CLEANSING and SUN THICKENING the UNREFINED Flax oil of his time. My book contains the method Pacheco used and surely it is the method he taught the 13 year old Diego Velazquez. Later in the book you will see my improvement of Pacheco's method, and will learn how his method of using Lavender flower buds and a very strong alcohol liquor, inspired me to create my 'Psyllium Husk-Alcohol method'. The fine preservation of Velazquez 350 year old paintings attest to the permanence and validity of Pacheco's method of oil cleansing and sun thickening, and it invalidates views of those misinformed "experts" of today who criticize the permanence of Sun Thickened oil.
In past centuries, many artists and art writers wondered how Velazquez achieved his results. Many intelligent artists with years of experience in painting, but lacking scientific analysis, published their erroneous views, believing Velazquez used only oil and pigment. None knew what the scientific studies published in 1992 have determined as fact: Velazquez added large amounts of Calcium Carbonate and a protein additive to his superior Flaxseed oil paint.

HIGH TEMPERATURE HEATING DECOMPOSES THE OIL
Modern science tells us that IF LINSEED OIL IS BOILED or if just heated past 230C., it becomes decomposed. This means the life span of the oil is shortened. This means the oil loses its pliability and flexibility far sooner. The oil begins decomposition when it reaches 230 degrees Celsius. Modern industrial LINSEED STAND OIL is BOILED OIL far past that temperature.
It is false advertising to name modern industrial Stand Linseed Oil as being a true "STAND OIL". The modern industrial oil has nothing in common with 'STANDING" and is simply boiled for several hours. Cennino Cennini, the Renaissance master, said that BOILED OIL was good for one thing – to be used as a mordant (an adhesive) - but NOT GOOD FOR OIL PAINTING!

The Old Masters made their superior oil by STANDING IT IN THE SUN for 15 to 60 days. Cennino said the best oil for painting was Sun Thickened oil. This is TRUE STAND OIL. Throughout history, artists have sought properly prepared oils, and for good reason.

In modern times Industrial linseed oil was sometimes boiled in large kettles and is called 'kettle oil or 'boiled oil' but it is not used for fine art painting. The higher the temperature and the longer it is boiled, the darker the oil becomes. Boiling will evaporate any moisture but at great cost because the oil becomes irreversibly darkened. Dark oil will lower color tone over time, because oil paint becomes more translucent with age. Oil boiled for extensive periods and at high temperatures will become rubbery, and dark, and becomes an extremely slow drying oil. This oil is called Lithographic oil, and is made for Lithography and Printing. It is also called 'Burnt Plate Oil'. in the 1950's Frederic Taubes wrote that Boiled oil wrinkled very badly when used in making paint.

Some moisture can be removed by giving the oil a 'water bath' in boiling water for a period of time. Uncap the jar and do not allow water to enter. Place the jar with the oil in tepid water, and bring the water to a boil (approximately 190 degrees Fahrenheit.). You will notice that the water will boil but the oil will not boil, but it does heat up enough to evaporate some moisture. One experiment took 5 hours for the moisture bubbles to stop rising. I noted that the oil became a brighter yellow color. A 30 minute experiment also made the oil become slightly brighter yellow. In contrast, Sun Thickening the oil will create a light pale, straw colored oil.

BOILING OR HIGH HEATING OF LINSEED /FLAX OIL is destructive.
200 Degrees Centigrade = The Old Masters use of a goose quill to indicate safe heating
230-236 Degrees Centigrade = DECOMPOSITION of the oil with a reduced lifespan
300 Degrees Centigrade = Bodied, Stand Linseed Oil, heated without Oxygen
300 Degrees Centigrade = Oil smokes and produces toxic Carbon Monoxide and Acrolein
343 Degrees Centigrade + = Oil begins to boil
343 Degrees Centigrade + = Oil Ignites
380- 425 Degrees Centigrade= Burnt Plate Oil also called Lithographers oil

The scientific paper given below cites the decomposition of linseed oil when heated above 236 degrees centigrade.
http://www.si.edu/MCI/downloads/articles/Tusoma_paper.pdf
Title: "The Influence of Lead ions on the drying of oils"
Authors: This academically peer reviewed and published paper is by Charles S. Tumosa; PhD, and Marion F. Mecklenburg; PhD.
It warns of OVERHEATING the oil. [See page 41, 3rd paragraph, left side for their Quote]:
[Paraphrased]: *Linseed Oil starts to decompose at 230-236 degrees Celsius.*

DO NOT BUY OIL THAT CONTAINS ANTI-OXIDANTS – IT WILL DRY VERY SLOWLY
REGARDLESS of what method you use to thicken your oil, the most important consideration is to buy the CORRECT OIL. You must buy COLD PRESSED, UNREFINED flax or Linseed oil. AND it must contain no additives of any kind. READ THE FINE PRINT ON THE LABELS!. Some sellers at health food stores will add ANTIOXIDANTS to the oil to preserve its sweet taste. The most common additives are Vitamin 'E' and ' C', Rosemary, Polypherols, Tocopherols, and mixtures with other oils that DO NOT DRY.
WARNING: Do not buy any flax oil made for pets, nor those with added LIGNANS.

ANTIOXIDANTS stop the oil from absorbing oxygen. The FLAX oil can only harden [*cure, polymerize, dry hard*] by exposure to oxygen. Health food stores keep the oil refrigerated- Artists DO NOT need the oil to remain refrigerated. Health food stores put the oil in dark plastic containers to keep out the light. Artists should transfer the oil to clear jars so the sunlight UV rays will begin the bleaching of the oil. As long as the lid of the container is kept on tight and no oxygen gets in, the oil will remain THIN. Once the oil is exposed to oxygen, it begins the polymerization process. ARTISTS want the oil to polymerize over time. It is the only way the paint will dry.

'AIR PUMP OIL'
THE MODERN METHOD OF THICKENING THE OIL

In about 2009 my friend Maurice Garson [see his extraordinary website www.askmaurice.com] wrote to me and suggested I try a method in which one can thicken the oil by means of an air pump. I did not follow up because my studies from 50 years before informed me that in the 20th century, the industry of Linseed oil had already done that. It was called 'BLOWN OIL'. Frederic Taubes had denounced that industrial oil as yellowing greatly and causing the oil paint to wrinkle badly on drying. The big difference is that the industrial BLOWN OIL was made with ALKALI REFINED linseed oil which already is a poor quality oil and used mainly in making house oil paint for painting wood houses. In addition the oil was also mixed with metallic driers and also turpentine. All these additives were used in order to get the oil paint on the houses to DRY FAST within hours. House paints usually lasted 25 years at most. The goal of the industry was not for FINE ART PAINTING which expects Fine art to last for centuries.

In the year 2000 when I pioneered the REBIRTH OF THE OLD MASTERS' SUPERIOR OIL, I was too occupied to attend to testing the AIR PUMP METHOD. After my friend Maurice, time passed and in late 2010, a lady wrote to me about her experiments. Still I did not act. Finally in early 2012, my friend Rene Benvennuti a fine artist from Puerto Rico came up with the idea independently on his own and told me of its success. Finally, I tested it in early June- July 2012.

I believe this extraordinary method will revolutionize the OIL used by Fine Artists and will make the current alkali refined boiled oils obsolete.

TESTS AND THE TEST RESULTS of AIR PUMP OIL

As the oil thickened by air pump exposure, I removed samples of the oil in increments of days. I tested the samples by mixing them with chalk to make CSO. Then I mixed the CSO with tube oil paints. Then I made a separate test where I did not use tube oil paints but instead the DRY PIGMENTS were mixed with the CSO made of the sample oils.

THE OIL I used was unrefined Flax oil that I had previously cleansed with the ' PSYLLIUM HUSK- ALCOHOL' method, over a ten day period. The AIR PUMP was a low cost low power pump that was hooked up to 6 feet of plastic tubing. The jar of oil was covered with a lid and three ¼ inch holes were made into the lid. In one hole I placed the tube all the way down to the bottom of the jar. The other two holes were left open for air circulation. A plastic cover was loosely placed over this to keep moisture from entering the oil jar. The electric air pump was kept constantly running both day and night.

THE JAR OF OIL BECAME fully bleached water-clear in 5 days. Recall the oil had previously been exposed to 10 days of sunshine as it was being cleansed.

5 DAY OIL: This oil was still limpid and thin. With CSO and tube oil paints it dried in thin paint between 20-25 hours. With dry pigments and CSO –it dried in 20 hours.

10 DAY, 15 DAY and 18 DAY OIL, became increasingly more thick and viscous.
When each of these three oils – 10/ 15/ 18 day AIR PUMP OIL samples - were mixed with chalk to make CSO and then mixed with tube oil paints the paint dried in under 14 hours. When the CSO was ground with dry pigments the paint dried in 5 hours.

THE WARNING OF OVER EXPOSURE – WRINKLING PAINT

The 10 day and 15 day oil did not cause any wrinkling with thin layers of paint. The 18 day oil caused THICK and THIN layers of paint to wrinkle, whether it was mixed with tube oil paints or made with dry pigments.
During my 12 year research, I discovered how Rembrandt was able to paint thick oil paint made with highly viscous Linseed/ Flax oil paint and NOT HAVE IT WRINKLE !. He did this by adding an emulsion of egg and oil to the oil paint. When a few drops are added, the Emulsion will cause the thick viscous flowing oil paint to STOP FLOWING and to hold its impasto textures. The Emulsion also allows the entire BODY of the paint to dry evenly together. WRINKLING is caused when the top layer dries first— forming an air tight skin- and the interior remains wet. Then, as the interior slowly dries, the top DRIED LAYER will wrinkle. The effect is similar to an apple left in a window sill. The outer skin peel will wrinkle and dry out, while the inside is still fresh apple. Wrinkling of oil paint is explained in my book.

ADDITIONAL TESTS OF 'AIR PUMP OIL' AND TRADITIONAL SUNNED OIL

Flax/Linseed oil is a miracle oil of nature. The seeds are tiny and the shell is very hard and glossy. The mucilage is crucial to the germination of the seeds and is a complex mixture of molecules. For artists the mucilage in the oil is a disaster and must be removed. Observing how the oil appears under a variety of circumstances tells many things about the oil. Oil with mucilage is very transparent in warm weather, but once the temperature drops, the mucilage in the oil causes the oil to become cloudy and non-transparent.

The Old Masters tried many ingredients to remove the mucilage safely. The one ingredient that did cause the mucilage to separate out of the oil is ETHANOL. Ethanol is a part of drinking liquors like whiskey, vodka, brandy. The amount of ethanol in liquor is determined by the PROOF of the liquor. Most liquors have 80 proof, so the amount of ethanol is half the proof. This means 80 proof liquor is 40% ethanol and 60 % water. Some liquors are sold with 101 proof and 175 proof and higher. Pacheco's 17th century recipe called for liquor with 87% ethanol. The CSO Psyllium Husk Alcohol recipe uses 80 proof or 101 proof. Proof above that is not recommended because the husk needs the water.

The FATTY ACIDS are important to the long life of the linseed oil paint and must not be removed.
Please see ARTHUR H. CHURCHS book, "THE CHEMISTRY OF PAINTS AND PAINTING "Published in 1890. Professor Church was a Professor of Chemistry at the Royal Academy of Arts In London England. Professor Church has written in the book section on Linseed oil the following: He wrote that Linseed oil has four main glycerides and each has their fatty acids. The OLEIN glyceride has the OLEIC fatty acid and it DOES NOT OXIDIZE, and as he wrote, "Its presence confers elasticity", to the hardened oxidized film of Linoxine [the term is also spelled today as Linoxyn and is the term to describe oxidized hard dry linseed oil]. The book is available from Google books online.

EIGHT different oils were tested in this study. The results tell us important things to be aware of. THIS STUDY used oil samples that were placed in the FREEZER portion of my kitchen refrigerator, and allowed to remain for several days. All tests are with FLAX-LINSEED OIL from various sources and ALL were fluid and fully transparent in warm weather before being placed in the freezer.

1. Yellow thin Oil from France, brand unknown, claimed to be purified = RESULT: Opaque, non fluid, solidly frozen.
2. Pale yellow, viscous oil from France, same unknown brand as #1 = RESULT: Opaque, non fluid, solidly frozen.
3. Barleans brand, cleansed by the CSO Psyllium husk alcohol method, sun thickened 60 days, viscous , pale, plus 9 days Air Pump treatment = RESULT: Fully transparent and fully fluid and flowing.
4. The same oil as #3 but without any air pump treatment= RESULT: Fully transparent and fully fluid and flowing.
5. An oil I tested in 2010 containing antioxidants, pale yellow, viscous, sun thickened, slow drying= RESULT: Fully transparent and fully fluid and flowing.
6. Famous brand name Alkali Refined Linseed Oil from Art store, thin not thickened, pale yellow = RESULT: Fluid and Translucent somewhat opaque
7. Same Famous brand as #6, Alkali Refined Linseed Oil from Art store, pale yellow, thickened with 18 days of Air Pump = RESULT: Fluid and Transparent
8. Sample from 2010, cleansed by Pacheco's method, kept in dark cupboard for past 3 years, thin, not sun thickened, pale yellow= RESULT: Fully fluid and transparent

CONCLUSIONS:
1. Oil kept in the freezer that became frozen and opaque to any degree, contains mucilage and moisture. Mucilage itself contains moisture.
2. The air pump treatment of the oil assists in evaporating any moisture as does the exposure of the oil to the direct hot summer sun rays.
3. Modern Alkali refinement of the oil, does NOT remove all mucilage nor moisture from the oil.
4. The CSO Psyllium husk-Alcohol and the Pacheco methods, both, DO remove the mucilage from the oil.

HOW NEW OR HOW OLD IS AIR PUMP OIL?
Many Old Masters were geniuses. Passionate and truth seekers, they used their OBSERVATION of the natural world to solve their problems. The VAN EYCK paintings are still here 600 years later. The important Rembrandt expert scholar, Ernst Van De Wetering, has stated that mixtures of oil and egg emulsions are AN UNRECORDED Old Master SECRET. He has reported this ancient knowledge was only recently discovered in the late 20th century!

SO, the question is: DID THE OLD MASTERS' KNOW OF AIR PUMP OIL?
I say, YES!
Since they had no electricity they found other ways to power the constant aeration of the oil. They knew of and used WATER POWER and WIND POWER. In wind power they used windmills to create MOVEMENT to grind grains and other things. In use of WATER POWER they created WATER MILLS, powered by the running river water to cause constant movement. I have NO DOUBT these ancient geniuses made contraptions to cause the oil to be CONSTANTLY lifted and poured out , much like we have garden wheels that will cause CIRCULATION of water. To my knowledge there is no record of this.

CHAPTER FIVE
MIXTURES OF CHALK AND OIL
'CALCITE SUN OIL'

GESSO IN EARLY PAINTINGS
The early oil paintings were comparatively small and painted on wood. The wood was prepared with several layers of Gesso, which is a mixture of Glue and Calcium Carbonate (chalk) or, Calcium Sulphate (gypsum). When the chalk is mixed with glue it results in a pure white opaque mixture.

Later, when larger paintings were desired, canvas became the support of choice because of its relative light weight. The canvas was sized (sealed) with a glue coat followed by a priming of lead white or with a mixture of lead white mixed with Calcium Carbonate. Painters had learned that when Calcium Carbonate is mixed with oil, it becomes almost transparent, and it has no coloring matter.

Eventually, inexpensive Calcium Carbonate was frequently used as an extender to more expensive white lead pigment, and used in priming the canvas. This then led to oil painters mixing the dry powder with their oil paints in order to make the oil paint thicker as Rembrandt and Rubens did.

20TH CENTURY SCIENTIFIC FINDINGS

The recent scientific studies of the paintings of Diego Velazquez clearly show he used mixtures of Calcium Carbonate **with ALL his colors in ALL LAYERS of his paintings** - not just in the priming. He did this to increase the translucency and to enrich the depth of his colors. Velazquez certainly recognized and used to advantage other benefits of Calcium Carbonate, as did Rembrandt who added Calcium Carbonate to his paint to achieve thick impasto that will not collapse. Besides increasing the body of the paint, Calcium Carbonate provides an important adhesive cement-like quality. This gives the paint durability and strength while assisting the paint to remain exactly where and how the artist placed it.

The internet offers us complete information on the fascinating subject of Calcium Carbonate. Reportedly, it covers 4% of the earth's crust and is widely used in many industries of our modern world, such as the making of cement, plaster, and in the rubber industry, as well as in the formulations of paint by large corporations, for "non-fine art" purposes. Calcium Carbonate is a natural substance found in nature and is millions of years old. It is known by many names in many different languages.

Calcium Carbonate powders can be purchased under various names: Chalk from Champagne, France - Marble Dust - Chalk from Bologna, Italy - Calcite, Aragonite, Mixtures of Chalk with Marble Dust. There are others, and many contain mixtures of other ingredients. They differ in various ways.
My preferred Calcium Carbonate powder is Chalk from Champagne, France. When mixed with the oil, it creates a mixture with the strongest adhesion and the greatest viscosity because of its softness.
'Calcite' is gritty, and separates from the oil when stored. The mixture with the 'Calcite' powder is whiter in color than the mixture of the Chalk from Champagne, which has a light beige color. Calcium Carbonate, when mixed with oil, is 98% transparent and has absolutely no coloring or tinting matter. The beige color of the mixture with Chalk from Champagne, is harmless. When mixed with tube white oil paint, it will create a slight off-white. This can be corrected by grinding in an addition of dry White Titanium Dioxide powder.

CALCIUM CARBONATE IN REMBRANDT'S and VELAZQUEZ' PAINT

Four very important books published in the late 20th century inspired me to learn more. In 1988, the London National Gallery of Art published its First Edition book, "REMBRANDT: Art in the Making", and it was updated in 2006; The extensive study of Velazquez, authored by Carmen Garrido-Perez, Chief of the Conservation department of the Prado Museum in Madrid, Spain, titled, " VELAZQUEZ: Tecnica y Evolucion" was published in 1992. "REMBRANDT: The Painter at Work", authored by the head of the Rembrandt Research Project, Professor DR. Ernst Van De Wetering was published in 1997. Finally, the book titled, "Velazquez: The Technique of Genius", co-authored by Carmen Garrido-Perez, was published in 1998, and is a much smaller reduced version, of Garrido-Perez' mentioned extensive research volume.
Please note: The extensive study on numerous Velazquez paintings show Velazquez used both, Chalk and Calcite in his paint mixtures. The smaller book on Velazquez studies just a small number of paintings and in these, studies show only the Calcium Carbonate Calcite was used as a paint additive, not chalk.

The scientific results show the paint of Rembrandt and Velazquez, both 17th century masters, contained Calcium Carbonate. Results show Velazquez surpassed Rembrandt's use, and used greater quantities and mixed it with all his colors. Previous masters had traditionally mixed Calcium Carbonate with their lead white oil paint as an extender. Both Velazquez and Rembrandt used it to impart translucency and provide body to their hand ground oil paint, in addition to providing other beneficial properties to the paint. Studies show Rembrandt used only Chalk and Velazquez used Chalk and Calcite.

Analysis of the paint medium binder of both masters, also show additions of a protein substance. This substance could be 'hide glue', egg, or milk, but the analytical equipment cannot state for certain which. Scientists using advanced equipment admit their conclusions are always open to debate because many unknown factors of the painting's conservation history may erroneously influence the results. A practicing painter will know the immense value the addition of this protein ingredient will have on controlling the viscous oil. It stops dripping, bleeding and distortion of the paint. In my book I explain why I believe the only appropriate protein additive was Egg Glair.

CALCITE SUN OIL (abbreviated as CSO)

The 1988 research by scientists inspired me to create a modern binding oil mixture of Chalk and the Superior Oil of the Old Masters. This mixture is called, 'CALCITE SUN OIL'.

'CALCITE SUN OIL', is a measured mixture of Calcium Carbonate and the Superior oil of the Old Masters. 'Calcite Sun Oil' allows painters to achieve excellent results, whether mixed with Hand ground paints or mixed with Tube paints. 'Calcite Sun Oil' allows today's painters to achieve the Old Masters' Paint Quality with complete Safety and Permanence. 'CSO' is an abbreviation of 'Calcite Sun Oil.

10 IMPORTANT BENEFITS of 'Calcite Sun Oil' (CSO)
The benefits offered by CSO are somewhat different with Hand Ground paints than with Tube Paints. The Emulsions must be used in conjunction with the CSO for some of the results to be achieved.

1. FAST DRYING: The highly siccative property of the Superior Oil of the Old Masters provides the painter with fast drying paint, allowing the painter to complete a painting in less time. CSO paint can dry within 30 hours depending on the 7 factors that impact all paint drying: The oil, The pigment, The paint thickness, The ventilation, The temperature, The humidity, The additives. CSO dries through safe, natural means, as the CSO has absolutely no hazardous driers added to it.

2. INSURES ADHESION: CSO paint eliminates the dripping or the beading, of thick or thin paint, but the CSO paint MUST be used in conjunction with the either of the two Emulsions. The cement-like quality of CSO and the stickiness of the Emulsion, insures adhesion of the paint in exactly the place the painter puts it, if applied properly.

3. FACILITATES BLENDING: The viscosity of the 'Oil' in the CSO, facilitates blending for those painters wishing to create smooth transitions of color or uniquely soft textural effects. Painters using a style of realism will especially find CSO to their liking.

4. TRANSLUCENCY and TRANSPARENCY: CSO creates sumptuous translucent paint, whether it is thick impasto that will retain its character and brush markings, or the thinnest of clear color glazes. This is accomplished through simple mixtures and methods of application.

5. THICK IMPASTO TEXTURES: By adding just a few drops of the Viscous Emulsion, the CSO paint can be made stiff and thick textures can be easily made.. To create thick impasto textures the sequence of adding and grinding is important.
FIRST grind equal amounts of tube paint and CSO together.
SECOND, add a few drops of the emulsion and grind it well into the paint.
THIRD, add, and grind well, dry Calcium Carbonate into the mix.

6. COLOR DEPTH and LUSTER: CSO gives the paint a translucent enamel-like, deep color luster, which dries to a hard silky finish.

7. MICRO-FINE DETAILS: The extremely fine lines like those found in many Old Master paintings will be retained as painted, without bleeding or spreading. Tube oil paints properly ground together with CSO, can create the fine micro-lines with the use of "Calcite Sun Oil" alone, without the use of an Emulsion. The details must be painted into a damp coat of paint, or a damp coat of emulsion 'oil out'.

8. THIXOTROPY: CSO promotes a 'Thixotropic' quality to the oil paint. This means it allows painting wet paint ON TOP of wet paint which is different from the current method of painting "wet-in-wet". The nature of Tube oil paints (without adding CSO) do not allow painting "wet-on-top-of-wet" paint because of the non-viscous quality caused by the non-polymerized oil and the additives they are made of. The Thixotropic quality is stronger with the Hand Ground paints mixed with CSO, than with the Tube paints mixed with CSO, because of the non-polymerized oil contained in the Tube paints is not as viscous.

NOTE: I would like to clarify that to apply wet paint on top of wet paint, using the Thixotropic quality, takes a certain amount of skill to achieve. To achieve the Thixotropic qualities to the fullest, the painter requires a skilled and deft touch, at times feather light, at other times gouging and rough, and requires paying very close attention to the viscosity of the paint. For one to reach a high level of accomplishment, the craft of painting requires a certain degree of eye-hand coordination, the skill of manual dexterity in the handling of brushes, and a great amount of dedication and time. Through proper use of materials, it is possible to achieve this wonderful thixotropic quality. Thixotropic paint is made possible by the ingredients in the binder. **The paint must be viscous and sticky for thixotropy to be possible.**

9. ELIMINATES THE 'SUEDE EFFECT': Tube oil paints have a disturbing optical quality called the 'suede effect'. This is most noticeable when the paint is used right from the tube. The light reflects off of the various brush marks, making it difficult to see the true color. Changing the lighting does not eliminate this disturbing visual effect. The paintings of the Old Masters do NOT have this disturbing 'suede effect'. Adding CSO to Tube paint will eliminate the "suede effect".

10. ELIMINATES WRINKLING: Oil paint made with fast drying, Polymerized, sun thickened linseed/FLAX oil WILL wrinkle if the paint is thick. This happens because the TOP FILM LAYER of the paint dries so fast, it blocks oxygen from entering the remainder of the thick paint film. As the lower layers dry, they cause tension and wrinkle the top layer as it dries. Adding and grinding either of the Emulsions with the paint will prevent wrinkling, because the egg moisture slows down the drying of the paint film. My tests show that when Emulsion is added to the paint, though it is dry to the touch within 30 hours, it takes three days to dry HARD. The prevention of wrinkling is one of the most important benefits of the Emulsions, and was Rembrandt's secret that prevented his thick viscous impasto from wrinkling.

HOW TO MAKE 'CALCITE SUN OIL' (CSO)
HEALTH WARNING
**Calcium Carbonate is NOT toxic but the fine powder can be an irritant to some people.
Always wear a dust mask when handling ANY fine dry powder or pigment.**

IMPORTANT: You must have a GRINDING TABLE and a PALETTE KNIFE
GRINDING TABLE: I use a glazed floor tile that is 18 inches X 18 inches. You can buy them very cheaply at a home improvement center. Make sure it is glazed so it will not absorb the oil out of the mixture. Buy a mid-tone colored tile. Do not buy a white one nor a black one because they make it difficult to accurately see colors.
PALETTE KNIFE: I use a straight blade metal blade that is about 6 inches long and about ½ inch wide. The blade is stiff yet flexible. It has a wooden handle. You do not need a muller. Mullers are used when making large amounts. I recommend making daily amounts of CSO.

RECIPE: I use a teaspoon or tablespoon to measure the amounts.
1 part Oil; Use only the Superior Oil of the Old Masters for optimum results. A level measurement.
3 parts Calcium Carbonate Chalk, packed tight and level

You will be tempted to add more oil. DO NOT ADD MORE OIL THAN CALLED FOR IN THE RECIPE.
The amounts of Calcium Carbonate and the Oil must be measured accurately. Once you learn how to make the CSO, you will no longer need to measure. I recommend 'Chalk from Champagne, France. It is superior to the white powder sold at some art stores called, "French Chalk"'. Because some artists do not have the superior oil I created alternate mixtures of Chalk and Oil. Please read in the text.

SMALL AMOUNTS: I RECOMMEND MAKING ONLY ENOUGH CSO FOR THE DAYS WORK.
Place the Chalk on the Grinding table. Add the Oil. MIX together until all dry powder is moist. This takes two minutes. You will notice the Calcium Carbonate has an enormous capacity to absorb the oil.

DO NOT add more Oil than the formula calls for. Once the mixture is MIXED it must then be GROUND well together **with pressure**. Use a firm but flexible palette knife. MIXING and GRINDING are different. IF your blade is NOT BENDING, you are NOT GRINDING. GRIND with pressure. GRIND until you see no more dry chalk. This takes a few minutes. If the CSO is too loose, add a bit more chalk then MIX then GRIND. My Oil Painting DVD has a live film 12 minute demo in 'real time'.

LARGE AMOUNTS: Some artists like to make jars of CSO for use later on. Use your grinding table and either a muller or a firm palette knife. Place the powder and the oil on the grinding table and first MIX them together. Then spread out the mixture thinly over the grinding table and then GRIND the mixture well.
NOTE: It is important to keep the edge of the lid and the jar clean. The CSO is like cement and very strong. It may become difficult to remove the cap if not kept clean. Here is a simple trick. Before placing the cap, use your finger and dip it into some NON-SUNNED linseed oil, then lightly apply it around the jar edge. This NON-sunned oil dries very slowly and allows the cap to be removed easily.

IMPORTANT: Tightly cap the jar, and store it upside down on its lid when not in use! Store the jar upside down so it rests on the cap and keep it that way until needed. If the jar is kept right side up, the surface of the CSO will skin over because of the fast drying polymerized oil in contact with oxygen, and you will need to perforate the skin. When you need some CSO, turn the jar right side up, pop the lid slightly to allow pressure to exit. Let the CSO settle before removing the lid. When CSO is needed, take what you need out of the jar and FIRMLY GRIND it on the grinding table. Do this with your palette knife for about ten seconds.

STORAGE CONTAINER – USE GLASS ONLY
The only container to keep the CSO in, for short or long term storage, is a glass jar, as all other containers were found to be deficient. Aluminum tubes expand, plastic bags leak air, plastic bottles react chemically. The CSO keeps very well in a glass jar, if the jar lid is kept tightly closed and the jar is kept upside down on its lid.

CLEAN UP
On conclusion of the day's painting do not discard the left over paint or the left over CSO on the Grinding Table or Hand Palette. Scrape it up and place it in a glass jar. Add a bit of non-sun oil and mix well. It will turn a brownish color. This paint is still a high quality paint and can be used in priming, under painting and over painting. Studies of Rembrandt's priming containing many colors, show he did exactly this.

CSO SUMMARY

'**Calcite Sun Oil**', is a carefully measured mixture of only two ingredients, the Superior Oil of the Old Masters, and dry Calcium Carbonate powder.
'**Calcite Sun Oil**', uses the exceptional qualities of the Old Masters oil in providing important benefits for today's oil painter. Used alone, ALL thickened Oils WILL drip and sag, causing distortions due to their leveling property. These defects are solved through the formulation of "Calcite Sun Oil" in the proper mixture, and with the addition of a few drops of an emulsion, and use of an Emulsion 'Oil Out". See the chapter on making the emulsion.

'**Calcite Sun Oil**', when properly mixed with Tube oil paints, eliminates all its deficiencies and greatly improves its working properties by radically changing its non-viscous quality to a HIGHLY VISCOUS quality while maintaining an appropriate consistency and body." Calcite Sun Oil" is made with FLAX Oil. However, it may be made with Walnut, Poppy, or other drying oils. Do not use sunflower seed oil, it dries soft and can easily be scratched. Do not use non-drying oils, such as Olive Oil.

Today's commercially sold THIN OIL= "Alkali Refined Linseed Oil" and THICKENED OIL= 'Stand Linseed Oil' are deficient because they are very slow drying oils and because they have been refined and treated with caustic lye chemicals and solvents and heat. These mass produced industrial 19th and 20th century oils were not available to the Old Masters.

ACADEMIC TERMINOLOGY IN FINE ART PAINTING

The Art of Painting is noble and deserving of respect.
The Old Masters used various Ochres and Umbers they obtained from the ground.
We call these important colors and ingredients 'Earths", not Dirt, nor Mud, nor Muck.
The name, 'Calcite Sun Oil" honors the archival ingredients of the Old Masters.

Slang terms have no place in Academic Art terminology in naming the mixtures of ingredients the Great Master artists used, as they painted their Masterpieces.
As many artists today experiment with various mixtures of oil and substances, they use slang terms such as: 'Gunk', 'Goup', and 'Putty''. Slang terms denigrate Painting and the Old Masters.
GUNK collects in auto radiators
GOUP is a glue
PUTTY is a water sealant used by plumbers.

'CALCITE SUN OIL' IS A REMARKABLE AND REVOLUTIONARY GRINDING OIL FOR OIL PAINTING AND IS BASED ON THE ANCIENT KNOWLEDGE OF THE OLD MASTER EUROPEAN PAINTERS.

CHAPTER SIX
EMULSIONS
THE VAN EYCK'S SECRET WONDER MEDIUM

The mixing of egg and oil is a true 'studio secret' of the Old Masters. A statement by Professor Dr. Ernst Van de Wetering from his book, 'REMBRANDT, The Painter at Work' [paraphrased]

THE EMULSION
An Emulsion is a mixture of an oily fluid and a watery fluid. Normally you cannot mix oily and watery fluids, but a chicken egg has unique qualities, that allows the mixing of an oily fluid and a watery fluid. Prior to the perfection of Oil Painting, Northern European artists in the 1300's were painting with egg tempera. This method uses a mixture of egg yolk and water, which is mixed with dry pigment. History informs us the Van Eycks were trained as egg tempera painters before they began painting with oils.

HISTORY OF EMULSIONS
JAN and HUBERT VAN EYCK , THE WONDER MEDIUM OF EMULSIONS

THE VAN EYCK BROTHERS, Hubert (b.? - d.1426) and Jan Van Eyck (b.1395 - d.1441), developed a medium that has eluded artists for centuries and has spawned numerous theories. Authorities agree the oil paintings made by the Van Eycks survive in an excellent state of preservation after almost 600 years. Because they did not leave us a manuscript to pass on their knowledge, we will never know the true methods and materials they used. In recent years, scientific evidence determined the use of egg-oil emulsion in their paint (see Bibliography; Van De Wetering).

History and modern scholarship tell us the 15th century Van Eyck brothers were trained as egg tempera painters. We know they did not invent, but rather perfected, the ancient oil paint method. I believe their egg tempera training and knowledge, gave them intimate knowledge on the characteristics and working properties of "egg" as a painting medium. I believe they adapted important procedures from the Egg Tempera painting method, to solve the problems of oil painting they encountered.

I believe the Van Eyck's and their followers DID NOT use Solvents, Resins, or Driers mixed with their oil painting method because they are not necessary and are detrimental. I believe the Van Eycks developed an effective 'paint medium' that was easily made and easily applied. A medium that was non-invasive, non-destructive, non solvent based and completely safe and permanent.

I believe the Van Eycks "secret" was made of TWO PARTS:
[1] Their use of a variety of egg-oil emulsions used throughout the entire oil painting process.
[2] A critical unique application method of the 'Oil Out'.

I do not know the exact contents or ratios mixture the Van Eycks used, but my experiments prove egg-oil emulsions do solve the many problems inherent in oil painting. My views and experiments are validated by recent scientific examinations that found slight amounts of Emulsions in the paint of Rembrandt and Velasquez and Van Eyck [see Bibliography; Van De Wetering and Garrido-Perez].

PROBLEMS OF THE OIL PAINTING MEDIUM
The Van Eycks had the same oil painting problems we have today.

1. SLOW DRYING NON-POLYMERIZED OIL
Painters found that paint made with non-polymerized oil, dries extremely slowly, therefore not conducive to either creative work or to the demands of commerce. In addition, the paint is stiff and difficult to blend, it dries matte with poor color depth, and dries with a comparatively 'soft' paint surface.

2. SAGGING POLYMERIZED OIL
Painters found that paint made with POLYMERIZED oil offered excellent results, but had serious disadvantages. It allowed easy blending, it increased color depth and luster, and dried fast with a hard tough gloss surface. But, it sagged and distorted the work. Also, tactile textures and fine line details were impossible because of its extreme leveling. Oil can be artificially polymerized within a few hours by boiling, but boiled oil yellows. Natural polymerization by exposure to the sun and air takes about 30 days.

3. LOSS OF DETAIL RETENTION
Paint made with POLYMERIZED oils alone, will NOT allow fine lines to remain sharp or clear. Details will flow, bleed and there will be distortions. Paint made with NON-POLYMERIZED oils will hold their detail, but need to be thinned to be brushed, this then causes some loss of sharpness of details.

4. POOR ADHESION
Any oil or oil paint glaze applied to a dry layer, of glossy hard oil paint, will "bead" up (also called "trickle" or "crawl"). The wet paint does not stick, it beads up into droplets indicating poor adhesion. This condition requires the dry surface to be "etched" through one of several means, in order for the new layer to adhere to it. The various "means", be it, sandpaper, pumice powder, urine, solvent, varnish, garlic, potato, do help solve the problem by softening or etching into the paint layer, but the nature of some of these are destructive to superficially-dry, fine detailed layers of oil paint. This is counter-productive to the creation of fine detailed work that needs protection, not destruction.

THE IMPORTANCE OF EMULSIONS TO OIL PAINTING

1. SOLVENTS ARE DISRUPTIVE TO PAINT
I believe the Van Eycks did not use solvents or solvent-resin mixtures for their medium because of the destructive effect of these types of media and more importantly, because they are not needed.

My experiments show that solvents are best used as a cleaning agent, and paint remover. The theory that solvents mixed with oil to thin it, reduces the amount of oil used, and therefore may reduce the yellowing of paint is a FALSE theory. The fact is, solvent will completely evaporate, leaving the SAME amount of the same oil. Also, other factors cause yellowing: i.e. quality of the oil, method of processing, contamination of seeds. Excessive use of solvents dangerously reduces the binding of pigment particles with the oil causing the paint to dry powdery and matte, and endangering the painting's permanence. For maximum permanence, the pigment must be completely encased in oil for protection, and the dried oil film of the painting surface must dry hard for maximum protection of the pigment. Solvents do increase drying of oil by evaporating, but the use of naturally sun thickened UNREFINED cold pressed linseed/FLAX oil, which dries under 30 hours and eliminates the need to add solvents or driers for accelerating the drying.

2. AN EMULSION IS NON-DISRUPTIVE TO SOFT PAINT
I believe the Van Eycks did not use the yolk and only the clear of the egg. The yolk is egg oil and cures at a different rate than does linseed/flax oil. The egg yolk cures in several months and the flax linseed oil does not finalize curing for hundreds of years. Once the egg white is converted to Glair, it was mixed with flax linseed oil to make an emulsion. These were either a viscous or a non-viscous Emulsion for 'oiling out' between paint layers, as a preparation layer for in-painting extremely fine micro-lines, and as a paint thinner to allow easier brushing, or to make thick impasto textured paint..

My experiments show the application of an Emulsion is non-disrupting to superficially dry, delicate work that was previously completed, no matter how hard one rubs it in BY HAND ONLY. An Emulsion makes painting fine details easy, and is an excellent thinner. IN CONTRAST,use of any solution containing a solvent will soften and smear paint, and will be damaging to a thin, fine, superficially dry paint layer, especially if any rubbing occurs.

3. BENEFITS OF VISCOUS PAINT
I believe the Van Eycks' ground their pigments in a highly viscous, Sun Thickened mucilage free Cold Pressed Linseed/FLAX Oil to make a highly viscous paint that offered many benefits.

My experiments show this creates an easily blending, enamel-like, lustrous, fast drying, tough skinned paint that will protect the pigments with a hard glossy surface.

4. VISCOUS PAINT PROBLEMS
I believe the Van Eycks solved the sagging, dripping, leveling problems inherent in viscous paint by adding a small amount of an Egg Glair-Oil Emulsion to it, and by painting in thin layers while avoiding impasto applications.

My experiments show that any paint ground in a polymerized oil alone, will become very leveling. This causes it to sag and drip whether applied in a thin glaze or thick impasto, and fine lines and details will blur and lose clarity. My experiments show that a small amount of Glair-Oil Emulsion mixed well into a viscous paint, will completely eliminate any sagging or dripping whether applied in a thin layer or a thick impasto, the impasto paint will not wrinkle, and ALL fine lines and details will remain sharply defined.

5. MICRO-FINE LINES and VISCOUS PAINT

I believe the Van Eycks used a thick, viscous paint to paint their extraordinarily fine micro-lines and detail. Their paintings and others of their school are characterized by extremely fine details and micro-fine lines. Their clarity caused Van Eyck's contemporary artists to wonder what paint medium was used to make them possible.

My experiments show that when thick, sticky, viscous paint is applied with a super fine soft hair brush into the correctly applied 'oil out' layer of an Egg Glair-Oil Emulsion medium, [or into an 'oil out' made of 1 part CSO and 2 parts Non-polymerized oil] the thick paint will create extremely sharp and extraordinarily fine micro-lines, that have an elevated body and hold their sharp clarity. This viscous condition of the paint is needed to paint in the fine micro-lines and details we see in their paintings.

6. VISCOUS EMULSION vs. NON-VISCOUS EMULSION in the 'OIL OUT'

I do not know the exact RATIO mixtures the Van Eycks used for making their Oil Out medium..
My experiments have been conducted with two Emulsions I formulated:
[1] A NON-VISCOUS EMULSION (NVE) = GLAIR mixed with NON-POLYMERIZED oil [thin oil].
[2] A VISCOUS EMULSION (VE) = GLAIR mixed with POLYMERIZED oil [thick oil].

My experiments show that the non-polymerized oil used in the NON-VISCOUS emulsion, reacts with the sticky, viscous polymerized oil used in the grinding of the paint, causing it to stiffen as in the 'resin effect', and one can argue that use of a NON-VISCOUS EMULSION , instead of a VISCOUS EMULSION, results in the very finest lines. However, one can use either Emulsion for the 'oil out'.

7. EGG and OIL RATIOS

I do not know the exact ratios or the exact mixtures used by the Van Eycks , but my experiments lead me to believe they used different mixtures for different purposes. Ratios I have experimented with are: (oil is the first number) 3:1 , 2:1 , 1 ½:1, 1:1, 1:2, 1:3. I am satisfied that the Emulsion mixture of 3 parts of oil to 2 part of glair is the best. More Oil than Glair makes a 'fatty' Emulsion. More Glair than Oil makes a 'lean' Emulsion.

My experiments show that too much oil causes adhesion problems. And, too much Glair causes a fragile film since Glair by itself is brittle. My experiments with the Glair were successful. My experiments with the yolk proved the yolk to be ineffective and unneeded.

I have not experimented with mixed oils called ' CO-POLY" oils, in the making of emulsions.

GLAIR- THE IDEAL EMULSION INGREDIENT

My experiments show that GLAIR, which is the white of the egg that has beaten to a froth and then distilled to a clear liquid, is THE ideal 'protein' ingredient for mixing with oil, to make an Emulsion for use with Oil painting (NOTE: Glair is not a desirable binder for Egg Tempera painting).

My experiments have shown that the use of GLAIR, meets the important requirements for use in oil painting: 1. It dries very fast even when mixed with oil into an emulsion. 2. It is transparent. 3. It is thin bodied.4. It is a sticky adhesive. 5. It is a natural binder. 6. It is archival permanent.

The reasons why neither GLUE nor MILK are desirable is because the glue would make the calcium carbonate opaque white, defeating its main benefit of creating translucency, and though the milk (non-fat milk) is excellent for making emulsions, it dries very slowly, which is another very undesirable property.

.

For Glair to be usable in oil painting it MUST first be mixed with the oil, thereby creating an Emulsion. Neither Glair nor Yolk alone without being emulsified with oil can be EFFECTIVELY mixed into oil paint, as egg will float and bead up no matter how hard one grinds. My experiments show that the yolk of the egg is not needed, nor desirable for mixing with oil paint, and is a hindrance for use with oil painting. Yolk is viscous, and is appropriately used as the best binder for Egg Tempera painting BUT NOT for oil painting. In Oil Painting, the polymerized linseed/Flax oil itself is sufficiently viscous and additional viscous ingredients are not desired. When mixed with oil, the viscous thick egg yolk dries slowly and remains soft for undesirable extended periods of time. For these reasons, Glair is the ideal egg ingredient because of its properties listed above.

Rembrandt's Binding Medium
I offer the following comments regarding Professor Dr. Van De Wetering's statements in his book, "REMBRANDT: The Painter at Work". These comments are made with the highest respect for the tireless work Dr. Van De Wetering has devoted to the study of Rembrandt's work. In his important and extremely valuable book, Dr. Van De Wetering devotes an entire chapter to Rembrandt's Binding Medium, see Chapter IX , pages 225 to 243. The entire chapter is of great interest to today's oil painters, yet, page 239 is the key page to study. I will paraphrase the points to be commented on, with accuracy.
Dr Van De Wetering says that egg in some form, saying it could be the yolk, or the white, or the entire egg, has "considerable" impact on oil paint, when it is included in the OIL PAINT. As a practicing painter I have performed experiments with glair that prove the truth of his statement and I will add additional information.

2. Dr. Van De Wetering cites use of ' some mixing techniques" as important to dispersing WATER into oil but he does not disclose them . Just prior to that statement, he describes EGG as basically being a WATERY substance. His written words are not clear, but his meaning is clear that he is referring to EGG and not WATER as the ingredient to be dispersed with the oil.
I note that in the book's section of Acknowledgements, expressed by Dr. Van De Wetering (see pages XIV and XV) he states that he is grateful to many translators [his text that is written in Dutch]. Dr. Van De Wetering is Dutch and he himself claims his English is "Pidgin English". He says he does not hold any of his translators responsible for [errors in] their translations.

3. Egg, which contains water, repels oil and oil normally floats on top of a watery substance. However, when oil and dry pigment are firmly mixed together into OIL PAINT, it is the watery egg that beads up and floats on top of the oil paint if one attempts to mix the egg into the oil paint.

4. Dr. Van De Wetering states that by mixing an ' oil/pigment mixture"(which is 'oil paint') with egg , using either the yolk or the entire egg, an emulsion can be easily made. This text statement is erroneous on two points. First, it is very difficult to mix (grind) egg into OIL PAINT because it will bead up and float. Secondly, the text is in error because in truth, an Emulsion is a LIQUID made by mixing egg with an oil together ---not by mixing egg alone with oil paint. His text erroneously claims the mixing of the egg with OIL PAINT (oil paint is a mixture of oil and dry powdered pigment) creates an emulsion. Though he correctly cites some historical uses of soaking dry pigment in water, and that water can be part of the emulsion. However, a practicing painter who has already ground oil paint (by mixing oil and dry pigment) CANNOT easily mix egg into the OIL PAINT, as it will bead up and float and resist all efforts to grind the two together. A simple experiment will prove my point.

5. Dr. Van De Wetering then calls the mixture of WATER, and EGG, and PAINT, a 'paste", and in the subsequent sentence he calls it an 'Emulsion", and in a subsequent sentence calls it 'paint'. He uses the three words as synonyms. Calling 'oil paint' a 'paste' is not incorrect, and is acceptable, but it is very unnecessary and confusing. I believe it is confusing for these reasons: 'Oil paint' is a mixture of oil and dry powdered pigment. An Emulsion is a liquid mixture of egg with oil (in this case). An Emulsion is an opaque white liquid, but becomes crystal clear when mixed into "oil paint". An emulsion is easily, very easily, mixed into oil paint. It does not float nor does it resist when mixed together. **This is the magic of the Emulsion, and the only way to mix egg with oil paint effortlessly, fully, and efficiently**.

6. Oil paint that has been mixed with an emulsion has very unique behavioral properties [the modern term is 'rheology'] that contrasts greatly to oil paint made of only oil and pigment alone, as Dr. Van De Wetering has correctly noted. Certainly, Rembrandt, Velazquez and the Van Eycks learned of this and used it to maximum benefit.

7. Dr Van De Wetering cites evidence of Van Eyck's use of mixing egg with oil paint, and cites the 20th century modern Dutch master, Karel Appel, as using the mixture. He cites that there is not known to exist, a 17th century manuscript of the uses of egg with oil paint, and calls it a true 'secret formula'.

NOTE: Dr Van de Wetering is missing a very important part of how Emulsions are used in Oil painting: THE METHOD OF APPLICATION. My own testing allows me to believe the secret VAN EYCK medium is in fact made of TWO PARTS: [1] The emulsion. [2] A critical application method, described elsewhere in this book.

I have the highest respect for Dr. Ernst Van De Wetering's work. I am honored to have met him in Los Angeles at the Getty Museum in October 2010. I take this opportunity to mention important aspects of oil painting that have NOT been discussed nor mentioned by Dr. Van De Wetering in his published works.

In his book on Rembrandt, Dr. Van De Wetering discusses the mixing of egg WITH the oil and paint. He states that modern tests cannot distinguish what part of the egg Rembrandt mixed with his paint, saying it could be either egg yolk, whole egg, or egg white.

My experiments show why the egg white, converted to Glair, is the ideal ingredient Rembrandt would have used.My experience as a painter led me to determine the NEED for, and then to develop two very different Emulsions which have, important different properties. To distinguish one from the other, they were given different names. One is the 'Viscous Emulsion', the other is the 'Non-Viscous Emulsion'.

Dr. Van De Wetering's published work makes no mention that an Emulsion can be made as either VISCOUS or NON-VISCOUS. My practical application of materials show that an emulsion of GLAIR and the Superior oil of the Old Masters with oil of different viscosities are needed for maintaining control of viscous oil paint, and for changing its consistency, and each Emulsion offers important and distinct uses in the paint application process. A painter MUST experiment and gain intimate knowledge of the subtle nuances and variations.

HOW EMULSIONS IMPACT OIL PAINTING

First: The mixture of Glair and Oil, into an opaque Emulsion mixture, allows egg to be efficiently and easily mixed with oil paint vs. trying to mix egg alone directly into paint, which is problematic if not impossible to do effectively.

Second: Either of the two Emulsions are invaluable as the 'oil out' preparation of the surface. This 'oil out" preparation insures adhesion, prevents trickling and dripping, and prevents the spreading of the viscous paint. They allow micro- fine lines to remain as clear and distinct as placed, and the paint retains its body. It can be argued that the non-viscous emulsion allows finer lines to be painted. The 'oil out" application must be as thin as possible, and must be rubbed in, and must NOT be applied with a brush. This 'oil out" procedure also allows the correct manner of applying a glaze, which uses thick viscous paint that has not been liquefied.

Third: Either of the two Emulsions, allow the creation of thick viscous impasto paint that is easily blended, yet holds all brush marks, or for creating extremely thin paint, that will remain as placed.

Fourth: Both of the Emulsions promote thixotropy, allowing wet paint to be applied on top of wet paint in one sitting. This does take skill.

Fifth: The addition of the Emulsions to viscous oil paint prevents the paint from wrinkling. <u>This is one of the most important discoveries I made</u> in regards to the value and use of the Glair-Linseed oil Emulsions. It explains Rembrandt's thick viscous oil impasto that has NO wrinkles. The slow evaporation of the moisture of the egg white mixed into the highly viscous oil paint, prevents the wrinkling

*****

AN EMULSION IS SUPERIOR TO RESINS

In ancient times, artists found out that some ingredients will stop the oil from dripping or sagging. One of these ingredients is use of a natural RESIN, either a soft resin like Mastic, or a hard resin like Copal or Amber. Today, some artists still use hard resins. Today we have synthetic SOFT resins like Dammar that will also keep the oil from sagging.

Master painters from the past also found that EGG will also keep the oil from sagging and dripping. The reason the EGG is superior to the RESINS is because mixing Resin with oil, only causes them to CO-MINGLE as they WILL NOT truly integrate. IN CONTRAST, EGG will integrate itself INTO THE OIL by nature of the emulsification process, on a molecular level and they become ONE SUBSTANCE. My experiments prove the crystal clarity of a properly formulated Emulsion.

Numerous Emulsion formulas are in old and new books. Generations of artists repeat the complicated USELESS mixtures, as they mix water, solvents, resins, driers and other ingredients with the oil, HOPING to create a workable Emulsion. The two Emulsions I formulated are SIMPLE, ARCHIVAL, and made in a matter of seconds. They are truly a 'WONDER MEDIUM' for oil painting. A later Emulsion I created is called 'ESPESO' based on my research of Rubens' methods. It also is a 'wonder' medium and allows maximum thixotropic painting effects. Thixotropy means that a WET layer of oil paint can be painted ON TOP OF A WET LAYER of oil paint without smearing the lower wet layer.

MAKING THE EMULSION

1. PARTS OF THE EGG

The egg has two basic parts; [1] The yolk which is very oily [2] The clear white which has only an extremely small amount of oil. In the Egg Tempera painting method (NOT the Oil Painting method), ONLY the yolk is used because it contains natural egg OIL, that gives pliability and permanence to the tempera paint made from it. The yolk is mixed with an equal amount of water because the yolk is an extremely viscous, sticky YOLK OIL. The addition of water creates a paint that is easy to brush. A less commonly used Egg Tempera recipe uses the whole egg in which the yolk and the white are beaten together.

2. ELIMINATING THE YOLK - USING THE WHITE

Since an emulsion is made of egg and LINSEED/FLAX OIL, I believe ENOUGH of an oily substance is in the Linseed/FLAX oil therefore there is no need to add more oil. My experiments show we can eliminate the oily yolk and use only the egg white. The egg white is very uneven, being thin and thick. Therefore, it must be beaten with a spoon to an even consistency. This process causes the egg white to froth. The froth is removed and allowed to sit and distill, and the clear liquid is called GLAIR. The Glair is sticky and it aids adhesion. The frothing method is demonstrated in my oil painting DVD.

GLAIR has an ancient history as a paint binder. It is fully permanent and archival. Archival permanence is relative. This means the material, if cared for properly, will last for hundreds of years. Nothing in this world has ABSOLUTE permanence, as all natural materials degrade with sufficient time.

Scholars agree on one fact: In one regard, EGG is the finest binder for Fine Art painting known to Mankind because it does not alter the color of the pigments. It is superior to any vegetable oil, be it Flax, Walnut or others. However in another regard, Flax Linseed oil is superior to Egg because egg is non flexible, it must be painted on a rigid surface. Flax linseed oil remains flexible for hundreds of years and can be painted on canvas.

All natural Resins become brittle and yellow over time. Scientists say that egg white glair becomes gray over time. They refer to the 'Tonality' meaning 'coolness' of egg, versus 'warmth' of resins. Science reports that Synthetic resins also eventually become a gray cool tonality. Natural resins become a warm tonality. Glair does NOT BECOME OPAQUE over time and in fact remains fully transparent. The paintings of the Van Eycks and Old Masters that used glair are proof of its absolute stability and archival permanence. Illuminated Medieval Books of the 1200's used glair as a pigment binder, and their colors are as accurate as when painted.

Egg white has an ancient history as a VARNISH for completed oil paintings and for completed Egg Tempera paintings. Old texts make positive and negative comments, contradicting each other. Egg white glair was used as a varnish for oil paintings because it will cover the 'sticky' oil film, and by doing so, prevents dust from sticking to the oil surface. The egg glair application dries within minutes, and any dust that lands on it is easily removed with a DRY rag. Any dust landing on a sticky oil film cannot be removed, and remains forever. However the Glair varnish is NOT waterproof until the Glair cures over a period of months and years.

The Native Americans used Egg White as a pliable sealant for their canoes. They learned that egg white, when heated by hot sun or by placing near a fire, the egg white becomes like rubber and seals against moisture. This explains why VAN EYCK, placed his completed Egg Tempera painting out into the sun. He wanted the heat of the sun to render the egg waterproof. The story goes that the sun was too hot and it burst the joints of his painting. VAN EYCK then sought out a medium that would dry WATER PROOF in the shade, and eventually made mixtures of egg and oil into what is known today as an EMULSION.

3. MIXING EGG WITH OIL TO CREATE AN EMULSION
You CANNOT effectively mix pure GLAIR into paint, as it will float on top of it no matter how hard you grind. To add GLAIR to paint, the Glair must first be mixed with Oil to make the Emulsion. As an Emulsion mixture, Glair can be mixed into the paint effortlessly and effectively.

4. FACTORS TO CONSIDER WITH RATIO MIXTURES
The ratio of Oil to Glair is important. My experiments show that use of a large amount more of Glair than Oil will result in a matte, fragile film. For purposes of improved working properties and permanence, it should have more oil than Glair. Too much oil in the mixture will create an Emulsion that will not adhere correctly and will 'bead' up on a dry surface. Too much Glair in the mixture will make it difficult to mix the Glair and the Oil together. An Emulsion with more Glair than Oil is called a 'lean' Emulsion and is not useful in Oil Painting. An Emulsion with more Oil than Glair is called a 'fat' Emulsion and is ideal for use in Oil Painting.
I have experimented with mixture ratios of 3:1, 2:1, 1&½:1, 1:1 , and, 1:2, 1:3, The first number is the oil, the second number is the glair- volume measurement. My tests show that an emulsion made of 3 parts oil and 2 parts glair is ideal for use in Oil Painting.

5. GLAIR VISCOSITY
Another factor affecting the results is the viscosity of the Glair, just as much as the viscosity of the Oil. Old manuscripts state that one-day old Glair is better than freshly made Glair. Non-refrigerated Glair dries hard into a brittle glob after a few days. Glair keeps well when refrigerated.

6. THIN PAINT vs. THICK PAINT
THIN paint made with sun thickened oil dries completely, throughout its body, but, THICK impasto paint remains wet and dries very slowly within a dried top skin. Any application of a fast drying layer on top of a paint layer not thoroughly dried WILL crack or wrinkle. The Van Eycks avoided these problems by painting with very THIN paint. A THIN paint layer made of UNREFINED Sun Thickened Cold Pressed oil, dries fast, does NOT wrinkle, and provides maximum color transparency. A small amount of an Egg-Oil Emulsion added and mixed well into thick paint will completely eliminate any wrinkling. Experiments show that adding an additional small amount of dry calcium carbonate to paint, AFTER the emulsion was mixed into the paint, will immediately create a body with an extremely firm texture that will NOT level out and can be piled high. Tests indicate this is what Rembrandt did to create his thick impasto paint. See the section titled, 'Rembrandt's White Oil Paint' for recreating his paint.

EMULSION UPDATES

Both emulsions, the VISCOUS EMULSION and the NON VISCOUS EMULSION play a crucial part in the CSO METHOD. My published book states it must be kept refrigerated because egg will spoil. Yet, experience shows that over weeks, it will spoil even when refrigerated. The Old Masters did not have refrigerators and use of egg led to a name called PUTRIDO in the Italian language. In Spanish [my first language as a child] the word PODRIDO is similar and means rotten or spoiled and we all know the odor of rotten eggs. Some added either liquor or vinegar to help prolong the life of the emulsion. I do not add either one to my emulsions.

Regardless if vinegar or liquor is added, the egg eventually goes bad with an odor and the emulsion turn brown. Science tells us vinegar contains ascetic acid and it impacts the Albumen which is Protein. Therefore, I do NOT recommend adding vinegar to the emulsion for oil painting, but with the new CSO-EGG TEMPERA medium and gesso that will be covered with oil paints, vinegar is needed in the mixture with the chalk. Some artists have told me that vinegar impacts certain pigments.

One problem I see with refrigeration of an egg emulsion is that the closed jar creates a certain amount of condensation of water. This is not helpful or desirable. Certainly the Old Masters did not have to deal with this factor of refrigeration. Possibly the best approach is to make the emulsion fresh for use, keep it capped tightly when not used and let it sit in a cool room at room temperature, discarding it after a couple of days. Always use a new unused jar for new egg emulsion mixtures. Egg tempera experts say no matter how much soap and water used to wash out a used jar, it contaminates new mixtures.

Two things are happening chemically to the emulsion mixture. One is the sun oil is very acidic. The other is the Glair is very complex in its structure as is the oil. Over time you will see a phenomenon. The oil will darken, as some of it separates and sits on the floor of the jar. YET. The emulsion that is fully emulsified and seen clinging to the walls of the jar remains fully transparent when thin, or when thick it is opaque with a clean pale white color. When used as an "oil out', the thinness of the emulsion is clear and as transparent as crystal glass. This transparency remains constant and once it dries, there is no color change nor decomposition over the years. It may be best to make the emulsions fresh every few days, and not let the water condensation nor the vinegar/alcohol impact the effectiveness.

CHAPTER SEVEN
THE "OIL OUT"

The use of an ' OIL OUT" in painting is a distinguished and important painting procedure well documented throughout the history of oil painting and was used by the GREATEST masters, such as Rubens, Rembrandt, Velazquez and Titian.

YET, misinformed 'oil painting experts' of the 20th century—criticize use of an 'oil out'. This is because some lacking SUSTAINED practical studio painting experience, and others ignoring the lessons and procedures of the Old Masters, and **all of them being ignorant of the superior true oil of the Old Masters** lack understanding. They are accustomed to using the inferior industrial linseed oil of the 19th and 20th century and have seen its inferiority. Ignorance coupled with improperly interpreting science, they have erroneously warned artists not to OIL OUT because they claim linseed oil will yellow.

They further warn the "LESS OIL THE BETTER". This is mistaken, misguided and ignorant advice from these 'experts'. It is reminiscent of the ignorant condemnation of the OIL PAINTING MEDIUM by 19th century French Academics who similarly warned artists of their day...saying all oil paintings will yellow. Saying these things, as they ignored the perfectly preserved colors and oil paint of the Van Eyck OIL paintings, and other 400 year old FLAXSEED/LINSEED OIL paintings in their famous LOUVRE museum.

CHOICE OF "OIL OUT" MEDIUMS
I HAVE CREATED THREE DIFFERENT EMULSION "OIL OUT" MEDIUMS. A FOURTH 'OIL OUT" MEDIUM IS NOT AN EMULSION. EACH WILL ACCOMPLISH A DIFFERENT PURPOSE.

THE CSO ' VISCOUS EMULSION [VE]- A medium to paint very fine details and micro-fine lines as Van Eyck painted.

The CSO 'NON VISCOUS EMULSION' [NVE] - A slower drying version of the Viscous Emulsion. It can be argued that this emulsion allows even finer details and lines than the VE.

THE CSO ' ESPESO' EMULSION - Use this to paint with MAXIMUM THIXOTROPY as Rubens and Rembrandt painted.

THE CSO ' AGUADO' [this medium is not an emulsion] For a more fluid paint and for large paintings as Velazquez and Rubens painted. The Aguado can be applied with a brush- the three Emulsions MUST be applied by hand and rubbed to an ultra-thin film.

ACADEMIC TERMINOLOGY vs SLANG TERMS

Art terms from different cultures and languages are used interchangeably and with appropriate respect for words of NATIONAL LANGUAGE ORIGIN.
Sfumato, Sgraffito = ITALIAN.
Mische, Mahlstick = GERMAN
Aguado, Espeso = SPANISH
Frottage = FRENCH

Each of these words have international meaning to an artist.
There is some confusion today in the TERMINOLOGY used in describing the OIL OUT medium.
Some MAL INFORMED English speakers refer to an OIL OUT...as a "COUCH" or a ' CUSHION".
This is a fractured form of the French word, COUCHE [phonetically pronounced KOO-SHAY]
which is a French word that means , 'a film of oil or paint'.

The English word 'COUCH' is a sofa, a piece of furniture.
The English word ' CUSHION' is a pillow
The English word 'COUCH' is,'Canape' in French.
The words COUCH and CUSHION are NON DESCRIPTIVE for painting, but VERY DESCRIPTIVE for furniture and bedding, sleeping or resting.

THE TERM, 'OIL OUT' IS AN ABBREVIATION FOR
*'OIL RUBBED IN AND OIL WIPED **OUT**'*
This term is descriptive, instructional, goal oriented and important for oil painting:
The oil is RUBBED IN and then it is WIPED OUT, in order to leave the thinnest film possible. The Emulsion 'oil out' mediums cannot be applied with a brush.

PURPOSES OF THE 'OIL OUT'
The important purpose of the OIL OUT is to act as a LUBRICANT for allowing easier brushing as well as to increase adhesion of layers. The composition of the OIL OUT LIQUID is very important. An OIL OUT liquid must not contain a SOLVENT since the OIL OUT liquid must be RUBBED IN in order to achieve an ultra-thin film. ANY liquid containing a solvent will loosen and weaken the lower paint film that is in process of drying. One can vigorously RUB IN an emulsion on a fragile oil paint film, without lifting, softening, or disrupting the paint film.

'PURE OIL' by itself is not an effective OIL OUT medium because pure oil by itself will
drip...even thin layers. One must never use PURE SUN OIL by itself because the OIL OUT will certainly cause the oil paint to drip and run. The old Masters added a PROTEIN such as egg to stop the drip.

EMULSIONS FOR OIL OUTS
The VISCOUS EMULSION, (VE).
The NON-VISCOUS EMULSION, (NVE).

They differ slightly when used as a thinner, but the difference between the two is important to understand. I believe the Old Masters knew the ratio mixtures and properties intimately, and how they functioned under different circumstances, but they did not record them. Therefore we do not know exactly how they mixed or used them. My experiments allow me to share my results. I have tried several ratios, and feel that 3 parts of oil, mixed with 2 parts of glair, is best. I use a teaspoon to measure the 'parts'

HOW TO MAKE the VISCOUS EMULSION, (VE)
Use THREE parts UNREFINED Sun Thickened polymerized cold pressed Linseed/FLAX oil, with TWO parts GLAIR. The sun oil is very viscous and thick—make sure you let all the oil drip off the spoon, each time. Place two or three penny coins or small pebbles in the capped jar to help the mixing. Shake vigorously a few minutes. Mixed thoroughly together, the solution becomes white and opaque. When rubbed onto a dry surface, the opaqueness disappears and becomes crystal clear. I no longer refrigerate to prevent spoiling of the egg as I previously said. This emulsion is recommended for TUBE paints or with hand ground paint made with non-polymerized oil because the viscous sun oil dries faster than the NVE.

HOW TO MAKE the NON-VISCOUS EMULSION, (NVE)
Use 3 parts UNREFINED, non-polymerized cold pressed Linseed/FLAX oil, with 2 parts GLAIR. Place both in a capped jar with a few pebbles or coins to help the mixing. Shake vigorously a few minutes. Mixed thoroughly together, the solution becomes white and opaque. When rubbed into a dry surface, the opaqueness disappears and becomes crystal clear. This emulsion is recommended for Hand Ground paint that was ground with sun oil. It dries slower than the (VE).

*****

HOW TO APPLY THE EMULSION 'OIL OUT'

THE EMULSION MUST BE APPLIED –ONLY- WITH THE BARE HAND OR FINGERS
NEVER WITH A BRUSH, NOR A RAG, NOR A PAPER TOWEL NOR A GLOVE
 [please follow this important procedure as stated].
IT MUST BE RUBBED IN FOR SEVERAL MINUTES, ONLY WITH THE BARE HAND
DO NOT USE A RAG OR OTHER ITEMS FOR THE RUBBING,
RUB UNTIL YOU FEEL A RESISTANCE TO THE RUBBING.
THE EMULSION 'OIL OUT' MUST BE APPLIED CORRECTLY OR IT WILL FAIL

The rubbing causes FRICTION which causes HEAT and AIR to enter the Emulsion. This causes the natural moisture in the egg to evaporate. Once evaporated, only the oil and the sticky Albumen of the Glair remain. The sticky Albumen causes the oil to stay in place. This is the secret of the Emulsion, and why it is truly a 'WONDER MEDIUM'. Also, for it to succeed, only the superior linseed/Flax oil must be used. Once applied correctly, the artist paints into the DAMP wet film of the Emulsion. Before painting again the next day, apply a new 'oil out' if the paint is tacky dry and will not smear when rubbed. Use it to 'oil out' any dry matte areas to restore the luster and color depth.

SMALL AREA: To apply the Emulsion to a small area, dip the fingers into it and rub a sufficient amount to the dry painted surface with a firm circular motion. The cloudiness will quickly disappear and becomes clear as glass. If your hand is flowing smoothly on the surface, you have too much emulsion. Stop and dry your fingers with a dry cloth and GENTLY, with a soft cloth or towel, wipe off any excess emulsion. DO THIS GENTLY. Then resume the circular rubbing and repeat. Continue until you feel a drag to the circular rubbing. Look at it in an oblique side light as you rub. You will see that at first, the emulsion beads up, but as you rub, it begins to stick, and becomes crystal clear. Once this state is achieved, the fine line details can be painted into the WET 'oil out', using thick, sticky, viscous paint. The emulsion film must be rubbed in to an ultra -extremely thin film.

LARGE AREA: Use your entire hand, not a brush. Apply it in a circular motion. Even a small painting 18X24 inches will require some effort and it may tire your hand. After you are done, lightly wipe the entire surface with a dry lint free towel, and re-rub the surface. It must be a very thin film of Emulsion, not one that is thick and soupy or it will drip.

NO NEED TO HURRY: There is No need to rush, as the emulsion layer will remain workable for many hours. This condition I believe was very necessary in allowing the Van Eycks to work on their highly detailed paintings. A very important key to the success of painting sharp micro-lines, is that the Emulsion be applied in the absolutely thinnest layer possible, or the lines will lose some sharpness of detail. It is important to keep the container of Emulsion capped and in a cool area when not in use. You can 'oil out' on top of a 'tacky dry' or dried surface time and time again. This allows you to make as many corrections as needed. If you oil out a very dried painting, the emulsion might bead up. You can place a finger into dry chalk and rub it into the wet emulsion that is beading up.

OILING OUT WITH TWO TYPES OF EMULSIONS
Either Emulsion can be used for 'oiling out' between layers. An Emulsion 'oil out' insures the adhesion of a new paint layer as well as lubricating the surface. The VISCOUS emulsion dries faster than the NON-VISCOUS Emulsion but to paint extremely fine micro-lines the choice might be the Non-Viscous Emulsion as it can be argued that the finest lines can be painted into it, instead, of into the Viscous-Emulsion.

MUST YOU 'OIL OUT'?
NO. If you want a DRY-BRUSH effect, you will not 'oil out', but if you want smooth blending effects, you must 'oil out'. You cannot paint fine details or micro-fine lines onto a dry surface that has not been 'oiled out'. You can apply an 'oil out' onto a surface that is "tacky dry" and has not dried hard.

ADDITIONAL INFORMATION

I do not know for certain if the Van Eyck's used Calcium Carbonate as a paint additive, though one source says Aragonite, a form of Calcium Carbonate, was found in parts of the Van Eyck's thicker paint. The Van Eycks mainly painted with extremely thin glaze applications avoiding thick impasto which would eliminate the need of Calcium Carbonate, unless they wished to add body to some parts of their paint. But, we DO KNOW Velazquez and Rembrandt did use it. Both Rembrandt and Velazquez combined thicker paint with thin glazes, with Rembrandt being the one artist who used impasto of exceptional thickness. Additions of Calcium Carbonate would explain the historical development, from the time when artist's used thin paint, to when artist's used thicker paint in oil painting. The Calcium Carbonate, like the Egg, adds body and provides stability to the paint, preventing sagging or dripping.

'Calcite Sun Oil', can also be used as an 'oil out', to be used to paint extraordinarily fine micro-lines. My experiments show the CSO can be thinned to a mixture of 1 part CSO and 2 parts NON-polymerized Oil. This creates a transparent "Oil Out" film that adheres to any dry surface and allows the painting of fine micro-lines equal to those as with Emulsion. And, like with an Emulsion "Oil Out", it is imperative to lay down the thinnest possible layer. Years after these tests, I created AGUADO which is one of the 'oil out' mediums. Aguado is a soupy CSO mixture, is much like using a thinned CSO as the oil out medium.

*****

EMULSION ADHESION PROBLEMS

The 'Oil Out" insures the adhesion of the next paint layer that is painted into the WET 'oil out'. It is possible that as you rub the emulsion in, in preparation for painting a new layer, you may find the emulsion to bead up. This can occur on a rare occasion because so many factors can cause this to exist.

As stated, the **Viscous Emulsion (VE)** is made with the fast drying Sun Thickened polymerized Oil, and the **Non-Viscous Emulsion (NVE)** is made with the slow drying Non-polymerized (not thickened) Oil. The two Emulsions have different properties that can be used effectively by a painter.

Assuming you correctly applied the Viscous Emulsion (VE) to the dry surface, and if the emulsion beads up, the following remedies are recommended:
1. Dip your finger tip into the (NVE) NON-Viscous Emulsion and rub that into the previously applied wet (VE) Viscous Emulsion layer. This combining of two different polymerizations may solve the problem.
2. Dip your finger into some dry chalk and rub it into the wet area. If it is still not solved, make a new batch of the Emulsion. The viscosity of Glair, and the settling of the Glair and oil does change over time.
3. You may also try using the Emulsion at a warmer room temperature, not in a cold damp room.
4. In basic terms, the egg is a food, and all foods, even if refrigerated decompose. Keep the Emulsion refrigerated when not in use. Even then, at some point, it loses its effectiveness. Discard it and make a new batch. But it is best to make small batches so as to not waste your oil.

IMPORTANCE AND PERMANENCE OF THE OIL OUT PROCEDURE

The use of an ' OIL OUT" in painting is a distinguished and important painting procedure well documented throughout the history of oil painting and was used by the GREATEST masters, such as Rubens, Rembrandt, Velazquez, Titian.

YET, misinformed ' oil painting experts' of the 20th century--some lacking SUSTAINED practical studio painting experience, and others ignoring the lessons and procedures of the Old Masters, **and all of them ignorant of the superior true oil of the Old Masters –** criticize this valuable time tested procedure. They are accustomed to using the inferior industrial linseed oil of the 19th and 20th century. Coupled with improperly interpreting science, they have erroneously warned artists not to OIL OUT because they claim the artist is using too much oil and the linseed oil will yellow. Their information and advice is erroneous.

They further warn the "LESS OIL THE BETTER". This is mistaken, misguided and ignorant advice from these 'experts'. It is reminiscent of the ignorant condemnation of the OIL PAINTING MEDIUM by 19th century French Academics who similarly warned artists of their day...saying oil paintings made with linseed oil will yellow--as they ignored the perfectly preserved colors and paint of the Van Eyck oil paintings, and other 400 year old FLAXSEED/LINSEED OIL paintings in their famous LOUVRE museum.

THE 'ESPESO' EMULSION FOR OIL OUTS

At the conclusion of my filming the DVD on Rubens' methods and hazardous materials, I cleansed and rid my studio of all the Hazardous materials Rubens used. I was going to miss some of the fine points of his method and materials. As I pondered the loss, I received an INSPIRATION that resulted in my creation of the new OIL OUT MEDIUM, I named 'ESPESO'. THE WORD, ' ESPESO' IS A SPANISH WORD MEANING ' THICK', AND IS THE OPPOSITE OF THE SPANISH WORD ' AGUADO'.

HOW TO MAKE 'ESPESO'

'ESPESO' IS A MIXTURE OF CSO'S VISCOUS EMULSION AND CHALK CALCIUM CARBONATE. THE RATIO IS ROUGHLY 50/50. THE CSO'S VISCOUS EMULSION IS MADE FROM MIXING 3 SPOON FULLS OF SUN OIL WITH 2 SPOON FULLS OF GLAIR. MY BOOK AND DVD GIVE ALL THE DETAILS ON ITS FORMULATION, USE , AND APPLICATION. TO MAKE 'ESPESO', SIMPLY GRIND THE CHALK AND THE CSO VISCOUS EMULSION TOGETHER. IT IS QUICK AND EASY TO DO

HOW TO USE ' ESPESO'

'ESPESO', IS A THICK CREAMY MIXTURE, AND IS APPLIED BY HAND. IT IS RUBBED ALL OVER THE SURFACE AND THEN WIPED DOWN TO A THIN FILM ---- IT IS NOT RUBBED TO AN ULTRA-THIN FILM AS WITH THE VISCOUS EMULSION -- JUST ENOUGH OF THE 'ESPESO' IS LEFT AS A THIN FILM TO IMPACT THE APPLICATION OF THE CSO OIL PAINT THAT WILL BE APPLIED ON IT. THERE IS NO NEED FOR VIGOROUS RUBBING AS HOW THE VISCOUS EMULSION NEEDS TO BE APPLIED. ' ESPESO' IS SIMPLY APPLIED AND WIPED DOWN TO A THIN LAYER....NO EXTENSIVE RUBBING IS REQUIRED. IT IS BASICALLY COLORLESS AND IF YOU WISH, OIL PAINT COLOR CAN BE ADDED TO IT.

WHAT 'ESPESO' WILL DO
YOU WILL FIND THAT WHEN THE CSO PAINT IS APPLIED TO THE WET FILM OF ESPESO, IT HOLDS THE CSO PAINT IN POSITION, AND ALLOWS IMPASTO, WHILE ALLOWING EASE OF BLENDING. YOU WILL FIND IT WILL IMPROVE THE THIXOTROPIC HANDLING OF THE PAINT. IT IS REMARKABLE AS YOU WILL SOON FIND IT TO BE. I SUSPECT RUBENS MUST HAVE KNOWN OF THIS MIXTURE --THO, THERE IS NO WRITTEN RECORD OF THAT. HOWEVER IT IS A RECORDED FACT THAT REMBRANDT PAINTED WITH A SIMPLE CHALK-OIL MIXTURE [EQUAL TO CSO] AS ONE OF HIS PAINTS. MY TESTS SHOW HOW EASILY THE ADJOINING COLORED OIL PAINTS BLEND INTO THE MIXTURE. I RECOMMEND ADDING A FEW DROPS OF THE VE OR NVE TO THE CSO MIXTURE TO PREVENT WRINKLING. I AM SURE REMBRANDT FOUND THAT TO BE THE CASE ALSO.

THE 'AGUADO' MEDIUM FOR 'OIL OUTS' [Aguado is not an Emulsion]
AGUADO was developed in July 2009 after I received a letter from a painter.. This expansion of the **Calcite Sun Oil/ Emulsions** method, complements and gives the painter increased power for painting large sized paintings. It can be used effectively for small sized paintings as well, and provides the PLEIN AIRE painter a simple effortless procedure. It does NOT eliminate the use of the CSO/EMULSIONS method as I will explain later.

WHAT AGUADO IS
AGUADO is an "OIL OUT" mixture - it is NOT a painting medium nor a paint thinner. Having said this, I know creative artists will experiment with their new CSO materials. It is true that if one wishes, one can dip the tip of a brush into the AGUADO and then mix it into paint that is on the hand palette. I WARN readers not to stick the entire brush into the AGUADO, because there will be too much oil put into the properly prepared CSO-oil paint. This excess of oil will cause the paint to drip. If sparingly used as a thinner, the AGUADO mixed into CSO paint glides effortlessly on the surface of the support, and stays as placed.

HOW AGUADO IS MADE
The AGUADO mixture is made of 2 parts of the fast drying Superior oil with 3 parts of Calcium Carbonate Chalk from Champagne France. It must be ground on a grinding table then can be stored in a capped jar.

HOW TO USE AGUADO
APPLY it to the support with a wide brush. WIPE IT DOWN evenly while gently removing all excess, with a rag. The AGUADO , when wiped down thinly becomes colorless. You will note that the chalk causes the fluid viscous oil to remain where it is placed. Extensive rubbing of the Aguado is not required because it contains no egg..

DIFFERENCES OF EMULSIONS and AGUADO

The early Flemish paintings by the Van Eycks and others were generally - not always- of small size and painted on wood panels. The smooth gesso wood support and the 'oil out' method used... allowed micro-fine details with great detail to be painted as photo-realistic effects.

The CSO/EMULSIONS method can duplicate those effects and the wonderful paint quality. This is done without any use of Driers, Varnishes, Resins or Solvents. It depends in great part on the SUPERIOR oil. This application method takes a bit of time to get it right. This application method is ideal for smaller easel paintings up to 24" X 30" .If an artist is faced with a 6 foot tall canvas, the task is daunting then the artist can use the AGUADO medium.

The huge Baroque paintings like those of Rubens required an easier method. These are the reasons for the development of AGUADO. A need for Speed, Efficiency, and Ease. The development of AGUADO occurred through the normal evolution of using the new materials. By using the perfected CSO and Emulsions method over several years and experiencing its specific requirements and needs it was then possible to understand the needs for expansion, then to think, then test, and develop.

AGUADO could not have been developed WITHOUT first having developed the CALCITE SUN OIL/ EMULSIONS mixtures, and its application methods, and proving its value by actual painting. I am very excited of this breakthrough development. I have painted with it and I am amazed at its power. Though there are some ratio mixture tests yet to be made, the method is simple and fool proof.

AGUADO : A HISTORY OF ITS DEVELOPMENT

Since the year 2000, when I unknowingly began this trek on developing the Calcite Sun Oil / Emulsions method, I have never HURRIED, nor even been concerned with the OUTCOME. Every step, every new DEVELOPMENT, each happened on its own time. After having painted almost 45 years with TAUBES' resin solvent method I had NO IDEA I was to write a book ,and less so, on even thinking of OIL PAINTING WITHOUT my beloved Frederic Taubes' SOLVENTS, RESINS, VARNISHES and DRIERS.

NOTHING could have been farther from my mind. YET, now here I sit with a book focusing precisely on those important issues. Since publishing my book privately in 2004, many very fine and great artists around the world, are now thinking more about the oil they use, and about the oil in their tube oil paints, and about the REVOLUTION happening now : OIL PAINTING WITHOUT Hazardous solvents and without the other hazardous materials still being taught today.

I HAVE met many fine painters across the globe because they bought my book and through numerous letters we became fast friends. I have only met 4 artists who had an axe to grind, but the rest were respectful, gracious and very knowledgeable about oil painting. One day, a fine painter, brought up one VERY GOOD QUESTION, about the CSO/EMULSIONS method. He asked how it would be used in large mural sized paintings. Of course he was referring to the method described in my book on the application method of the ' OIL OUT' with the EMULSIONS, which he considered to be tiring and tedious. I agreed.

MY FIRST RESPONSE was that the Old Masters had WORKSHOPS with working students to do the menial labor. They were in the business of earning money, and teaching. They hired their finest students to help them complete commissions. Rubens had a huge WAREHOUSE studio in Antwerp, Belgium. I have visited his studio in Antwerp and seen it inside and out. The grinding of colors, preparation of paint, preparation of canvas and panels ...was NOT done by master Rubens...as neither was the grisaille under painting. OF COURSE there were paintings he did on his own -and his letters show he offered them at a higher price. SO, I explained that the laborious jobs went to student assistants.

I TOOK the comment serious. There is a huge difference--in SIZE--between the normally small paintings of the Flemish masters of the 15th century, and those HUGE paintings by the BAROQUE master RUBENS in the 17th century. THIS FACT, led me to develop an EXPANSION of my original CSO/EMULSIONS method, which uses the EMULSION as the 'OIL OUT". Those who do not know, this EMULSION must be applied correctly. The application takes time and one works on relatively smaller areas. a 30X40 inch painting appears very HUGE with this method. YET, the original CSO/EMULSIONS method is a method of perfection, allowing the finest detailed work and an ease and CONTROL of the paint not equaled by the SOLVENT-RESIN oil painting methods. Thanks to this inquiry, AGUADO was born.

CHAPTER EIGHT
THE VAN EYCK'S SECRET MEDIUM

History records the words of Giorgio Vasari, as saying the excellence of the Van Eyck paintings were due to a 'secret medium'. My account here serves to inform those who are new to the subject and to shed light on the Sun Thickened Unrefined cold pressed linseed/FLAX oil and the two Emulsions used in my book.

GIORGIO VASARI and the VAN EYCK SECRET
In the year 1550, Giorgio Vasari (1511-1574) first published his multi-volume book," **Lives of the Most Eminent Italian Architects, Painters and Sculptors".**

In book Eight, titled, " Antonello Da Messina ...", Vasari wrote that John of Bruges (Jan Van Eyck) had invented painting with oils. Modern scholarship shows oil painting is an ancient art, existing centuries before the Van Eycks. It is clear Vasari meant to say, Jan Van Eyck 'perfected' oil painting. Born over 70 years after the death of Van Eyck, Vasari accurately wrote that Van Eyck's oil paintings far exceeded the quality of the paintings of his (Vasari's) day.

Vasari says the following, (paraphrased in brief): ***Before Van Eyck, artists used 'distemper' [a glue or egg medium]. Many artists all over Europe tried to find a way to paint more realistically. They tried different liquid varnishes and colors but did not succeed. Jan Van Eyck made a secret varnish that he would not share.*** The full story from the actual text is available at the Internet.

Not only does the quality of the Van Eyck's paintings stand out amongst those of their era (1385-1441) (there were two brothers) but when compared to paintings of recent centuries and of today, the Van Eyck paintings are held by conservators as being STILL in the most remarkable condition. The paintings have sharply defined micro-fine details and lines, with hard lustrous paint and great depth of brilliant color. Frequently they are referred to as being "jewel-like". These extraordinary qualities cause one to ask,
"What medium did the Van Eycks use to do this"?

QUESTIONS and ANSWERS

Since Vasari did not know the 'secret medium', then what oil painting method did Vasari and his peers use? Vasari and his colleagues used a method of oil painting still in use today and taught at all academic levels around the world. This method OBLIGATES USE OF several hazardous ingredients, each serves a specific purpose and it can be called the **'solvent-resin-varnish-drier' method of oil painting.**

1. SOLVENTS: Different types of solvents such as Turpentine were used. The main purpose was to thin the paint. It also helped the paint to dry faster. Solvents evaporate completely except old turpentine leaves a sticky residue that does not dry well. Solvents have another purpose, which is to liquefy resins. The defect of solvents is that they break the bond between the pigment powder and the oil. The extreme health hazard of solvent fumes to humans has been firmly established by medical science.

2. RESINS: Resins are hard **or** thick gummy substances. This stickiness helps oil paint stick where it is placed, and prevents the oil paint from dripping down. When a resin is mixed with a solvent, it becomes thinned enough to be easily mixed with oil. Painters using these solvent-resin mixtures frequently have to add more solvent to the oil paint as they paint, because as the solvent evaporates, the paint becomes stickier. The defect of resins is that they become yellow and brittle with the passage of many years.

3. DRIERS: Non-polymerized oil (oil that is not thickened) when used to make paint, dries very slowly, taking 6 to 12 days. Driers are powders or liquids that accelerate the drying of paint. The defect of driers is that they cause colors to become dark and cause paint to become brittle over many years because driers accelerate the drying of the paint into a hard dry mass. Driers cause browning and cracking of oil paint.

WAS THE OIL OF THE VAN EYCKS DIFFERENT FROM THE OIL OF TODAY?
Yes, The Van Eyck's oil was different from today's oil in that they had cold pressed, UNREFINED linseed/FLAX oil. Today's modern industrial oil is heat extracted, chemically cleansed Alkali REFINED linseed oil. Also, all linseed oils are not the same, even today. Linseed oil is pressed from the seeds of the flax plant and the quality of the plants and their seeds vary according to different geographical regions. Much like grapes to make wine, the unique environmental conditions impact the quality of the flax seeds.

The Van Eyck's used ancient press equipment that extracted the oil by pure pressure and without any heat. It is called Cold Pressed oil, and it was pure, natural and UNREFINED. It was not refined by chemicals as is done today. Today's chemical treatment of linseed oil has produced a linseed oil that is slow drying. This slow drying property requires artists to use driers and solvents to accelerate the drying of the paint. This extremely slow drying condition was documented in the year 1100 by Theophillus.

DID VASARI HAVE ACCESS TO THE SAME OIL AS THE VAN EYCKS?
Yes, Vasari and his colleagues did have the same SUPERIOR oil that was common to artists of his and Van Eyck's day. They never wrote about it because it was not an issue. It was the only Linseed/FLAX oil they had.
It is: UNREFINED, Cold Pressed Linseed/FLAX oil that was slowly thickened in the sun. It was Vasari's use of this SUPERIOR oil that would allow minimal use of any additive ingredients. Yet, even he knew his solvent-resin based method did not give him the full control of the paint as the Van Eyck's method. Vasari did not know that the Van Eyck 'secret' medium required an important ingredient to control the flow and drip of the polymerized viscous oil. Vasari experimented with emulsions and wrote that they were not successful. **This emphasizes the importance of the correct application method of the emulsions**. Apparently Vasari was unable to discover the correct application method that is required for success of Emulsions use.

DO TODAY'S ARTISTS HAVE ACCESS TO VAN EYCK'S SUPERIOR OIL?
Yes, it is abundantly available, and it is LESS expensive than the linseed oil sold in the art stores. But it has to be processed at home as it is not for sale in art stores. This book gives information on this oil, and its preparation.

Today, Art stores sell Alkali REFINED linseed oil in one of two conditions of viscosity. (1) Alkali Refined Stand linseed oil, which is thickened (polymerized) through high heat. (2) Alkali Refined Linseed oil, (not polymerized), meaning it is thin and not thickened. Both are slow drying oils.

Alkali Refined LINSEED oil, with its drying defect, requires the "solvent-resin-varnish-drier based method" to make it effectively usable. As a youth, I learned to oil paint with this solvent-resin based method and alkali refined linseed oil, and it did not allow me to have full control of the paint. Although Van Eyck's SUPERIOR oil is available today, few artists are aware of its important properties or of how to CLEANSE it or of how to process it. This ignorance causes them to settle for the slow drying chemically refined linseed oil sold in the art stores.

SHOULD WE DISCARD MODERN TUBE PAINTS?
No. Alkali Refined linseed oil and modern tube paints made with it are here to stay...forever. In fact, the modern tube oil paints, regardless of their deficiencies, are very usable if they are conditioned properly. This book goes into detail on that point. Modern tube oil paints are convenient, relatively inexpensive, and available everywhere. Of course they vary in quality from one manufacturer to another. Informed artists can make wise choices, and once they read this book, many of them will.

DO SOME STORES SELL UNREFINED COLD PRESSED LINSEED OIL?
Some art stores do sell Cold Pressed linseed oil, but the labels do not say UNREFINED, because some type of refinement or solvent treatment has been done to it. Some of the labels of American produced oil, downplay the importance of TRUE COLD PRESSED LINSEED OIL, and even denigrate it as an 'inferior' oil. This is simply misleading 'Market Advertising' and is designed to promote the sale of the inexpensively mass produced Alkali REFINED oil. Alkali refined linseed oil offers the artist of today two things: convenience and low price, and it provides the manufacturers with two things: convenience and profits. Generally, European produced cold pressed linseed oil is much more expensive than the American brands.

HOW IS THE VAN EYCK SECRET MEDIUM MADE?
We will never know EXACTLY. They did not leave a document with their formula, however, historical facts, logic and studio experimentation and experience allow me to say the following with confidence:

The Van Eycks were trained as EGG-TEMPERA painters. The Egg-Tempera method, (NOT the oil method), uses a mixture of egg YOLK and water with the dry pigment. Egg-Tempera is an ancient method still in use today. Artists have always experimented with their materials, and at some point, Van Eyck, or someone before his time, mixed some part of an egg and oil and found out the unique properties of this mixture which we call an egg-oil Emulsion. Like in anything else, the exact RATIO of materials creates the result, making it useful or not. In ancient times, lacking science and mass media, results of experiments were known and kept by a few. With 19th century Industrialization, the Old Masters' art studios disappeared and art students were trained in colleges. The mass production of artist's materials produced materials of varying quality, and much studio knowledge was lost. Linseed oil was mass produced, heat extracted and cleansed with chemicals, to the detriment of the oil and the art. This poor oil has led many intelligent researches astray as they fruitlessly tried to reconstruct the Old Masters' methods.

WHAT IS AN EMULSION AND HOW IS IT MADE?
An Emulsion is the mixing of two NORMALLY unmixable liquids, one being water-based and the other oil-based. Vigorous shaking and certain components of the liquids allow the two to mix. An Emulsion can be made with a variety of natural substances that contain natural water in their make-up, but not all are successful. For example, mixing casein and industrial oil creates an emulsion that becomes dark over time, as well as being an extremely slow drying emulsion which is a hindrance.

The more common aqueous substances for mixing with oil are these:
1. The whole egg. 2. The Egg Yolk only. 3. The Egg White only (glair). 4. Casein. 5. Glue. 6. Others.
There are many recipes for making Emulsions. Some are complex requiring the addition of more water, different oils, resins, and or solvents. **None of those recipes are necessary**, some are hazardous, and some cause impermanence.

GLAIR is the one ingredient that has all the requisite and important properties for use with mixing with oil, in the making of an Emulsion with extraordinary properties. Glair is colorless transparent, it is a strong archival binder adhesive, it dries very fast and hard, it is permanent, it is fully compatible with oil, and it mixes quickly and easily with oil. This Emulsion serves several important functions in oil painting.

My experiments support my belief that an Emulsion medium having extraordinary properties is made of TWO very basic ingredients, but they must be mixed in specific RATIOS.
INGREDIENT #1: The SUPERIOR Linseed/FLAX oil THAT WAS Sun Thickened in the sun SLOWLY.
INGREDIENT # 2: Glair in the proper ratio to the oils. There are two different Emulsion mixtures, each with the SUPERIOR oil, but of a different viscosity. [note: This is now revised to include ESPESO]

IS THE VAN EYCK METHOD OF OIL PAINTING OF VALUE TO TODAY'S ARTISTS?
Yes it is, for these reasons. Our world is very different from the world of the Van Eycks.
We live in a fast paced, scientific, technological age. Our age is characterized by a demand for instant gratification , intolerance of anything that 'wastes' (requires) our time, and accustomed to using disposable items. Modern styles of painting reflect this energized anxiety with splashes, drips, and broad wet-in-wet painting methods that are 'best' done within a few hours. Many painters have discarded 'troublesome' slow-drying traditional oil paints and use only fast drying acrylic paints that allow faster and greater freedom, and the creation of multi-media works. Acrylic paints and their clear synthetic emulsion adhesive, allows use of collage, with additions of paper, wood, crayon, ink, and other substances. Even now, in the 21st century, artists have discarded the 20th century acrylic paints in favor of faster computer graphics, which when combined with high resolution printing presses, can create exciting visual art of huge proportions within minutes or hours by piecing together photographs.

The oil paintings of the 14th century Van Eycks and of other Masters of the era, were made slowly by hand, with natural materials, and with methods guided by experience and understanding. Almost 600 years later, they are still here in an extraordinary condition of preservation. Their paintings took weeks, or months, to complete with use of a layering process. The artists had understanding of thixotropic properties of their oil and the properties of natural emulsions. These paintings have brilliant color depth, hard lustrous surfaces, extremely fine minute micro-fine details, sensuous textural applications and have been called "jewel-like" by experts throughout history.

   In our fast paced world, there are still many artists who wish to use the methods and materials of the Van Eycks, Bellini, Rembrandt, Velazquez, and other Old Masters. I am confident the information in this book, will allow them to accomplish this as the numerous Testimonial letters I receive, indicate.

DID THE VAN EYCKS USE MIXTURES OF CALCIUM CARBONATE WITH THEIR PAINT?
I have read that some Aragonite, which is a calcium carbonate powder, was found in some parts of the Van Eyck's paintings. The source was on the internet. How accurate or complete this is I cannot say. But, there is much scientific evidence from several highly qualified sources (see bibliography) that Rembrandt and Velazquez added calcium carbonate powder to their oil paint. Of the two, Velazquez used it the most, adding it to all his colors. Velazquez' paintings are in remarkable condition, with translucence and brilliance of his colors, in addition to sumptuous textures. Science found an Emulsion in the paintings of the Van Eycks, Rembrandt and Velazquez. Van De Wetering called this a 17th century studio secret because, he said, no document from the era has ever been found that mentions it.

WHAT ARE YOU OFFERING TODAY'S OIL PAINTERS?
In two words: SAFETY and PERMANENCE, but also ease of painting and total control of paint. Sharing knowledge, facts and accurate information with artists is important so they can make wise choices. I also offer my invention, 'Calcite Sun Oil", which changes and improves modern tube oil paint giving it the properties and control, like that of the Old Masters' paint. My 'Calcite Sun Oil' formula was patented by the US Patent and Trademark Office in November 2006. It is patent # 7141109.
My book also discuss the important uses of the "wonder medium" of Emulsions in oil painting which allow us to eliminate ALL hazardous Solvents, Resins, Varnishes and Driers.

*****

CHAPTER NINE
TUBE PAINTS
and HAND GROUND PAINTS

TUBE OIL PAINTS
In its normal state, TUBE PAINT is not viscous, meaning it is not sticky. Properly mixing the tube oil paint with 'Calcite Sun Oil' will radically change the non-viscous quality of tube paint to a HIGHLY VISCOUS QUALITY. Artists using Tube oil paints will recognize the important benefits 'Calcite Sun Oil' will give their paint, and the advantages gained in mastering the oil paint medium.

MIXING 'CALCITE SUN OIL' WITH TUBE PAINT
Tube paints properly conditioned with 'Calcite Sun Oil' require no hazardous solvents, resins, varnishes, driers, and paint mediums containing these ingredients, as thinning of the paint is generally not necessary. IF thinning is desired, it is important to use either of the two Emulsions as the thinner.

Using *'Calcite Sun Oil'* with Tube oil paints is easy and pleasant, because the work of 'grinding' is already done. However, tube paints must be properly mixed with CSO for it to be effective. This is effortless and takes seconds. The resulting paint is not as thick as Hand Ground paint but is much easier to brush on.

The SAFETY and the PERMANENCE claimed in my book is related to the specific 'Calcite Sun Oil', Oils, and Emulsions I describe. I recommend painters carefully read the labels on tube paints and dry pigments and avoid ALL hazardous materials. "The Artist's Complete Health and Safety Guide", by Monona Rossol , provides excellent information on toxicity and hazardous materials. Even though the dry Calcium carbonate powder is not toxic or hazardous, use a dust mask when handling ANY finely ground powders or pigments, and always wash your hands afterwards with soap and water.

GRINDING TUBE PAINT WITH "CALCITE SUN OIL"
Normally you need to mix an approximate equal amount of CSO as the amount of paint. Some oil colors need more than others. Use good judgment. You do not have to measure accurately. My DVDS demonstrate this. The CONDITIONING of the Tube oil paint is correctly done when the paint becomes more enamel-like and sticky. For the Thixotropic quality to even be possible with Tube Oil paint, the paint must be RADICALLY changed to a viscous and sticky condition. Add as much CSO as needed to bring about this change. The amount of CSO to add varies because different manufacturers add different amounts of non-polymerized oil found in their tube paint. Always use a palette knife to firmly grind the CSO and paint. To make thick impasto paint, additions of DRY chalk and the emulsion are needed. The sequence of the mixtures is important. FIRST, grind CSO into the tube paint. SECOND, add a few drops of the Viscous Emulsion and grind, THIRD, grind dry calcium carbonate and grind it well.

PREPARATION OF IMPASTO WHITE OIL PAINT
The section titled, REMBRANDT'S WHITE OIL PAINT instructs you on how to duplicate Rembrandt's white oil paint by using *'Calcite Sun Oil'*, an Emulsion, and some dry Calcium Carbonate powder.

DEFICIENCIES OF TUBE OIL PAINTS
Tube oil paints, regardless of their deficiencies, are here to stay...forever because they are convenient. I use their slower drying quality to my advantage. The current principle of 'FAT ON LEAN' is used only by those artists who use solvent-resin-drier based 'painting mediums'.
THE CSO METHOD DOES NOT NEED TO FOLLOW THE " FAT ON LEARN" PRINCIPLE because CSO uses NO solvents nor Resins nor driers.

The Old Masters used the principle of **'SLOW DRYING paints on top of FAST DRYING paints'** to prevent cracking of the paint film. I hand grind a limited number of oil paints for the under painting because dry powder pigments ground with CSO, dry much faster than Tube paints. I use my TUBE paints mixed with CSO in my top layers because they dry slower. Mixing CSO with Tube paints will accelerate their drying, yet, it is important to know which are your fast and which are your slow drying paints.

The problem is not so complicated. The paint layer you applied yesterday is already 24 hours into the drying stage as compared to the paint layer you are applying today. Also, all painters know that UMBER is one of the fastest drying pigments. Because of this many Old Masters under painted with colors mixed with UMBER, especially the colors they knew to be slow drying. ALSO, the painters knew that a THIN paint layer dried faster than a THICK layer, so they were careful not to use excessively thick paint in the under layers, unless it contained additional UMBER mixed in. I have seen Titians that were under painted in UMBER and WHITE monotones, with the jewel-like transparent color glazes on top.

There is a myth that UMBER should not be used in the lower layers because it is a pigment that is 'thirsty' for oil and it reportedly will suck oil out of other colors. This is not a concern if you think of the UMBER as a sponge, and a sponge can only soak up so much water, at which time it gets saturated and will not soak up any more. UMBER is the same. IF you paint on a **non-absorbent ground**, the UMBER will not lose any oil to the absorbent ground, and in turn will not soak any oil from the other colors.

Tube oil paints used straight from the tube, have many deficiencies, causing problems for the painter, but grinding the Tube paint with "Calcite Sun Oil" and used in conjunction with the Emulsions, will eliminate these deficiencies which are listed here: 1. SLOW DRYING OIL: The non-polymerized REFINED oil used in Tube oil paints, causes paint to dry extremely slowly, taking as much as six to twelve days, or longer, even for thin layers of some colors. This limits the method of application to a "direct" wet-in-wet painting method. This deficiency discourages the exploration of color and textural qualities that are only possible through a layering process. It also encourages use of harmful driers. *Tube oil paints conditioned with 'Calcite Sun Oil' dry within 30 hours without the use of any hazardous driers, if thinly applied and with a favorable environment. [UPDATE NOTE: The newly created AIR PUMP OIL thickening method, when mixed with chalk to create CSO will dry tube oil paints in UNDER 14 hours and if mixed with chalk and dry pigments, the paint will dry in about 5 hours].*

2. PROBLEMATIC ADHESION: One of the most disturbing technical problems encountered by an artist is insuring that subsequent layers will adhere to a dried paint layer. Since use of Tube paints is limiting to the 'wet-in-wet' technique the need for corrective over paintings will be needed. Artists need to be assured that subsequent layers will remain firmly attached. The methods recommend to solve this problem are many, but all are deficient in one way or another. *The combination of 'Calcite Sun Oil' and the Emulsions 'oil out' is an easy, permanent solution to this major problem.*

3. POOR BLENDING: Manufacturers grind the dry pigments with slow drying non-polymerized oil, insuring a long shelf life. Most paints in air tight tubes can last indefinitely. To insure the pigment does not separate from the oil, a stabilizer is added - usually aluminum stearate, which is a fluffy colorless powder. It creates the "buttery like" consistency of tube paint – but with the disadvantage of creating difficult blending. *'Calcite Sun Oil' added to tube oil paint increases the viscosity and allows ease of blending.*

4. DECREASED TRANSLUCENCY and TRANSPARENCY: Tube paints dry matte and with a relatively soft film, as well as having low color depth without luster. *'Calcite Sun Oil' added to tube oil paint vastly increases the color depth, luminosity and luster of tube oil paints, and dries to a hard durable shiny surface.*

5. LIMITED IMPASTO: Tube oil paint normally has a limited range of impasto and glazes are normally without body. *'Calcite Sun Oil' added to tube oil paint, and by following simple instructions, a variety of impasto and textures can be created, and thick bodied transparent paint films can be easily created.*

6. LIMITED APPLICATION METHODS: Tube paint used straight from the tube, is limited to a simple 'wet-in-wet' application. This limited method stifles creativity and imagination, and slows down the completion of the painting. These defects, are what caused artists to seek out 'painting mediums' containing hazardous ingredients that would rectify the defects. These ' painting mediums' are normally a mixture of various ratios of Solvents and Resins to help control the drip. Solvents to thin the paint for easier brushing and to increase drying, and Driers to accelerate the slow drying paint. *'Calcite Sun Oil' added to tube oil paint will give the artist FULL CONTROL of the paint without any HAZARDOUS ingredients.*

7. LIMITED DETAILS: It is IMPOSSIBLE to replicate the micro-fine lines and details seen in the Old Master paintings when using tube oil paints straight from the tube. *Calcite Sun Oil' added to tube oil paint gives FULL CONTROL of the paint, and allows the painting of these micro-fine lines and details.*

8. NO THIXOTROPY: Thixotropy is the term used that describes the painting of WET paint...ON TOP OF WET PAINT, without drastically disturbing the wet paint below. This important quality allows the painter to create extraordinary effects, textures, color combinations and fine line details, all IN ONE STEP. *'Calcite Sun Oil' added to tube oil paint, promotes this quality, BUT, because the tube paint has been made with slow drying, non-viscous oil, the thixotropic quality is not as strong as with Hand Ground oil paints, but it is improved.*

9. 'SUEDE EFFECT': Tube paint has powdered aluminum stearate or another stabilizer added to give it a firm consistency. Tube paint is non-viscous, it does not flow nor blend easily, remaining firm even as it is applied. This causes a very disturbing condition called, "the suede effect". As the paint is brushed, it holds every brush mark and the light reflects off the different angles of brush strokes, making it difficult to see the TRUE color of the paint. It makes the painting appear "spotty" and changing the light source does not solve this disturbing visual condition. *'Calcite Sun Oil' eliminates the disturbing suede effect. The paint of the Old Masters does not have the optically disturbing "suede effect" problem, and neither does tube paint properly mixed with CSO.*

10. HARMFUL DRIERS: The pigments used in making oil paint, dry at different rates. It is believed some manufacturers of tube oil paints add minute quantities of driers to the slower drying colors, in order to give painters the advantage of colors drying at the approximate same time.
'Calcite Sun Oil' added to tube paint allows colors, whether fast drying ones or slower ones, to dry at an increased rate without the use of hazardous solvents or driers. Temperature, Humidity, and Ventilation are some environmental factors affecting drying. The pigment color, its thickness of paint, and the oil used, are the technical factors that impact the drying.

*****

BENEFITS OF HAND GROUND OIL PAINTS

WHY SHOULD I MAKE MY OWN PAINT?

It almost seems ridiculous to make your own oil paint in today's modern times. But, once you learn of the benefits, you will become a believer and will do it more often. These are the reasons: (1) It is more economical (2) The vast variety of ready ground dry pigments in all values, colors, chromatic degrees, is staggering (3) You control the oil and other ingredients that go into the paint (4) You create fast drying paint for the under painting layer. (5) You control the fluidity or thickness of the paint.

If you do choose to Hand-Grind, I recommend you only hand-grind a few colors, and also make use of the tube paints for their convenience. For Hand-Grinding, 'Calcite Sun Oil' (CSO) is an ideal grinding oil for making Hand Ground Oil Paints. However, CSO used as the grinding oil, creates a very thick viscous paint that must be thinned. I recommend thinning the Hand Ground oil paint with the NON-VISCOUS EMULSION, as it will insure that it will not drip. Grinding should always be done with a palette knife and never with a brush.

The Old Masters made their own paints. Raw sources of minerals or other natural substances were carefully processed by a variety of ways, to isolate the pure color grains or liquids. As apprentices, these artists really did "Grind" the powders to achieve the desired particle sizes. Eventually, ready pulverized dry pigments were bought from 'color men' specialists, whose business it was of grinding the color pigments.

The old Masters had a small number of colors, as Velazquez and Rembrandt are known to have used but a handful of colors. Studies of Velazquez and Rembrandt's paint show they used mixtures of different sizes of particles of dry pigment. Sometimes the grind was very fine, and other times it was very coarse. These differences impacted the aesthetic plasticity of the final effect, and the manipulation of the paint.

Today, we have an immense number of finely ground dry pigments, available in a huge variety of colors. The painter who grinds (mixes) their own paint will know exactly what the paint contains. This is not true of store bought, ready-made oil paints sold in tubes. In addition, the artist can choose from a great variety of values, hues, or intensities of all colors. Another benefit is the paint can be ground as thick or thin as one wishes. Once an artist grinds their own colors and is aware of the benefits, such as faster drying, it becomes an important and valuable part of their painting process.

CAUTION: Always wear a dust mask when grinding fine powders. Read the labels and avoid toxic pigments or paints.

SUMMARY

Hand Ground paints simply require more effort and time. The mixing of oil and dry pigment is not difficult and the skill can be mastered within minutes. Yet, it requires time to set up the palette each time one wants to paint. Oil paint in tubes is ideal for modern people who value convenience and time. One can use both types, using the hand ground paints in the under painting because they dry faster. Ready-made tube paints save us a lot of time. Grinding the Tube paints with 'Calcite Sun Oil' creates an excellent paint and the use of the Emulsions is very important. Hand Ground paints can be made to dry faster and have a stronger Thixotropic quality than the Tube paints. The choice is in the oil used for grinding.

GRINDING TOOLS REQUIRED

The Old Masters did not attach 'liquid filled oil cups' to their HAND PALETTE, as today's artist are taught to do. The Old Masters used a small – not huge- HAND PALETTE as seen in their representations of artists working in the studio, and one frequently sees the "GRINDING TABLE also represented. It was on the Grinding Table that the CONSISTENCY of the paint was carefully changed to thicker or thinner paint. Once the desired consistency was achieved for the purpose at hand, it was transferred to the Hand Palette.

The practice of dipping the brush into an oil cup, to thin the paint on the hand palette, results in poorly mixed unbalanced paint. However, some modern artists aim for using DRIPS and other random effects in their painting as part of their style. However, **one single drop of emulsion** added and mixed well with the palette knife, to a glob of paint, will greatly change the consistency.

1. GRINDING TABLE: I use a GLAZED floor tile about 18 inches by 18 inches. Use a tile that is a mid-value tone of a brown or gray color. This helps to see the colors accurately. It is more difficult to see colors accurately on pure white or black. Make sure the tile is glazed. A glazed tile will not absorb the oil from the paint.

2. MULLER: Glass mullers cost between $50 and $75. You do not need one unless you will be grinding large amounts of materials. I use ONLY a stiff but flexible palette knife.

3. PALETTE KNIFE: I use a palette knife to grind my 'Calcite Sun Oil. My palette knife has a 5 inch long, ¾ " wide, straight bladed with a rounded end that is firm yet flexible.

4. HAND PALETTE: Use any size or shape you like. They are designed with a hole through which you stick your thumb and it rests on your forearm. I use a glazed floor tile which sits on top of a small table in front of the easel. This frees my left hand, so I can hold a 4 foot long wooden stick in my left hand. I lean it against the easel to steady myself when painting small details.

CLEANING THE BRUSH WHILE PAINTING

When an artist is actively painting on a picture it frequently becomes necessary to clean the brush when a different color is going to be used. All you have to do is dip your brush in a jar of NON-polymerized linseed oil. Then swirl the brush in the oil and then using a rag to squeeze out the color. You might have to do this a couple of times. Then, when the brush is clean, wipe it off thoroughly with a clean dry rag. Try to get all the SLOW drying non-polymerized oil out of the brush then continue to paint.

CHAPTER TEN
PAINTING METHODS
THINNING OR THICKENING PAINT

OIL PAINTING METHODS
GLAZES, SCUMBLES, and IMPASTO are achieved through a variety of additive [adding by means of brushes, knives, fingers etc.] or deductive [removing by scratching, scraping, wiping] methods, through manipulations of painting brushes, knives, rags, fingers, and anything else imaginable.

GLAZES are applications of thin transparent or translucent paint. Oil painting has traditionally been greatly admired because of the purity and transparency and translucency of the paint colors. The paintings of the 15th century Flemish masters, such as the Van Eycks, have the appearance of jewels. The surface of these 500 year old excellently preserved paintings is shiny, as **a healthy film of oil paint is always shiny**. Glazing a bright red color over a dull red color will create a unique dimensional color effect, and painting a bright red color over its opposite, a dull green, will create a contrasting color effect. The combinations are endless.

THE CORRECT WAY TO APPLY A GLAZE
DO NOT make the paint liquid as is taught by many teachers. In watercolor painting artists normally add large amounts of water to the paint. In oil painting, the paint should be kept very firm and very viscous. The area to be glazed should first be properly 'oiled out', with the correct Emulsion. The thinnest possible film of Emulsion should be rubbed onto the surface with the hand. All excess 'oil out' must be carefully removed with a gentle wipe of a rag if necessary, and re-rubbed with the bare hand. Once this 'oil out' is correctly applied, then, the firm viscous oil paint is applied. To correctly apply a soft glaze you need your fingers and/or brushes, or a soft rag. To create a glaze having less concern with softness, the palette knife can also be used.

One Art writer of today wrote that glazes are out of fashion as today's artists prefer to paint in the "direct manner" with opaque oil colors. A study of many of these contemporary paintings allows us to see the dryness, dullness and dead opacity of the paints that lack luster and color depth. These poor effects are caused by using oil paint mixed with large amounts of solvent to create a flat matte surface. Home decorators prefer this appearance because the painting has no disturbing shine, but the permanence of the painting has been compromised.

SCUMBLES are applications of thin layers of opaque paint. Scumbles can be applied on a wet paint layer - or on a dry paint layer that has an 'oil out'. Like Glazes, their purpose is to modify or heighten the color effects of another lower layer of paint. They also add to the textural quality of a painting. Allowing the under color to bleed though the scumble creates what is known as "optical grays", which appears as 'shading'.

MAKING THICK IMPASTO PAINT
Physical Tactile textures can add to the aesthetic interest of the painting, as Rembrandt's exploration of a variety of textures demonstrates. Rembrandt frequently scratched into his impasto for additional effects of plasticity. You can increase the "thickness" of your paint easily by following simple instructions to avoid problems common to thick paint.

IMPASTO PROBLEMS: Thick paint piled high has a tendency to wrinkle IF it is made with a polymerized, fast drying oil. The wrinkling is caused by the fast drying of the outer skin of the paint glob, while the interior stays wet for several days or weeks due to lack of oxygen. Wrinkling can be eliminated by adding several drops of an Egg-Oil Emulsion, and mixing it well with the paint. My experiments indicate Rembrandt added an Emulsion to his thick highly viscous paint to keep it firm, and to prevent it from dripping or wrinkling. See the chapter on Egg-Oil Emulsions.

One important benefit of 'Calcite Sun Oil' and the Emulsions is the ease with which one changes the consistency of the paint. One can make thin paint or thick paint, and maintain complete control. A summary of how to make thick WHITE impasto paint is described here.

THE MIXING SEQUENCE IS VERY IMPORTANT
FIRST grind CSO and the tube oil paint together using equal amounts of each. SECOND, add a few drops of the Emulsion to the mixture, and grind together well. You will have noted that the more Viscous Emulsion added to the paint will stop the flow. THIRD, if you want even thicker impasto, add dry Calcium Carbonate to the mixture and grind it well using a stiff palette knife.
Do this in small increments because as more dry Calcium Carbonate or dry pigment is added, the mixing is more difficult, and **you must avoid** making a paint that is under-bound, meaning lacking sufficient oil binder. A more detailed explanation follows here as Rembrandt's impasto paint is recreated

REMBRANDT'S THICK IMPASTO WHITE OIL PAINT
The color 'white' is one of the most important colors used by artists. Achieving a pure white color has been a challenge for the greatest of artists. With Tempera paints (egg tempera), and Acrylic paints, this is not a problem because their binder medium dries colorless. With Oil Painting, maintaining a pure white color has been a concern because white linseed oil paint, under storage conditions, causes the white oil paint to lose its color purity and become tinged. Master painters sought out vegetable drying oils that were lighter in color. Many master artists experimented with Walnut Oil, which is a golden yellow color.

Today, some white paints are ground in poppy oil because this oil has a pale color. Rembrandt used lead white pigment ground with sun thickened, cold pressed Linseed/Flax oil. Since I do not recommend use of this or any poisonous lead pigments, we cannot duplicate Rembrandt's paint exactly. We can use non-toxic Titanium Dioxide white dry pigment powder and create a satisfactory substitute.

THE UNIQUE QUALITY of REMBRANDT'S WHITE PAINT

Rembrandt is the first Old Master to apply his white paint thickly with a palette knife as an aesthetic form of expressive paint quality. His paint is thick, viscous, and flowing, just like paint that is ground with highly viscous, polymerized linseed/flax oil, and yet, the textures in his thick paint are sharp and clear. Every brushstroke or palette knife mark is firmly and clearly preserved as he put it. The perplexing fact is that paint made with viscous polymerized oil, should have dripped, and it should have flowed and spread out so much that any details or sharp edges should have disappeared. **This perplexing condition of Rembrandt's thick paint has stymied artists for centuries, and even today.**

How did Rembrandt make his paint behave in a manner, other than how it should have? Professor Ernst Van De Wetering has written (see bibliography) that the addition of an egg-oil emulsion changes the rheology of oil paint that was made with polymerized linseed oil, to where it remains long and flowing and easy to blend, but, that it becomes firm and holds its shape once the brush stops moving. It is also known that Rembrandt's white lead pigment varied randomly in granular sizes, in contrast to today's finely and evenly ground pigments. I do not consider the granular variety of sizes important because my experiments show modern ground pigments are satisfactory. My personal discovery, confirmed by testing, is that the wrinkling of thick viscous oil paint is prevented by adding a few drops of the viscous emulsion. Once well mixed together, the surface will harden in equal time of the paint without the emulsion – but the interior and surface dry out at an equal time- thus, preventing wrinkling.

HOW TO REPLICATE REMBRANDT'S WHITE PAINT

With CSO, and the Egg-Oil Emulsion, artists using Tube Oil Paints, or by hand grinding, can duplicate Rembrandt's paint quality and create wonderfully expressive effects of paint quality.

1. Use non-hazardous Titanium White TUBE oil paint that was ground in non-polymerized linseed oil, or use dry powdered Titanium Dioxide powder and grind it with non-polymerized oil. Rembrandt used poisonous Lead white. We do not need to use it, and though the many purists will disagree, I believe lead white is not worth the health risks involved. **WARNING:** I recently purchased what should be non-toxic Titanium White tube oil paint, from a brand I never use. The fine print said it was carcinogenic because some Zinc White had been added to it. Carefully read the fine print on the labels!

2. Use a grinding table, not the hand palette. Place a quarter sized thick blob of tube white paint or hand-ground paint. Add an approximate equal amount of 'Calcite Sun Oil'. Grind the two well, applying firm pressure with a palette knife, not with a brush. You will notice the Tube paint has become more flowing. By conditioning your Tube Oil Paint with 'Calcite Sun Oil', you have changed the tube paint from a non-viscous condition, to a paint with a great amount of viscosity. An additional beneficial condition, called the 'resin effect', is achieved without the use of any resins. See the section that describes this beneficial condition.

3. Now add several drops of the Viscous Emulsion to the CSO-oil paint. See the section on making the Viscous Emulsion. Mix well with the palette knife, not with a brush. You will notice the condition of the white paint becomes more liquid, but then it becomes 'streaky' and appears to separate. Take several more minutes to grind (mix together) this very well **with pressure** in circular motions, until the paint is creamy again. You will notice the paint is soft but firm.

4. Divide this paint into 3 equal parts. Place one part onto the hand palette. This will be your thin flowing paint that has a loose consistency but yet, remains firm. It can be used for special effects.

5. Mix the remaining 2 parts on the grinding table together and add one level teaspoon of dry calcium carbonate, and mix it all together. Wear a dust mask when handling any powder. Grind them firmly with a palette knife until it is creamy and the dry powder is well mixed. Notice the paint becomes less liquid and thicker, yet it spreads easily and holds any markings of the palette knife. Divide this into two equal parts and place one part on the hand palette next to the first mixture.

6. With the remaining paint, add another level half teaspoon of dry calcium carbonate. Mix it well with the palette knife. You will notice the texture becomes more firm, and may be difficult to mix. Grinding the paint with a continuous pressure in a circular motion will relax the mixture. Continue to grind it until it is a pliable paint. If it is too firm, add a drop of the first mixture into it. Once finished grinding, place this paint on the hand palette next to the other two white paints. You now have white paint in three consistencies.

THREE CONSISTENCIES OF WHITE PAINT
You now have a choice of white paint. Each consistency will serve a different purpose. You can create white paint that is even thicker and more firm by adding more, dry calcium carbonate. Like Rembrandt's paint, you can easily apply it, easily blend it, apply it thinly or thickly, and it will hold its brush strokes and palette knife markings. The egg-oil emulsion prevents the thick viscous paint from wrinkling. Artists who Hand-Grind paint, should first grind the white with non-polymerized linseed oil and with the least amount of oil needed. Then, add an equal amount of CSO, and follow these instructions. It is not necessary to do this to the other colors but you can if desired. White is prepared this way as the other colors will mix with it during the painting process.

FASTER DRYING WHITE PAINT: If using the paint for the under painting stage, add a little DRY umber to the white paint. It will make it look slightly brownish, but it will greatly accelerate its drying.

EMULSION 'OIL OUT'
An 'Oil out' is the application of an EMULSION to a surface area, in preparation for painting a new layer of paint. It insures adhesion and aids blending. It is not mandatory and can be ignored, but if painting fine details, such as the hairs in a portrait it MUST be done. In either case, a very thin layer of Emulsion is placed on the surface of the painting, lubricating it so the brush can spread paint effortlessly. It is only applied to a dry or 'tacky dry" surface. Apply it with your bare hand or finger.

DO NOT 'OIL OUT' WITH PURE OIL
Pure oils, without a Calcium Carbonate addition, or without an Emulsion, will bead up, drip and sag even if thinly applied or rubbed in hard for a long period. POLYMERIZED thickened oil is the WORST when used pure, due to its excessive leveling quality. The Emulsion stops the 'drip, sag, bleed' deficiency of pure oil.

BEAD-TRICKLE- CRAWL MEANS POOR ADHESION
The beading up of a layer of paint on a dry surface indicates the adhesion of the two layers is NOT complete, and the permanence of the painting is endangered. Old and modern instruction books discuss this 'beading up' problem and offer many solutions, **but many are objectionable and troublesome.**

INADEQUATE SOLUTIONS TO BEAD-TRICKLE- CRAWL
There are many inadequate recommendations to solve this problem. One is to brush turpentine on the dry surface before painting the next layer, but this can ruin, partially dry completed work by softening it. Another is to apply a spirit varnish, which is nothing more than Turpentine with some Resin, with the same dangers as turpentine. Other solutions are to rub the surface with a potato, or garlic, or urine, or sand paper. These various inadequate processes try to get the paint to stick to the dry surface.

The best solution is safe, permanent and non-destructive, and is the use of either of the Emulsions. Rub in an extremely thin layer until you feel tension to the rub. It causes no destructive action on the still 'tacky dry' incompletely dried surface, and the paint sticks and remains where it is put with permanent adhesion. One can rub in either Emulsion mixture to restore sunken dry matte colors to their original brilliance, and can also be used as a final permanent non-removable varnish.

PROPER THINNING of OIL PAINT

DEFECTIVE METHOD: Oil painters today are taught to keep a small "oil cup" attached to their hand palette. The cup is filled with turpentine, or a solvent based painting medium, and as they paint they dip their brush into the liquid and add the liquid to their paint and mix it on the hand palette. Because brushes suck up oil, this procedure causes an uncontrolled amount of the liquid to mix with the paint causing the paint consistency to vary, and loss of control of the paint.

EFFECTIVE METHOD: To properly thin oil paint, the key word to always keep in mind is - consistency. The consistency of the paint will determine how it will be applied and how it will behave and dry. It cannot be stressed enough. One must add ONLY one drop of emulsion at a time to thin the paint. DO NOT LIQUIFY, nor over thin the paint. It is not necessary for the paint to be 'fluid' for easy brushing of paint. There is a great difference between an undesired watery consistency that may sag, and a properly "thinned" yet firm consistency that will brush easily and not sag.

THIN THE PAINT CORRECTLY: Add one drop of Emulsion at a time and mix it well into the paint until you get the desired consistency. Use your grinding table and your palette knife to grind. Do not use a brush to grind the paint and the Emulsion. If the paint is still too thick, repeat the process of adding ONE MORE DROP of Emulsion and mix it well. You will be amazed the difference only ONE DROP of Emulsion will make, in changing the consistency of a blob of paint.

THE PERFECT THINNER is an EMULSION
Addition of a few drops of EITHER emulsion to the oil paint accomplishes more than thinning of the paint. It prevents thick paint from wrinkling, and it causes the paint to stay put and prevents sagging and dripping. Either Emulsion can be used at any time. Familiarization with both will guide you on which to use.

THE NON-VISCOUS EMULSION (NVE) IS BEST FOR THINNING HAND-GROUND PAINT.
The Non-Viscous Emulsion (NVE) is best for thinning Hand-Ground paints that were made by grinding dry pigments with CSO, because it contains enough viscous oil. The 'Non-Viscous Emulsion" will help create a firm consistency while still retaining control of the paint, and while not losing any of the benefits. The 'NVE' will not dramatically slow down the drying. If faster drying paint is desired, thin this paint with a drop of the Viscous Emulsion but, only a drop at a time.

THE VISCOUS EMULSION (VE) IS BEST FOR THINNING TUBE PAINT MIXED WITH CSO.
This is because the tube paint already contains enough non-polymerized oil. Normally the tube paint mixed with CSO, needs NO THINNING. If the dry pigments are ground with THIN OIL, then mixed with CSo, then use the VE for thinning, by adding one drop at a time and grinding well.

RUBBING PAINT INTO A WET EMULSION 'OIL OUT'
One effective way TO THIN PAINT is to add nothing to the paint, but rather to apply the paint as THINLY as desired by briskly RUBBING the paint with a stiff bristle brush, or your fingers, or a leather pad, into a WET FILM of the Emulsion 'oil out'. The gel-like quality of the CSO in the paint will produce a clear glaze as thin as one wishes. The Thixotropic property of CSO paint allows the painting of wet paint ON TOP of wet paint, if done so with care. It is the viscous quality of CSO that allows this Thixotropic quality of painting wet paint on top of wet paint. See the Rubens DVD and section in this book to read about Rubens' recipe for making a THIXOTROPIC MEDIUM.

DO NOT THIN YOUR PAINT WITH PURE SUN THICKENED OIL
Pure Oil can be used to thin paint, but I do not recommend it. If you decide to thin your paint with pure Sun Thickened oil, add ONLY One drop at a time to the paint and mix well. It will have a tendency to cause the paint to sag and drip. Adding Sun Thickened oil to paint gives it a leveling effect. DO NOT add this pure Sun Oil to Hand-Ground paint of dry pigments ground with CSO. The better choice to thin Hand-Ground paint is with the "Non-Viscous Emulsion". The Non-Viscous Emulsion will SLOW DOWN the drying of the paint slightly, but will prevent it from sagging or dripping.

*****

THE RESIN EFFECT
Before mixing CSO with the tube paint, check to see if the tube paint has an excess of thin oil. Sometimes you see this the moment the cap is removed. If your tube paint has excess oil, blot out a large portion by placing the oil paint on a paper towel. Then, mix the blotted paint with CSO. Generally speaking, it is not necessary to thin Tube paint once it is properly conditioned with CSO. IF thinning is desired, use the Viscous Emulsion, adding and grinding one drop at a time. The Tube oil paint is correctly conditioned when the non-viscous state of the Tube Paint is radically changed to a HIGHLY VISCOUS CONDITION.

Mixing CSO with Tube paints has a positive effect called, the **RESIN EFFECT**. This beneficial condition occurs when POLYMERIZED and NON-POLYMERIZED oils, were previously mixed separately with a powder, and are now mixed together. A later chapter discusses this interesting subject in detail.

For the Thixotropic quality to even be possible with Tube Oil paint, the paint must be made viscous and sticky. Add as much CSO as needed to bring about this change. The amount to add will vary because different manufacturers of tube oil paints add different amounts of Non-polymerized oil, as well as different amounts of stabilizers. And, they produce various grades of quality, such as 'student' oil paints and 'professional' oil paints, each using different measurements of oil and powders. A faster way to create thixotropic paint requires use of a BALSAM additive, and is discussed in the section on Rubens.

*****

HAND GROUND PAINT - IMPORTANT THINNING CONCERNS

DRY PIGMENTS ground together with 'Calcite Sun Oil', creates a paint that is thick and viscous, and can be difficult to brush, depending on the consistency it was ground to. It can be easily and quickly thinned for easier brushing. Normally, its best to use the Non-Viscous Emulsion to thin this Hand Ground paint. DO NOT thin with pure SUN THICKENED polymerized oil alone, as it will cause dripping.

To thin paint, use your palette knife and add a few drops of the emulsion to the thick CSO paint. Use the palette knife not a brush, and mix them well together on the grinding table. If still too thick, add another small amount of the emulsion. Repeat the mixing. Add more until you reach the brushing consistency you desire - but keeping it firm enough and not watery or runny. If thinned correctly, you will find that the paint becomes very easy to brush and that it holds and retains a firm body texture that is easily blended and the paint does not drip down the vertical support.

VERY IMPORTANT – VERY THINNED PAINT:

To thin any type of oil paint to a VERY THIN consistency, the ONLY choice is the Non-Viscous Emulsion because paint thinned to a very liquid state with the Viscous Emulsion WILL SAG.

PAINTING MICRO-FINE LINES

One quality we admire in many Old Master paintings are the fine details and micro-fine lines. These results are possible with Hand Made paint or with Tube Paint conditioned with 'CSO'. Fine details can be painted into wet paint, or into a dry surface that has been "oiled out with an Emulsion. Fine details CANNOT be painted on a dry surface that has NOT been 'oiled out'.

Daniel V. Thompson's book, (see bibliography) cites the need for a paint to flow easily if a painter is painting on a small scale. THEN he cites a fact that is of great interest for the use of very viscous paint, like the paint 'Calcite Sun Oil' will create. **Thompson says the EXCEPTION to the free flowing non-viscous paint that is used to paint on a small scale, is when an artist wishes to paint very MINUTE works with extremely small details, it is necessary to use a 'very viscid" medium, and Thompson describes paint made with this highly viscous medium as having the characteristic of, " ...it pulls out like very fine threads ...".** I cite this very important observation by Thompson, because it corroborates MY claim, that use of a Glair-Oil emulsion 'oil out', and an extremely viscous oil paint are BOTH necessary to paint the finest micro-fine lines and details.

PAINTING MICRO-FINE LINES INTO A WET SURFACE
To paint extraordinarily fine micro-lines, you must paint into wet paint or an 'oiled out' surface. Use a very fine, LONG-HAIRED soft hair brush and you must use viscous paint. **When you dip your brush into the very thick, viscous paint, as you pull the brush away, you will see an extremely fine "tail" of sticky paint falling from the brush that quickly disappears.** Apply the thick viscous paint into the wet layer of the paint, or the wet 'oil out' you just applied. You will notice the edges of the thin line will have a firm clear body and this clarity will remain exactly as painted.

USING CSO LIKE A PAINT
REMBRANT is known to have painted with a mixture of Chalk and Oil, but we do not know his ratio mixtures. The "Calcite Sun Oil" mixture can be used like one of the paints on the palette. Dipping the brush into the CSO, you can apply it like paint. Its gel-like quality immediately mixes in with the paint colors on the canvas, creating a highly translucent effect. It blends with all colors it touches, and has a thick sensuous quality. You will note it stays where it is placed. If used as a paint it is **VERY IMPORTANT to grind a few drops of the NON-VISCOUS emulsion to avoid any wrinkling or sagging.** It must be ground together very well with a palette knife on the grinding table.

When a jar of CSO is empty and finished, do not discard the crusty remains. You can apply it with a palette knife, to create unique thick rough textures. Professor Van De Wetering, advanced the theory that Rembrandt used crusty half-dried paint to help achieve some of his thick impasto effects as seen in his painting titled, "The Jewish Bride". I too have used this technique successfully.

'ROUNDS' ARE EXCEPTIONAL BRUSHES
Many different styles of brushes for oil painting are on the market. They have names like, filberts, flats, brights, fans, blenders, script liners. The versatility of round ferrule brushes, called 'rounds', makes others unnecessary. I only use brushes made of natural hair, not brushes made of synthetic hair. I use two main types of 'rounds'. The first type is made of stiff natural hog hair bristles. The second type, are those made of soft natural hairs. Soft hair brushes are available in many degrees of "softness" or 'firmness'. The firm ones have a spring and give me better control as I apply the paint.

I use different sizes of 'rounds'. Some have hairs that are very thick and wide, the hairs of others are very thin, and some have only a few hairs. Some have sharp pointed ends and others have ends that are round and fuzzy. Some have very short hairs and others have very long hairs. Only experience will tell you which brush is needed for the specific job in the area you are working on.

Brushes are only 'tools'. These tools wear out and must be replaced, but even a 'worn out' brush can be of some use, so I don't discard them. I use my brushes roughly because I do a lot of rubbing, and twisting, daubing, hard stippling. Sometimes I apply so much pressure that the metal ferrule strikes the painting surface, and hairs are bent and lost.

I also cut off a portion of the long wooden handles of the brushes to make them shorter. This gives the feel of having a pencil in my hand. I have read of 19th century artists using brushes with 6 foot long handles. This supposedly allowed them to stay in one place and enabled them to 'see' the composition better. I prefer to back up and walk away from the painting to judge my progress.

I do not wash my brushes after every day of painting. I place them in a level tray with enough non-polymerized oil to cover the hairs. This very slow drying oil keeps the brush hairs from drying out for months. The tray is slightly inclined at the end opposite the hairs so the handles are out of the oil. I am careful not to have the hairs get bent. Only when using umber do I make sure I squeeze all the paint out of the hairs, as this color will cling to and dry on the brush hairs even if the brush is submerged in oil.

*****

SUPERIORITY OF EMULSIONS
OVER SOLVENT RESIN PAINTING MEDIUMS

Modern books and University Art classes today, teach the use of Solvents, Resins, Varnishes, Driers and other additives in the form of a PAINTING MEDIUM. Old Manuscripts show SOME artists used solvents, resins and driers in oil painting. Whether in Olden days or modern days, these materials are used for specific reasons.

The Resins serve to keep the paint from sagging. The turpentine serves to liquefy the resins so it can be mixed with the oil and the oil paint. These mixtures of solvent, oil and resin, are called a PAINTING MEDIUM and are mixed with oil paint so it spreads easily. The driers are added to accelerate the drying so the painting can be completed faster. Various ratio mixtures of these three are used to make 'painting mediums' as paint additives, and as varnish for finished paintings. Experts warn that excessive amounts of resins, driers or solvents will be detrimental to the painting's permanence and should be avoided, and that excessive use of certain metallic driers will cause paint to darken and crack. Excessive use of driers have the opposite effect and slow down the drying.

Modern Tube oil paints have many deficiencies because they are made with slow drying ALKALI REFINED oils, and other additives. The deficiencies cause the oil painter to use the hazardous "painting mediums" to correct the deficiencies of tube paints. Doctors warn that exposure to solvent vapors, including vapors of LOW ODOR solvents, can cause serious health issues.

Today's oil painter do not need Painting Mediums containing hazardous and toxic ingredients because of the important benefits offered by the ingredients of "Calcite Sun Oil" and the Emulsions.
- Sun Thickened UNREFINED FLAX Oil dries fast and hard, eliminating need for Driers or Varnishes.
- Calcium Carbonate's cement-like quality and the Emulsions eliminates need for Resins and varnishes.
- Egg-Oil Emulsions thin the paint making it easy to brush, eliminating need for Resins or Solvents.

The Emulsions I formulated are superior to the 'resin-solvent-drier' painting mediums for many reasons, but the most important reason and explanation is this:

When resin and solvent and oil and driers are mixed together, they simply CO-MINGLE.
The solvent evaporates in a short period of hours, the resin remains side by side with the oil and the drier, each one curing at a different rate of time in their own way. When the Emulsions I formulated are made correctly, a molecule of the Glair ENTERS INTO a molecule of the Oil in the process called EMULSIFICATION. The two become one. There is no separation ever.

CHAPTER ELEVEN
THE 5 STEP PAINTING METHOD
P-D-U-O-F = Prepare - Draw – Underpaint – Overpaint - Finish

My method of painting a picture, developed from many sources and years of experience, is illustrated by the letters, "P- D- U- O- F ". The five letters in effect, separate and represent the FIVE steps I generally follow in painting a picture. At times I may deviate from this procedure. You will find these five steps, offer an intelligent, efficient, and easy method of painting, allowing you to express your aesthetic ideas to the fullest, and with safety and permanent results.

STEP ONE: "P" = PREPARE
The 'support' one uses will be a personal choice but it must be prepared correctly before you begin to paint. The surface must be fully non-absorbent.. Read the section 'Isolating the Support'. Apply either an OPAQUE TONE, called a 'toned ground', or a TRANSLUCENT TONE called an 'Imprimatura', or paint on the white ground color. The pure white of the gesso, or a mid-value gray, or a certain color, will result in different effects in the final work.

*****

STEP TWO: "D" = DRAW
One can do this step in a variety of ways. It will depend on the style of the artist. Van Eyck used a meticulous under-drawing using an ink-like substance. Rembrandt ignored it, preferring to use a direct under-painting instead. Any of a number of methods can be, and were used. Some used DRY media, such as charcoal, or pencil. See the page on safe Fixatives. Others used some type of WET media, such as ink, egg tempera, or fast drying oil paint mixtures. The KEY requirement was for it to be FAST DRYING. Others scratched the drawing into the wet paint.

METHOD ONE , USE NO IMPRIMATURA: Once the drawing is done and fully dry, apply a thin coat of the clear Viscous Emulsion all over the drawing, and begin to paint into the wet surface. OR: Use the next method.

METHOD TWO, USE AN IMPRIMATURA: Once the drawing is done and fully dry, apply a thin coat of the Viscous Emulsion mixed with a color such as dry umber and let it DRY. This is called an Imprimatura and is applied transparently. It will dry "tacky" and you do not have to wait for it to dry hard. As soon as it is 'tacky dry' it can be 'oiled out' again and one can begin the painting.
NOTE: If in a hurry, apply a thin Acrylic paint medium-tone wash on the gesso. It dries in 20 minutes. Then 'oil out' with the emulsion and begin to paint into the wet emulsion 'oil out' with oils.

WARNING: It is important to know oil paint layers become more translucent with the passage of time, and is the reason old paintings may show some dark images, like a horse with an extra set of legs. These are called "pentimenti", as they were design alterations covered up by the artist with a layer of paint. Not visible to their contemporaries 300 years ago, they have become disturbingly visible today. Because of this characteristic, it is important during the DRAWING stage, to wipe away ANY dark marks you would NOT want to become visible as the painting ages.

*****

STEP THREE: "U" = UNDERPAINT
YOU MAY SKIP THIS STEP. IF YOU USE THIS STEP DO THE FOLLOWING.

PAINT WITH A GRISAILLE. You can use dull muted colors, or paint with grays only. Painting with grays is called a Grisaille. Tube Paint mixed with CSO, takes about a day to dry, whereas Hand Made paint may dry within a day. Choose dull muted colors plus black, white and umber -or - restrict to painting in gray tone mixtures of white and black. If you paint with thick paint, you may have to wait longer for it to dry before over-painting other layers. The Old Masters knew that use of thin paint in the under layers, and the addition of the color UMBER to the various mixes, vastly hastens the drying, allowing for a quicker finish.

IF USING TUBE PAINT, ALWAYS CONDITION IT WITH "CSO" BEFORE PAINTING
Place the tube paint on paper towels to drain away the EXCESS non-polymerized oil, but do not drain it completely dry. With the palette knife, condition the tube paint, by adding enough 'Calcite Sun Oil" to change the viscosity from a NON-VISCOUS paint, to a HIGHLY VISCOUS paint. Use your dull colors plus black, white and umber for under-painting in muted colors. Read the section
titled: "Rembrandt's White Oil Paint" for instructions on how to recreate Rembrandt's thick white paint.

USE A BRISTLE BRUSH: Use a bristle brush- not a soft sable brush - to apply the paint in this step. Round brushes allow you to twist and turn the bristles in any direction you want, and you always get the mark you desire through subtle changes of pressure. A round bristle brush, wiped clean and flared out with use of your fingers, allows exceptionally easy blending.

CARE OF BRUSHES: It is not necessary to clean your brushes with Turpentine or soap and water. Read the section titled, "Never Wash Your Brushes Again ".

THREE IMPORTANT REASONS FOR UNDER-PAINTING
When the Old Masters applied a gray or muted color in the sub-strata, with or without the under-drawing, they called it the 'dead coloring' or a 'monotone', or a 'grisaille'. The under-work makes the painting process easier and more effective. Artists use these two very similar stages of the painting, the under-drawing or the under-painting, for several very important reasons:

DIVISION OF LABOR: The under-drawing or under-painting allows the painter to divide the main labor between COMPOSITION and COLOR - with the concern for TEXTURES also separated, allowing contemplation and time to make calculated aesthetic decisions.

STIMULATE THE IMAGINATION: The under-work stimulates the creative mind and allows the painter to VISUALIZE the development of the image inside the artist's mind, in a very creative and exciting manner. In other words, the DESIGN and the IMAGE grow of its own, unencumbered by other concerns such as texture or color. It is well known that CREATIVITY is made possible through associative images. A good example is this: Put a dot on a paper and a person will say they see a 'dot' and nothing more. Put another dot next to the first dot, and an imaginative person will say they see "a pair of eyes".
Artists know this, and through the application of a monotone 'haphazard scribble', of oil paint the artist will have 'flashes' of images that can be explored, in turn creating more stimuli, thereby creating additional "flashes" of imagery. Such are the workings of creativity, an ability all humans have, though most people do not know how to access it or have had it stymied.

INCREASED COLOR AND TEXTURAL EFFECTS: The under-painting in muted colors or gray tones creates a unique method to increase the color effects in the final work that CAN NOT be accomplished by the "direct" 'Alla Prima' method. Under-painting provides an important foundation for Glazes, Scumbles, and Textures. The creation of varied textures, are not possible through today's DIRECT painting method. Velazquez, Rubens, and Hals are considered to be the greatest virtuosos in the manipulation of paint, and their classic "Alla prima" method ALWAYS systematically used some form of under-work, upon which to place their sensuous applications of thin and thick paint.

IF YOU DID NOT USE THE UNDERPAINTING STEP you left out important color effects and textures you cannot obtain any other way. But, by skipping it, you can finish a painting faster, and sometimes the final painting will have a much fresher appearance. Your experience will guide you on choices. If you chose not use it, go on to the next step, in which we paint in a direct method, called 'alla prima' painting, a method in which we use all the colors, directly, and in one operation.

STEP FOUR: "O" = OVERPAINT (IN FULL COLOR)

IF YOU DID NOT USE THE PREVIOUS UNDER-PAINTING STEP, DO THIS: 'Oil Out' the surface with the Emulsion, and begin to paint in FULL COLOR using all the colors available to you. Before painting, always condition your tube oil paint with an approximate equal amount of 'Calcite Sun Oil' and grind the two well together using a palette knife and grinding table

.
IF YOU DID USE THE PREVIOUS UNDER-PAINTING STEP, DO THIS:
If you did under-paint with thin paint it will dry faster than thick paint. Let the paint dry sufficiently to where you can apply an Emulsion 'Oil Out'. You can 'oil out' a 'tacky dry' surface. Then use the very same mixing, application and thinning methods previously described. The goal is to paint the purest and brightest colors over the dull, muted or gray colors used in the under-painting step. Extraordinary color effects and textural effects, not possible by the "wet-in-wet" direct painting method, are easy to achieve.

If you did under paint with thick paint, it must be allowed to dry well. Frequently, we create a variety of textures when using thick oil paint in the under-painting step. The thick paint must be given extra time to dry hard enough, then we can apply glazes over it and then WIPE them off, allowing the glazes to penetrate the crevices of the paint. This CANNOT be done on paint that has NOT hardened sufficiently. If the thick paint is wet inside a dry outer skin, it will crack any over paint applications. The best procedure is to paint thinly in the under layers or be prepared to wait a long time.

*****

STEP FIVE: "F" = FINISH (IN FULL COLOR)

On a technical level, it is simple to finish a painting. We use the very same mixing, application and thinning methods already described. However, the finishing of a painting is the most difficult and time consuming step ONLY because the artist is faced with a multitude of aesthetic choices. Rembrandt said an artist is finished with a painting when the artist achieved the desired effect. This is good advice, as only you can decide when a painting is finished. Rubens painted many paintings without any assistance however the great demand for his work caused him to use assistants. At times his assistants did the under work based on his DESIGN, then he would use his "master's touch", to finish it.

Though you can use any of your colors, this step is where you use final glazes to alter a color, or to use as pure color accents. This is also the stage where you can use your PURE black and PURE white. BLACK is the depth of a painting and WHITE is the sparkle. Paintings that do not use both of these colors, lack both effects. I advise you to forget the concept by the Impressionists that BLACK should never be used because there is no black in nature. The fact is, we paint with paint, not with light rays, even though we see by light rays.The greatest of painters - Michelangelo, Rembrandt, Titian, Velazquez, and all the others, used BLACK. Black is especially effective when used as a transparent thin, or translucent thick glaze. When Ivory black is mixed with white, it creates cool pearl-like tones. Mars black produces warm tones.

The Thixotropic quality of *'Calcite Sun Oil"* paint allows you to immediately paint ON TOP of a wet glaze or scumble. The key is to first paint thinly, a VISCOUS glaze or scumble onto the dry surface. Then you can apply the next layer of paint on top, blending and brushing as needed. Your skill level will determine your level of success. To apply <u>wet paint on top of wet paint</u>, stroke it on gently.

PAINTING MICRO-FINE LINES OR SMALL DETAILS

In this step, artists MIGHT switch from the use of stiff bristle brushes to softer and smaller soft-hair brushes. These allow the fine line details appropriate to certain styles requiring fine detail finishes, like the hairs in an Albrecht Durer portrait. With a LONG fine haired sable brush, and without any thinning of the CSO conditioned Tube paint, fine micro-lines can be painted into wet paint or on a surface having an Emulsion 'oil out'. Please read the section on the use of EMULSIONS, how they are made and applied.

*****

ADDITIONAL COMMENTS

CORRECTIVE OVER PAINTS
Once you are 'finished' with the painting, place it in a place where you can OBSERVE it throughout the day for several days as you 'live' with it. You will see things you are not satisfied with. You can make corrections easily as long as the surface is fresh or at least 'tacky dry', meaning that when you rub in the emulsion 'oil out' the rubbing will not smear the paint. Also, any impasto thick paint should also be dry inside. Many master painters would repaint parts of their paintings over and over, and Rembrandt is known to have reworked one painting 10 years after it was 'finished'. When you want to make changes, 'oil out' the dry surface with the Emulsion, making sure the 'oil out' coat is very thin. Prepare your paints as before and make the corrections. You can make corrections and repeat this process many times. Corrective over-paints may dry out matte. Rub in a thin film of the Viscous Emulsion with your finger to restore the gloss.

STEPS IN PAINTING
Creative artists resist 'steps and regulations' so you can freely disregard my five step method. My goal in teaching the 5 step method is to give newer artists a logical approach to painting. Sometimes I paint in full color without an under painting. Sometimes while painting in full color, I might paint an area in 'grisaille' using only black and White. Artists need freedom of choice in technical as well as in aesthetic issues.

WHEN IS A PAINTING FINISHED?
I agree with Rembrandt's view that a painting is finished when the artist says it is finished.

The old statement, **"Beauty is in the eye of the beholder"**, is not acceptable to me because it gives the viewer the right to judge and decide whether an artist's work is beautiful or not. Personal opinions in judgment and criteria are subjective, and they vary from person to person. This old statement disregards the artist's views.

I wish to improve on that statement, by saying, **"Beauty is in the eye of the ARTIST"**.
I say this to empower the artist who has made the artwork. It supports the individual aesthetic sensitivity of the artist, and supports my belief that the view of the artist is what matters the most in any artwork ... not the opinion, or belief of the beholder.

*****

CHAPTER TWELVE
THE RESIN EFFECT and other CHALK OIL MIXTURES
The 'Resin Effect'
Alternate Mixtures of Calcium Carbonate and Oils

INTRODUCTION
I believe 'Calcite Sun Oil' is the very best Grinding Oil for Oil Painting because of the many benefits it offers users of Hand-Ground paints and users of Tube paints. I believe this chapter will stimulate experimentation by others.

THE 'RESIN EFFECT'
The much discussed *'resin effect'* is reportedly created by the mixing of two oils with different drying rates, one Polymerized, the other Non-polymerized. This mixture is supposed to cause a 'reaction', and the paint supposedly 'stiffens', with the aim of eliminating sagging or dripping when the painting is held in a vertical position. It is easy to prove this is NOT TRUE. If this stiffening were to happen, past artists would have eliminated the use of resins and egg as additives altogether. Frederic Taubes' formulations in the mid 20th century combined Polymerized and Non-polymerized oils, an indication he believed the mixing of the two oils could cause or promote the "resin effect".

My experiments show the mixing of these two oils – by themselves - does not create the 'resin effect'. It does NOT cause any stiffening, nor does it prevent dripping of the oil.

However, besides formulating painting mediums, Taubes also recommended grinding one pigment with a polymerized oil, and SEPARATELY, grinding a second pigment in an non-polymerized oil. Then, Taubes said, the artist could "properly balance" the plasticity of the paint by mixing portions of one paint with the other (Studio Secrets, 4th ed.,1946, p.25). Taubes correctly found out that for the unique reaction to occur between the two different oils – THEY MUST FIRST BE each be ground SEPARATELY with solid matter. This will create the 'resin effect', a stiffening that prevents sagging, without the use of resins.

When we mix TUBE PAINT (dry pigment matter mixed with non-viscous Non-POLYMERIZED oil) with 'CALCITE SUN OIL' (dry calcium carbonate mixed with highly viscous POLYMERIZED oil), we can duplicate Taubes' properly balanced paint plasticity and create the condition known as the "resin effect". Without any resin additions, this mixture does give the paint stability against sagging. This mixture has unique characteristics, depending on the different ratios of the two oils used in the mixture.

TEST RESULTS ON CREATING THE 'RESIN EFFECT'

1. Drying oils, refined or unrefined, whether cold mixed, or mixed and heated, when mixed together without any additives of DRY MATTER, WILL NOT of themselves, create the 'resin effect'. These oil mixtures will drip and sag when applied on a vertical surface.

2. Mixing a drying oil with dry pigment(dry matter)will create a paint.
   Mixing a drying oil with dry calcium carbonate (dry matter) will create a cement-like mixture [CSO].

3. Mixing a Polymerized oil with dry pigment to a firm consistency creates a very viscous, very fast drying paint that will dry within 30 hours, but it will sag and drip a great deal.

4. Mixing a Non-polymerized oil with dry pigment to a firm consistency creates a non-viscous, very slow drying paint that will dry in 6 days or more, but it does not sag and it remains firm.

5. The 'resin effect' is created by mixing equal parts, of the two separately mixed paints, each containing one of the two mentioned different oils above, OR, by mixing CSO with the Tube oil paint containing the non-polymerized oil. If the consistency is firm, this creates a paint that will not drip or sag when on a vertical surface, as the two distinct mixtures react and stiffen. Only if each oil is first SEPARATELY mixed with 'dry matter', be it pigment or calcium carbonate, and then when the two are mixed together, the 'resin effect' can be achieved.

RESINS: PRO and CON

Artists disagree on the use of adding resins to their paint, though it increases color depth, adds luster, assists adhesion of layers, and improves blending. Artists mainly add resin to the paint, to stop the paint from sagging and dripping. My own paintings from the late 1950's through the 1980's in which I used Taubes' copal mediums with Tube Oil Paints do not appear to have lowered in tone, do not have cracks and appear to be in stable condition, BUT they are relatively young.

I own several original Taubes oil paintings on canvas, with the oldest being from the late 30's or early 40's. One is very dry and the paint is cracked. Another has small cracks in several places. Another has numerous cracks in all the impasto thick areas. One is in excellent condition. The preservation of any painting is dependent on several factors, paint medium, support, application methods and VERY IMPORTANTLY- the care it has received. One of my Taubes originals had been relined and retouched, as it had a few tears in the original surface. Another had been in a fire as the entire back side was filled with blackened soot. The ones on hard board are in better condition than those on canvas.

Some artists believe resins, whether soft resin or hard resin, are injurious to the paint film over time, possibly causing the paint to become brittle, to darken, and to crack after many years. Others disagree and believe resins added to paint actually strengthens it making it more resistant to moisture and wear. Frederic Taubes, the formulator of the famous Taubes painting mediums of the mid 20TH century wrote in his famous book, ' The Mastery of Oil Painting', that copal resin **did not** make the paint tougher - using his 16 year old tests to form his opinion.

'Hard' resins like Copal or Amber are dark in color, and some believe they eventually darken the colors, so, they advocate the use of "soft" resins which are light in color. 'Soft' resins, like Mastic, or Dammar, are light in color, but paint concocted with a soft resin, creates a weak paint film that can be softened by a mild solvent, no matter how old the painting. Mayer wrote that a soft resin does not create a soft film but all my tests prove Meyer to be in error. Old paint films containing dammar can easily be wiped off with a rag and turpentine. This solubility creates a problem when a decayed dammar varnish is removed. As the solvent softens and removes the old dammar varnish, it also softens the paint film and removes delicate thin glazes and thin paint applications. My own experiments have confirmed this solubility of soft resin in paint.

Today, oil paintings are commonly varnished with a soft-resin, **'spirit varnish'**. This varnish is nothing more than soft resin like dammar dissolved in turpentine. Or, paintings are varnished with the new synthetic varnishes. Neither is permanent, but during their 40 to 50 year life they do protect the painting from grime, moisture and abrasion. The varnishes eventually decay, acrylics changing color and natural resins turning yellow that become brittle, and must be removed and replaced.

In summation, I do not know from my own experience whether any HARD RESINS do or do not make the paint tougher, or whether they do or do not cause the paint to eventually crack, or whether the dark hard resins will change or lower the tone over time. I believe a fully dry oil painting **can be given** a TEMPORARY removable, 'soft resin' spirit varnish. This will protect the paint surface from abrasion and grime, as well as to give it luster. I believe it is better to give the finished oil painting a permanent, non-removable film of the VISCOUS EMULSION as the final 'varnish'. See the section titled: 'Final Permanent Layer for Completed Paintings'.

*****

ALTERNATE MIXTURES of CALCIUM CARBONATE and OIL

'CALCITE SUN OIL' is THE VERY BEST Grinding Oil for mixing with Tube paint and for mixing with Hand-Ground paint because its fast drying quality offers many important benefits for the professional oil painter. 'CALCITE SUN OIL' is formulated with the superior oil of the Old Masters. I have previously explained why the Old Masters' oil makes a superior paint with many benefits. Until the Old Masters' superior oil is available on the market, artists can use the slow drying substitute linseed oil, sold as 'STAND LINSEED OIL', and by following instructions, can make 'CALCITE STAND OIL', also called 'CAL-STAND'.

Modern ALKALI REFINED OILS are fully embedded into our culture and are here to stay even though they lack important qualities of the carefully prepared oils of the Old Masters. 'CALCITE STAND OIL' is a slow drying mixture, but it is effective in many ways, especially for those artists that prefer a slow drying medium.

'CALCITE STAND OIL' (CAL-STAND)

Many artists are frustrated by the scarcity of the true Old Master oil described in my book. The use of the art store Linseed Stand Oil can be used as a substitute. It allows the Artist to approximate SOME the benefits of CSO. The 'Viscous Emulsion' can also be made with this Alkali Refined STAND OIL, but it will lack the fast drying.

FORMULA: Mix 3 parts of Calcium Carbonate to 1 part Linseed Stand Oil . Mix it well.
RECOMMENDED USE: Mix an equal amount of 'CAL-STAND' with tube oil paints to create a sensuous paint. 'CAL-STAND' is ideal for any artist, Professional or Beginner, who prefers slow drying paint. Tube Oil Paint mixed with an equal amount of 'CAL-STAND' creates the beneficial 'resin effect' without any resins. The paint mixture will still be a slow drier because both oils are alkali REFINED. Today's Stand Oil is made by boiling Alkali REFINED Linseed Oil at high temperatures without oxygen. This lack of oxygen prevented the oxidation of the oil. Almost all tube oil paints are ground in slow drying Non-polymerized Alkali REFINED Linseed Oil.

Thin this paint with an Emulsion. Make the Emulsion as described in the book, but substituting the slow drying STAND LINSEED OIL for the fast drying Old Masters' oil. Thinning can also be done by mixing ONE drop of Non-polymerized Linseed oil with the paint. This creates a glaze that holds firm if it is not too liquid. Thinning should always be done by adding one drop at a time, then mixed well with a palette knife, to insure a 'balanced' mixture. In my experiments, correctly thinned paint did not sag nor drip, and it kept the brush marks. The thick impasto kept its sharp textures. The paint gained in color depth and luster. The mixture is slow drying and dries even slower when thinned by adding more Non-polymerized oil. For faster drying DO NOT add additional oil. DO NOT THIN with Polymerized STAND OIL, as the paint will sag and drip.

'CALCITE RAW OIL' (CRO)

FORMULA: Mix 5 parts of Calcium Carbonate and 2 parts of Non-polymerized REFINED or UNREFINED Oil to create a mixture I call, " CALCITE RAW OIL", also known as CRO.
RECOMMENDED USE: 'Calcite Raw Oil' offers no benefits when mixed with Tube Oil Paints because the CRO and the tube paint both contain Non-polymerized oil. Neither the drying nor the viscosity are improved. 'Calcite Raw Oil', is a very slow drier. Thick impasto has a tendency to wrinkle. The addition of a small amount of an egg-oil Emulsion with the paint will completely eliminate any wrinkling. See the section on Emulsions.

'CALCITE MIXED OIL' (CMO)

'Calcite Mixed Oil, also known as CMO.
FORMULA: Use any type of oils
1 part Non-polymerized Linseed Oil.
1 part Polymerized Linseed Oil.
6 parts of dry Calcium Carbonate
Mix the Non-polymerized oil with 3 parts of the Calcium Carbonate.
Separately mix the Polymerized oil with 3 parts of Calcium Carbonate.
Once each mixture is separately mixed well, mix the two together, using equal amounts.
This mixture is added to any oil paint in equal amounts. The interaction of the two mixtures causes the 'resin effect' which is a reaction that gives stability to the paint as well as body and ease blending. Use it as an experimental mixture.

'CALCITE SUN OIL' and WATER

CSO [or any oil paint mixture containing chalk] when kept in a jar will skin over. This is due to the fast drying of the oil and the oxygen in the jar. If water is poured over the mixture, it will not skin over and the jar cap can be left off. However, the mixture absorbs the water causing the mixture to lighten as it blanches out. This causes it to become opaque and lose translucency, and when mixed with oil paints it acts as if it were white paint added to the color. The paint becomes viscous, easy to blend and easy to brush. One can paint EXCEPTIONALLY HIGH FIRM TEXTURES and they do not level as with regular CSO oil paint. There is no sag or drip. Extremely fine micro lines can be in painted into it while wet. When grinding with dry pigment, the water is expelled to the side. It is unknown how much water remains in the paint body or what final effect it has on the paint structure. The Old Masters frequently kept their fast drying oil paints like Lead White, UNDER WATER, so they would not dry out. This is an experimental mixture.

CHOICES of CALCIUM CARBONATE and OIL

1. CALCITE SUN OIL (CSO): The ideal and very best Grinding Oil for BOTH, Tube paint or Hand Ground paint. It eliminates the problems of Tube paints while giving them increased benefits. This mixture allows all painters to, "achieve the Old Masters' paint quality with Safety and Permanence".

2. CALCITE STAND OIL (CAL-STAND OIL) : USE AS A SUBSTITUTE FOR CSO.
Use as a Grinding Oil for Tube oil paint. Mixing the two different viscosities promotes the resin effect.
This is a slow drier that will dry even slower if thinned with more Non-polymerized oil.
Thinning with Polymerized oil will encourage sagging and dripping.

3. CALCITE RAW OIL (CRO): This mixture dries slower than CSO alone.
When mixed with CSO, it will sharpen textures and make them more firm. Use with Hand Ground paint ground with CSO, not with Tube paint as the Tube paint has sufficient Non-polymerized oil.

4. CALCITE MIXED OIL (CMO): An experimental mixture.

5. 'CALCITE SUN OIL' and WATER: An experimental mixture.

CHAPTER THIRTEEN
STUDIO PRACTICES

This chapter contains practical information to help the reader master the oil painting medium and to make life easier in the studio.

p.113   Materials List- the essentials of the equipment you will need
p. 115 Burnt Plate Oil - an extremely slow drying oil. It is made for Lithography, not Painting
p. 117 Drying Times of Paints - clearly shows the importance of the Old Masters' oil
p. 119 Acrylic Paints vs. Oil Paints - discusses the modern and the old media
p. 119 Isolating the Support - discusses the importance of this preparatory step
p. 122 Care of the Palette, Hands, Excess Paint - valuable studio information
p. 123 Never Wash Brushes Again – this will save many hours of tedious unnecessary work
p. 124 Final Permanent Layer - discusses the difference between temporary and permanent protection
P. 125 Fixative - describes a safe spray so your drawings do not smudge when over-painting
p. 126 Practical Ways to Paint a Picture – a summary of simple procedures.
p. 128 Umber oil and Half-White - fast drying oil and paint for under painting
p. 129 Example of painting with Aguado – example one
p. 131 Example of painting procedure
p. 132 Preparing the support

MATERIALS LIST

Most advanced artists have these materials. Some items are NEW even to experienced painters, such as the Grinding table.

1. CALCIUM CARBONATE: I recommend 'Calcium Carbonate Chalk from Champagne, France' because it does not separate when stored. Available online at: kremerpigments.com   NON-toxic, but one must ALWAYS wear a dust mask when handling all fine powders.

2. GRINDING TABLE: You must have a Grinding table. Do not try grinding your paints on your hand palette. Use a large sturdy table with a non-porous surface about 18"X18" or any size. I Use non-absorbent glazed floor tile with a smooth surface.

3. HAND PALETTE: Transfer the prepared paint from the mixing table to the hand palette as needed. I place my hand palette on a small table placed in front of the easel to free my hands.

4. SUPPORTS: WOOD PANEL; I use high quality cabinet grade ½ inch birch plywood that has a smooth surface. Oak plywood is harder, but it has a noticeable grain that if not filled, will be noticeable in the finished surface of the painting. Wood supports that are ready-prepared are expensive. It is easy and much more economical to prepare your own.

CANVAS; Ready-prepared canvas with acrylic gesso sometimes has too much tooth that will ruin your brushes as well as require more paint. Apply a layer of acrylic gesso, using a palette knife to scrape it on and fill in the weave. Do not apply this gesso layer with a brush because it will not fill the weave. If you want to stretch your own, it takes effort to get it right, plus other bits of equipment and tools are needed. Manufacturers provide instructions. The Old Masters mainly used Linen canvas. Today we have a choice of Linen or cotton or some synthetic fabrics, with linen being more expensive. The cotton weave surface can be mechanical and monotonous, whereas the linen weave surface is more random and lively. The Acrylic gesso is very absorbent and must be sealed before applying oil paint.

NON-ABSORBENT SURFACE: Without any doubt the surface on which you paint, must be fully sealed and 100% non-absorbent. Ready prepared wood and canvas supports are already primed. They are ready to paint on but they should be sealed/isolated first. If you are preparing your own surface from raw canvas or bare wood, you FIRST need to seal the raw wood or canvas with an appropriate liquid SIZE, and SECOND, the gesso must be isolated too. See: Isolating the Support.

5. TUBE OIL PAINTS and DRY PIGMENTS
One can under paint with Hand ground paints because they dry faster but you do not need to use these. Painting thinly with tube oil paints mixed with CSO will accomplish a fast drying film if one is using the Old Masters' superior oil The Non-polymerized oil in the tube paints slows down the drying but the addition of CSO will greatly improve the drying. If you do hand-grind, you only need a few dry pigments, such as umber, sienna, ocher, black and Titanium Dioxide white.
One can paint with a limited palette of tube paints, 6 basic colors; a bright Red , a bright Yellow, a bright Blue, a bright brown Burnt Sienna, Mars Black, and Titanium White. With these few colors you can mix many other colors, shades and tints. Hand ground paints and tube paints can be mixed together.

HEALTH WARNING: My claims of safety are restricted to the elimination of hazardous materials. It is beyond my control if artists choose toxic tube paints or dry pigment powders. See the book by Monona Rossol, titled: "The Artists Complete Health and Safety Guide" for hazardous colors.

6. BUY FLAX OIL OR LINSEED OIL : As described in the Introductory Chapter
Cleanse the Flax oil per instructions. Once cleansed it has many uses. Use it to clean your grinding table, your hand palette, your hands and to make the NVE emulsion. Also use it to clean your brushes. Sun thicken the rest for making the CSO.

BEWARE! A major brand sells 'SUN THICKENED LINSEED OIL'. The oil used is alkali refined LINSEED OIL that was later exposed to the sun. This art store oil has a label saying it is "sun thickened linseed oil". It is not the true oil of the Old Masters and it is a very slow drying oil and will not achieve the results of the CSO method. See the section on Alternate Mixtures of calcium carbonate and oils.

7. PALETTE KNIFE: Buy a straight blade that is flexible, about ¾" or 1" inch wide and about 5 inches long with a round tip. Use it to grind paint and to also to paint with. Grind paint mixtures with a firm pressure.

8. BRUSHES: I use brushes with ROUND METAL FERRULES known as 'Rounds'. Use natural, not synthetic, hog bristle brushes and soft-hair brushes of several sizes. Rounds allow all manner of application movements and techniques and do not leave unsightly markings. HOWEVER, flat haired brushes can add MODERNISTIC appearances to the painting. Artists should try both.

9. PLASTIC TRAY. Add oil to the tray and incline one end. Use for holding brushes after painting is completed. Keep the hairs in the oil, but not touching the edge or the hairs will bend permanently. It can be messy but it was the way the Old Masters kept their brushes. It saves time.

10. OPAQUE WHITE PORCELAIN CONTAINER: Use this for thickening the oil in the summer sun. My tests show an opaque white porcelain container, instead of a clear glass container, will reduce the time needed to polymerize the UNREFINED oil from 60 days to 30 days of direct sun exposure. Cover with a clear glass that allows air to enter, and keeps out dust and moisture.

11. MEASURING CUP, SPOON, BOWL, WEIGHING SCALE: Use for measuring and mixing the ingredients of the "Calcite Sun Oil", and beating the egg whites for the ingredient of the Emulsion.

12. PAPER NAPKINS or RAGS and WASTE BASKET: For general cleaning. CAUTION: Oily rags and papers are a fire hazard. Dispose of daily, kept outside in a metal container or immersed in water.

13. EGGS: For making the Emulsion. Four egg whites makes a sufficient supply for many paintings.

14. OPTIONAL ITEMS: A folding French easel is very good for small and medium sized paintings. It is easily adjustable if you sit or stand, and its built-in box holds your other items. Use a "paint stick" to steady your hand as you paint details. A 5 foot long, ½ inch dowel, with a rubber or leather pad on one end will do. Non-Fat skim milk, to make acrylic gesso non-absorbent. Wide flat brushes to apply the skim milk onto a charcoal drawing as a fixative. Drawing pencils, Ink, Vine charcoal, Hand soap, Towels.

BURNT PLATE OIL
ALKALI REFINED LINSEED OIL HEATED TO EXTREMELY HIGH TEMPERATURES

In modern times, Rembrandt's methods and materials have received much attention by world renowned and lesser recognized scientists using the most advanced equipment available. Scientists using these tools are many times in disagreement and some results are debatable. Scientists are human and make errors, poor guesses, perform incomplete or defective experiments, just like persons in any profession,

Anthony Bailey's book on the Rembrandt Research Project discloses the effect that ego and the position of the scientist on the 'pecking order', had on settling the disagreements as the seven members determined which Rembrandt paintings were authentic and which were not. Later RRP groups made of different members, have reversed de-attributions made by an earlier RRP group.

Recently, I reviewed a website in which two contemporary scientists THEORIZE that since Rembrandt was an etcher, that it was POSSIBLE that he used the extremely thick linseed oil used in that art form, and mixed it with his oil painting medium. The two scientists used old recipes and by boiling linseed oil at high temperatures they attempted to recreate what they theorize was the thick oil used by Rembrandt for his etchings. Their report calls this oil, "BURNT PLATE OIL".

Rembrandt was the first of the Old Masters to apply his paint in thick, high impasto by using a palette knife. I will be the first to say that Rembrandt's inventive, creative approach to his use of materials in oil painting makes the possibility of Rembrandt having made a ONE TIME 'experiment' with his etching oil. But, after making my own experiments with this Burnt Plate Oil, I concluded that it had important drawbacks and that Rembrandt would NOT have used it as his standard grinding oil.

TESTING THE THEORY AND CONCLUSION
I was asked by a friend to try out the theory. I painted a painting using BPO and simultaneously painted a painting using 'Calcite Sun Oil'. After testing BPO as a painting medium, I concluded that Rembrandt would NOT have used this medium in his oil paintings ...except for a one time experiment. This one time experiment would have demonstrated to Rembrandt the important reasons why he would not have continued its use. Rembrandt followed established methods of mixing smalt (ground glass) with his paint to accelerate the drying and Rembrandt added dry Calcium Carbonate powder to create high thick bodied impasto textures. At the conclusion of this essay I will expand on additional reasons supporting why Rembrandt would NOT have used BPO as his standard oil painting medium. I begin with a review and research of BPO.

RESEARCH ON BURNT PLATE OIL

I conducted research on the Burnt Plate Oil I purchased from a local Art store. For privacy at their request, I must leave out the names of the company representatives I spoke with. In fact, I was told by one contact person, that they were not allowed to give out information on their suppliers. It was only through perseverance and reaching a person in a higher position and after explaining the purpose of my inquiry, I was able to get the leads I needed. I was asked not to divulge the information.

BPO is used in the industrial commercial Printing industry, and in the fine arts of Etching, and Lithography. BPO can be bought in various degrees of viscosity from thin to thick. Various blacks and colors can be mixed with these BPO oils for desired colorist effects. The Art store where I purchased the BPO said that they do not MANUFACTURE the BPO but buy it from a SUPPLIER, and only resell it. I was given the names of two Suppliers, from which they purchase the BPO. Price considerations cause this art store to buy the #00 (very low viscosity) and the #3 (medium viscosity) from one supplier, and the #8 (very viscous) from another. I had a lengthy conversation with the representative of the supplier of the #00 and the #3 BPO.

In brief he stated (paraphrased): We do not manufacture this product. We buy it from the manufacturer and re-sell it, but I do not have their name. We don't call it Burnt Plate Oil, we call it dark bodied LITHO OIL (made for the Lithography printing industry). Though we do not make it, I can answer some of your questions. The oil used is linseed oil. I do not know if it is refined oil or not. Alkali refinement removes all the fatty acids by treating the oil with a caustic chemical called Sodium Hydroxide. After it removes the fatty acids, the chemical is washed out. This lightens the color and removes the impurities from the oil. The oil is boiled under a nitrogen blanket to keep oxygen out. The longer it boils the darker and thicker it gets.

Another representative informed me of the following (paraphrased) : Burnt Plate Oil and Litho Varnish are actually exactly the same product. We do not manufacture the BPO. We buy it from a supplier and re-sell it. They do not have solvents or driers mixed into them. I do not know what method of refining of the linseed oil is involved. Linseed oil is boiled and then at the end of the process an ignition source is added to the varnish kettle to flash off (or burn) the light ends. The light ends are the naturally occurring solvents in the linseed oil. The difference between raw linseed and bodied linseed (which is what burnt plate oil and litho varnish are) is the removal of the solvents – and the fact that by cooking the material for longer periods of time, the resulting oil gains body (viscosity). As the body of an oil increases the oil tends to darken. Varnish kettles accommodate approximately 20-30 drums of 55 gallons each

TEST PAINTINGS COMPARING BPO and CSO

I made a test by painting two paintings on the same date, and each took about 45 minutes to complete. The BPO painting was painted first and the CSO painting was painted immediately thereafter. Five DAYS after completion, the BPO painting was still wet in the thin blue paint area, and in the thicker paint, impasto areas. Some areas of the paint surface were able to be smeared by gentle rubbing. and many areas were still soft. The BPO dry time required was 5-6 days

Thirty HOURS after completion, the CSO painting was solidified to the touch in all areas. The drying was sufficient that gentle rubbing in all areas did not cause any smearing. The dry time was 30 hours.

ADDITIONAL TESTING OF BPO: Two samples of amber colored BPO were placed in direct sunlight for 40 days. They remained the same dark color and would not bleach. Other tests showed dried BPO to be brittle, showing the oil having lost its important flexibility.

CONCLUSION: REMBRANDT WOULD NOT HAVE USED BPO

Rembrandt would not have used the BPO because of the extremely slow drying quality. Like all the Old Masters, Rembrandt knew that Sun Thickened, UNREFINED cold pressed linseed/FLAX oil was a sufficiently fast drying oil. It dries within 8 to 30 hours or less, when used to make oil paint, depending on the pigment choice, thickness of film, and environmental factors. Rembrandt also knew that the addition of driers - to unnaturally accelerate the drying of oil paint made with linseed oil - was a dangerous practice that resulted in darkening and cracking of the paint film over time. Both of these reasons, combined with Rembrandt's knowledge of paint application methods (thin paint dries faster) and use of naturally fast drying pigments (umber dries fastest), and his use of inert natural ingredients that can impact drying by natural means (smalt and Calcium Carbonate) would eliminate Rembrandt's use of extremely slow drying BPO as a standard oil painting medium.

ADDITIONAL BPO INFORMATION: The #8 dark thick BPO has a strong odor. Though I painted in a well ventilated open garage, the fumes of BPO gave me a headache. The fine art craft of oil painting as practiced by the Old Masters required much time for preparation of their materials. Today, we have industrialized production and readily available oil painting materials in great quantity and variety of quality and price. One can still prepare the very IMPORTANT Unrefined linseed oil easily and efficiently, as explained in my book. Some artists want convenience. I do not fault artists for seeking easier ways to obtain their materials or for settling for inferior products because of their personal circumstances and needs. I support the experimentation of all art materials, as Rembrandt himself paved the way for us to follow.

Some artists have found the use of BPO to be an effective and fun way to oil paint. Artists that want an inexpensive, readily available, extremely viscous linseed oil , much thicker than standard 'STAND LINSEED OIL' might want to experiment with all the various viscosity grades of BPO and with a variety of inert additives such as calcium carbonate, ground glass, marble dust and others

.

DRYING TIMES OF PAINT
PAINT MADE WITH HANSA YELLOW DRY PIGMENT AND THE NAMED OIL

I conducted tests to determine the drying time for hand-ground paint. I did not use commercially available oil paint in tubes because some manufacturers add small amounts of driers to their paint, except for one test to demonstrate its drying time. I used a different oil for each mixture, but the same dry pigment color, Hansa Yellow, for all the tests. I made the consistency of each sample the same, and the thickness of the paint application was the same, thin and not an impasto. To describe paint, the term "short" means non-leveling, non-viscous, and firm. The term "long" means viscous, flowing, and leveling. The first three tests used Non-polymerized oils, the last four tests used Polymerized oils.

TEST RESULTS of paint containing Non-polymerized oil

1: **UNREFINED LINSEED/FLAX** OIL
  (NON-POLYMERIZED OIL)
  = 12 days to dry = It dried matte and is short

2: **REFINED** ALKALI REFINED **LINSEED** OIL
  (NON-POLYMERIZED OIL)
  12 days to dry = It dried matte and is short

3: **REFINED** TUBE OIL PAINT/ Made with Alkali Refined LINSEED OIL (major brand)
  (NON-POLYMERIZED OIL)
  6 days to dry = (indicating manufacturers addition of a drier) It dried matte and is short

****

TEST RESULTS of paint containing Polymerized oil

4. **REFINED** STAND **LINSEED OIL** - ALKALI REFINED LINSEED OIL (major brand)
  (BOILED, POLYMERIZED OIL)
  7 days to dry = It dried glossy, long

5. **REFINED** SUN THICKENED ALKALI REFINED **LINSEED OIL** (major brand)
  (POLYMERIZED OIL) Unknown number of days exposed to the sun:
  6 days to dry = It dried glossy , and is long

6. **REFINED ALKALI REFINED LINSEED OIL** (sun thickened by myself)
  (POLYMERIZED OIL) It took 90 days for it to polymerize equal to the UNREFINED oil
  3 days to dry = It dried glossy, and is long (Notice it is slow drying)

7: **UNREFINED LINSEED/FLAX OIL** (Sun Thickened by myself)
  (POLYMERIZED OIL) It took only 30 days to polymerize sufficiently
  30 hours to dry = It dried glossy , and is long (Notice it is fast drying)

ACRYLIC PAINTS vs. OIL PAINTS

The experts tell us we can underpaint with Acrylic paints and overpaint them with Oil paints, and the end result will be permanent. However, experts tell us we cannot paint Acrylics on top of Oils if we want permanence. The main reasons for using Acrylics as the underpainting, is to take advantage of their super fast drying and their flexibility when dry. Within minutes the Acrylic paints dry enough to overpaint with Oils. Quick drying in the under painting is important to creative work. With a strict Oil paint procedure, one must wait many hours or a day before one can overpaint, since Oil paint takes time to set firmly.

To accelerate drying of OIL PAINT, some artists add metallic driers to the paint. Experts tell us driers cause darkening, and cause the oil paint to become brittle, leading to cracking. Solvents like turpentine, added to oil paint do accelerate the dry time, but solvents weaken the binding power of the oil, leading to a flat, dry, powdery, weakened paint. Solvent-varnishes are also added to the oil paint for the same reasons, but a varnish is nothing more than a weak mixture of solvent and a resin. A natural resin is nothing more than non-distilled solvent in its thick natural state. Dammar resin varnish is completely impermanent.

Some experts say you can safely use small amounts of solvents, varnishes and driers. My experiments prove hazardous materials can be completely eliminated. This book teaches you how to paint with oil paints, with safety and permanence, without the use of hazardous solvents, resins, varnishes and driers.

*****

ISOLATING THE SUPPORT AND PRIMERS

The permanence of a painting will depend on several factors:
(1) Quality of materials. (2) Sound painting procedures. (3) Care of the painting. (4) The support.
The SUPPORT of the painting is the material the paint is applied to. (1) Canvas (2) Wood (3) Metal
(4) Plastics (5) Glass (6) Others I will only discuss two of these, Wood and Canvas. The page titled, Materials List, sufficiently describes them. This page focuses on the isolation of the painting surface.

An ABSORBENT support surface will absorb oil binder out of the wet paint layer. The paint will dry flat without a sheen, lose color depth, and will have a relatively soft surface. The Old Masters dried paint surface was never flat nor soft. A healthy dry oil paint surface is shiny and hard, from the oil that fully encompasses the pigment particles.

Studies of Old Master paintings on wood show pure white gesso under the oil layer, meaning the gesso absorbed no yellowing oil. The Old Masters isolated the absorbent wood or the canvas with an aqueous glue SIZE before they added the oil or gesso Primer Ground. This is because wood and canvas are porous and absorb liquids like a sponge. Oil paint that is painted on UNSIZED wood or fabric will cause oil paint to lose its binder through absorption. Many glues were used, but today we have modern options.

My experiments show that a dried layer of acrylic gesso (major brand) is very absorbent . All three liquid sizes here mentioned will isolate and seal a dried layer of Acrylic Gesso so it will not absorb oil. Only one of these will isolate and seal bare wood so it will not absorb oil. The liquid choices are; Skim Milk, PVA size, Acrylic Varnish. They each have different properties. Some dry faster and others are problematical to brush on. SKIM MILK (non-fat milk): Inexpensive cow's milk from the grocery store is excellent. Robert Massey's book (bibliography) tells how this pure casein has been used traditionally as a fixative. * When applied to bare wood, Skim Milk will NOT isolate the bare wood from absorbing oil, even if two coats are applied and allowed to dry over 12 hours.* Acrylic gesso adheres to this size when the size is dry.
* It will NOT lift or disturb the gesso layer when gently applied on acrylic gesso that has dried for 1 hour. Apply the skim milk liberally on the dry gesso with your hand. Then after it has been absorbed for a few Minutes, squeegee it off with the edge of your hand or a rubber squeegee. Though the gesso absorbs the milk, leave only a thin coat. It dries to the touch within 1-2 hours. Let it dry hard before oil painting.
*One coat of Skim Milk applied on dry acrylic gesso, WILL isolate the gesso from oil absorption.

PVA SIZE: PVA stands for Poly-Vinyl Acetate. A major brand manufactures this modern liquid size. It has the consistency of non-fat milk, and is spread on the bare wood or fabric, where it is absorbed into the support. The support remains damp for at least 2 hours.
* When applied to bare wood, PVA size will NOT isolate the bare wood from absorbing oil. Not even if two coats are applied and allowed to dry over 12 hours.
* Acrylic gesso adheres to this size when the size is dry.
*One coat of gesso is insufficient because, the PVA does NOT fill the wood grain, and the application dampness expands and raises the wood fibers, leaving them stiff and visible. Apply another gesso coat.
* It WILL lift or disturb the gesso layer when rubbed on acrylic gesso that has dried for 1 hour. It must be brushed on once, quickly, and without any rubbing, because it will "lift" and cause a freshly dried gesso layer to crumble. It will cause even well dried gesso to lift if rubbed briskly.
* One coat of PVA brushed on top of dry gesso WILL isolate the gesso from oil absorption.

ACRYLIC VARNISH: This liquid is manufactured by a major brand. It is clear and thick, and looks like a film of plastic. It is the same liquid used in making acrylic gesso. It lays on top of the support, leveling the pores of the support. I do not know if absorption occurs. It dries fully within 20 minutes. It must be brushed on once, quickly, and without any rubbing, because it will "lift" itself and cause separation and scabs of acrylic varnish to form, making an unpleasant plastic-looking surface.
* When applied to bare wood, it WILL isolate the bare wood from absorbing oil.
* Acrylic gesso adheres to this size when the size is dry.
*One thin coat of gesso applied over this dried size is sufficient.
* It will NOT lift or disturb the gesso layer when rubbed on acrylic gesso that has dried for 1 hour.
* One coat of Acrylic Varnish brushed on top of dry gesso WILL isolate the gesso from oil absorption.
(As stated: It will "lift" itself and cause separation and scabs of acrylic varnish to form, making an unpleasant plastic-looking surface).

GESSO PRIMERS ON CANVAS
WHITE OIL PAINT: White oil paint used as a Primer Ground, will not be as brilliant white as the gesso, especially if a small amount of umber is added to increase the drying. Scientific examinations by the Getty Museum in Los Angeles, California, of an excellently preserved Titian, shows that after the raw canvas was given a glue size, a thin Gesso layer was applied to fill the spaces between the canvas weave. The gesso was not applied as a continuous film, as that would have been inflexible, resulting in cracking. Titian achieved a fast drying primer and a brilliant white for maximum reflective properties, making his thin colors brighter. His impasto colors used the white oil paint to give vibrancy to the glazes. The Old Masters applied colored oil paint grounds as well as white oil paint grounds.

'CALCITE SUN OIL' PRIMER
This mixture with Titanium Dioxide White dry powder, will create a fast drying paint that can be applied on top of the size layer. It will not be as brilliant white as the Gesso, but if a toned ground is desired, this is an excellent choice. Adding dry Umber powder to the mixture will greatly shorten the drying time required. On canvas, Rembrandt would frequently use a double ground, with a dull dark red oil paint applied on top of the size, then a pale brownish gray oil paint applied very thinly to let the red color bleed through. This added a certain liveliness to the finished painting.

APPLICATION METHODS
To apply these liquids and gesso, I use my hand and rub them in. Brushes leave troublesome hairs and bubbles. It is easier to wash my hand than a wide brush. Textures can be created with the gesso if desired, as a smooth surface might be needed for fine details, but not for other effects. Skim milk rubbed into your hands, will easily remove dry gesso from your hands, and acrylic paint with some scrubbing.

ISOLATION TESTS AND RESULTS
SUPPORT: ½ inch Birch Plywood. SIZES: (1) Acrylic Varnish Glossy (2) PVA Size (3) Skim Milk

TEST CONCLUSIONS
The raw bare support must be isolated from the gesso. If not, it absorbs the glue binder from the gesso. The gesso must ALSO be isolated from the oil. If not, it absorbs the oil binder from the paint.

RECOMMEND PROCEDURE: The results of tests indicate a safe and efficient procedure to follow. FIRST: Isolate the bare SUPPORT with one thin coat of Acrylic Varnish. It dries in 20 minutes. The traditional size is a hide glue, such as 'rabbit skin' glue.

SECOND: Apply 2 thin coats of acrylic gesso. They each take about 20-40 minutes to dry. The traditional gesso is made with a hide glue, not modern acrylic medium.
THIRD: Isolate the acrylic Gesso with Skim Milk. Skim milk is casein, and is absorbed. It does not lay on top of the gesso in a continuous film. (See scraping test #6).
NOTE: IF any layer of gesso or size feels damp or sticky, or tacky - it needs to be allowed to dry hard.

TEST#1: 1 thin coat of gloss Acrylic VARNISH, applied to bare wood, dries hard, in 20-30 minutes.
RESULT: It fully seals and isolates. The oil drop did not spread and was not absorbed.

TEST#2: 1 thin coat, of PVA size, applied to bare wood, dries to touch, but not hard, in about 1-2 hours.
RESULT: It does NOT isolate from oil drop. A second coat of PVA was applied. It did NOT isolate.

TEST#3: 1 thin coat of Skim Milk, applied to bare wood, dries to touch in about 1-2 hours.
RESULT: It does NOT isolate from oil drop. Same result with 2 coats of Skim Milk.

TEST#4: 1 coat PVA applied to Bare wood, then Acrylic gesso was applied. Skim Milk was applied on the dry gesso.
RESULT: Skim Milk fully seals and isolates. The oil drop did not spread and was not absorbed.

TEST#5: 1 coat Acrylic Varnish applied to Bare wood, then Acrylic gesso was applied. Skim Milk was applied on the dry gesso.
RESULT: Skim Milk fully seals and isolates. The oil drop did not spread and was not absorbed.

TEST #6: 1 coat of Skim Milk on top of acrylic gesso applied to bare wood. Then when dry, scraped briskly with a palette knife.
RESULT: It fully seals and isolates. The oil drop did not spread and was not absorbed.

TEST #7: 1 coat of PVA size on top of acrylic gesso applied to bare wood. Then when dry, scraped briskly with a palette knife.
RESULT: It fully seals and isolates. The oil drop did not spread and was not absorbed.

TEST#8: 1 coat Acrylic Gesso applied to bare wood. No size was applied to the gesso.
RESULT: Oil drop was absorbed immediately. Acrylic Gesso does not seal nor isolate wood from oil.

TEST#9: Bare wood sized with 1 coat PVA. 1 coat Acrylic gesso was applied. No size on the dry gesso.
RESULT: The oil drop was slowly absorbed by the gesso over a 24 hour period.

TEST#10: Bare wood sized with 1 coat Acrylic Varnish. 1 coat Acrylic gesso was applied. No size was applied on the dry gesso.
RESULT: The oil drop was slowly absorbed by the gesso over a 24 hour period.

TEST#11: Bare wood sized with 1 coat PVA. 1 coat Acrylic gesso applied. No size on the dry gesso. Hand ground paint in thickened oil, in black, brown, red, yellow, blue were swabbed on with palette knife. ALSO, Tube paint in black, brown, red, yellow, blue were swabbed on with palette knife.
RESULT: All the paint swabs show oil spot around the paint swab, caused by absorption by the gesso. Tube oil paint dried completely flat, matte. The oil paint hand ground in thickened oil dried glossy in impasto, but flat, matte in thin areas.

TEST#12: Bare wood sized with 1 coat Acrylic Varnish. 1 coat Acrylic gesso applied. No size was applied on the dry gesso. Hand ground paint in thickened oil, in black, brown, red, yellow, blue were swabbed on with palette knife. ALSO, Tube paint in black, brown, red, yellow, blue were swabbed on with palette knife.
RESULT: All the paint swabs show oil spot around the paint swab, caused by absorption by the gesso.
Tube oil paint dried completely flat, matte. The oil paint hand ground in thickened oil dried glossy in impasto, but matte in thin areas.

TEST#13: The same sizing and applications as above. One coat of Skim Milk was applied onto the dry gesso.
Two colors were hand ground in thickened oil and applied with a palette knife.
RESULT: The paint did not sink, and there was no oil spot from gesso absorption.

PROPER CARE OF THE PALETTE

CARE OF YOUR HANDS and EXCESS OIL PAINT
CARE OF PALETTE: When finished painting for the day, it is important to clean the Palette and the Grinding Table. You do not need turpentine or solvents to do this. First, scrape all the paint off the palette and the Grinding table, and save it in a jar that has enough non-polymerized oil to cover the paint . Apply non-polymerized oil and scrub the palette and the grinding table. Wipe clean with a disposable paper towel. Then apply some dry Calcium Carbonate and rub until dry. Wipe with wet cloth.

EXCESS PAINT: The left over oil paint is kept in an uncapped jar with enough non-polymerized oil to cover the paint. The oil keeps it from drying out. The Old Masters did not have the convenience we have of buying our paint ready made. They saved all the excess wet scrapings in one container with non-polymerized oil. The different colors mixed together, resulting in a mud colored paint. Scientific examinations find the lower layers of many Old Master paintings are made up of these scrapings.

CARE OF HANDS: Place some of the non-polymerized oil on your hands and rub them together. It will lift the oil paint easily with gentle rubbing. Wipe your hands with a clean disposable paper towel and then wash your hands with soap and water. Olive oil will also clean the paint off your hands. Skim Milk will remove dried acrylic gesso from your hands, with simple rubbing.

*****

NEVER WASH YOUR BRUSHES AGAIN

Brushes are expensive. Some pure sable brushes can cost hundreds of dollars depending on size. Painters use many tools to paint with; brushes of various sizes, shapes and materials, palette knives, rags, their fingers, and anything else that helps them get the effect they want. Rembrandt's late work from the mid 1600's shows he used a flexible knife to apply thick paint to his canvas. Care of brushes is important, but washing them each day is not necessary.

NON EFFICIENT 21ST CENTURY METHOD: Contemporary teachers and books say that after painting for the day, one should squeeze out the excess paint from the brush, swirl in turpentine, and wash with a special (expensive) soap sold in art stores. They teach you to scrub the brush in the palm of your hand under the running water. In the past they taught you to stick the clean hairs in your mouth so your spittle would keep the hairs together, but the health concern of contaminated brush hairs has stopped that advice.

VERY EFFICIENT 16TH CENTURY METHOD: Neither the waste of water nor the expensive soap is needed, much less the time lost in cleaning a dozen brushes. After finishing painting for the day, wipe the excess paint off the brush. Then, dip the brush into an uncapped jar, half full of non-polymerized oil. Scrub the brush on the palette to squeeze out more paint. Wipe it again. Dip it in the oil again, and do not wipe off the oil. Just place it in a jar with the hairs up. That's it. The non-polymerized oil will not dry for over 6 days, so the next day, just wipe the brush off and begin to paint again. CAUTION: Any brush with Umber paint must be scrubbed extra well, because umber dries so fast, it will cause the hairs to stiffen.

IF you are not going to paint for 5 days or more, then you can do one of two things.
(1) Use a long plastic tray and raise one end up with a small block. Add just enough non-polymerized oil to keep the hairs immersed in the oil, but without the hairs touching the end so they do not bend. They can stay like this indefinitely. Just wipe off ALL the non-polymerized oil before painting.
(2) Wash your brushes in warm soap and water, and put them away.

MY BRUSHES

1. MY BRUSHES ARE MERELY TOOLS AND DISPOSABLE TO SOME POINT BUT THEY ARE STILL VERY IMPORTANT TO MY WORK.
2. I MANHANDLE MY BRUSHES---I TWIST, GOUGE AND TURN THEM AS I PAINT.
3. MANY OF MY BRISHES ARE RAGGED AND FRAYED. SOME HAVE BUT FEW HAIRS LEFT.
4. I NEVER THROW A BRUSH AWAY, EVEN WHEN IT HAS NO HAIRS. I KEEP THE WOODEN STUB HANDLE AS A SCRATCHING TOOL.
5. I NEVER WASH MY OIL PAINTING BRUSHES WITH SOAP AND WATER. I SOAK THE HAIR TIPS IN THIN SLOW DRYING OIL.

6. CSO-EGG TEMPERA [GLAIR MIXED WITH CHALK] WAS INVENTED TO CREATE A FAST DRYING UNDER LAYER FOR OIL PAINT ON TOP. THE SUN OIL IMPREGNATION IS EQUAL TO A "DRY/WET EMULSION" IN THAT THE OIL GETS ABSORBED BY THE GLAIR / CHALK MIXTURE [CHALK IS ABSORBENT], CREATING A CEMENT-LIKE DURABLE MATERIAL.

7. I WASH MY CSO-EGG TEMPERA BRUSHES UNDER THE SINK WITH A FLOW OF WATER, WITH NO SOAP, JUST TO GET THE MATERIAL OUT OF THE HAIRS. THEN I PAT THEM DRY IN A TOWEL AND PLACE THEM IN A CUP WITH THE HAIRS UP.

8. WHEN I DO OVER LAY CSO EGG TEMPERA WITH CSO OIL PAINTS, ONCE I AM FINISHED OIL PAINTING, I JUST SOAK THE HAIR TIPS IN THIN OIL.

9. ONLY ONE COLOR IS A PROBLEM...BURNT UMBER--IT DRIES SO FAST AND HARD THAT EVEN WHILE SOAKING IN THE THIN OIL IT WILL DRY HARD. TO PREVENT THIS, I DIP THE BRUSH IN THE THIN OIL, THEN I PRESS OUT THE BURNT UMBER FROM THE HAIRS. THEN I CIRCULATE THE HAIRS IN MY PALM WITH PRESSURE AND I REPEAT THIS A COUPLE OF TIMES. THEN I SOAK THE HAIR TIPS IN THE THIN OIL.

FINAL PERMANENT LAYER FOR COMPLETED PAINTINGS

DRYING IS IMPACTED BY THE ENVIRONMENT. A finished oil painting may take several weeks to dry without a tacky surface. The materials used, the method of application, and the environment play a part in how long it takes the paint to dry. Keep the painting in a well-ventilated, dry warm, dust free environment. Some factors affecting drying are Ventilation, Temperature, Humidity. Other factors are the thickness of the paint, the pigment itself, and of course the oil with and without additives.

I believe a finished painting should be given an extremely thin **permanent** protective layer once it is finished. This gives it an even gloss and restores sunken colors. I recommend one of these two permanent layers, and I consider them as an important step of the painting process. Do not confuse this permanent layer with a subsequent, removable non-permanent solvent based resin varnish that is applied to a finished DRY painting. I recommend using one of the two methods described here:

EMULSION, (Permanent non-removable coat). Do not apply with a brush. Use an EMULSION created by the mixture of THREE parts of UNREFINED Sun Thickened Cold Pressed Linseed Oil and ONE part of GLAIR. IT MUST ONLY BE APPLIED TO A WELL DRIED PAINTING. Do not apply this over thick paint that is dry on the surface but still soft inside. DO NOT apply with a brush- use your hand. RUB it on thinly. It must be a very thin coat. Wipe off all excess with a dry rag and re-rub again.

'CALCITE SUN OIL' (Permanent, non-removable coat) Do not apply with a brush. Make a mixture of one part of "Calcite Sun Oil" with three parts of the superior Linseed Oil. Mix well together. IT MUST ONLY BE APPLIED TO A WELL DRIED PAINTING. Do not apply this over thick paint that may be dry on the surface but still soft inside. It will cause cracking. Apply with your hand. It must be a very thin coat. Wipe off all excess with a dry rag and re-rub.

EITHER OF THESE mixtures bring out the sunken colors and protects the surface of the painting from moisture and wear. Apply with the palm of the hand, rubbing in the thinnest layer possible. Rub in the solution with a circular motion. STOP. Wipe the excess solution off with a dry rag. Repeat the process until you have the thinnest layer possible. NOTE: Oil films dry slowly. They MUST be protected from DUST as they dry.

A HISTORICAL OPTION:
In the past, some painters applied a thin coat of GLAIR to the entire surface. This coat dried in minutes. The main benefits were that any dust that landed on the tacky dry oil painting – would not STICK to the oil- and the dust was easily removed with a feather duster or dry rag. Another benefit was that the coat of GLAIR gave an overall silky sheen to the painting. The main problem is that egg glair requires up to a year to solidify hard. Glair will become hard and water resistant after much time passes. Heat and circulating air will help accelerate the curing of Glair. This 'varnish' is considered to be a permanent part of the painting and not removable.

REMOVABLE VARNISH: Whether or not you wish to apply a **removable** picture varnish is your choice. If you do, wait six months then wipe off the dust from the surface and then apply either a synthetic resin, or a natural dammar soft resin solvent based picture varnish. This varnish is TEMPORARY and lasts about 50 years. Over the years it will become discolored, yellow and brittle and must be removed and replaced. As of this writing, conservators say we do not yet have a permanent picture varnish that will not discolor. This temporary REMOVABLE solvent-resin based varnish is the kind the masterpieces in the museums are coated with. They do protect the painting's surface from moisture, abrasions, and any dirt the painting accumulates over the decades, and it can be safely removed and replaced.

*****

FIXATIVE (non-hazardous)
DO NOT USE NON-FAT MILK ON AN OIL PRIMING, USE ONLY ON A GESSO PRIMING.

Some Old Master's used vine charcoal to draw directly on the primed support. Vine charcoal has a grayish tone and it is easily wiped off when corrections are made. Many hazardous solvent-resin based fixatives in spray cans are sold to artists. They have to be used outdoors because of the harmful fumes. A traditional and SAFE fixative is inexpensive SKIM MILK, which is non-fat milk bought at the grocery store. The Skim Milk will seal and isolate the acrylic gesso and the traditional true gesso of hide glue and chalk. This sealant stops the gesso from absorbing oil from the oil paint. The milk coat will dry and is oil proof, but it is not waterproof. After you draw with the charcoal drawing.
ONE: Place the drawing flat on a table.
TWO: pre-dampen a thin cotton fabric with skim milk. Squeeze out any excess milk
THREE: Place the damp cloth carefully on top of the charcoal drawing and pat it down gently.
FOUR: Use a wide 3 inch flat brush to apply a bit more milk on the cloth and press the brush down gently.
FIVE: When finished , immediately remove the damp cloth carefully
Milk takes about 40 minutes to dry in a warm well ventilated room. Damp weather slows drying.

ONE CAN ALSO use the flat soft-haired brush without the dampened cloth and CAREFULLY apply the milk in gentle sweeps of the brush. NON-FAT MILK will fully seal the gesso. Do not use the milk on an oil ground. I sometimes draw with charcoal very expressively on the gesso and as I do, I gently apply the milk. I let this milk dry, and then continue to draw with the charcoal. Again, when I like the drawing, I apply more of the milk. Since the milk solidifies quickly, I can continue to develop the under drawing over several hours with corrections made easily.

PRACTICAL WAYS TO PAINT A PICTURE

There are an unlimited number of ways to paint a picture. These four methods offer a logical approach.
NOTE: If you are in a hurry, you can do the 'grisaille' or any under drawing or under painting in acrylic paints, they dry fast and one can safely paint with oils for the top layers.

METHOD 1. DIRECT PAINTING: Use any and all colors directly.
NOTE: The 'Direct' method does not use a 'PLANNED' under painting. One can also not make a drawing. Van Gogh would draw a rough outline in bright blue oil paint and then apply his thick oil paints on the wet blue oil paint drawing.
1. Draw freehand with charcoal - or trace the image with graphite and transfer.
2. Prevent smudging of the drawing by applying a Fixative- see instructions.
3. Oil out with the 'Viscous Emulsion" or AGUADO. Always paint INTO the wet 'emulsion 'oil out'.
4. Paint directly with all colors desired.
5. Let dry until tacky dry and the paint does not smear if rubbed.
6. Oil out with the 'Viscous Emulsion" or AGUADO.
7. Paint corrections and changes with all colors desired.
8. Oil out with the 'Viscous Emulsion" or AGUADO before applying additional corrections or layers.

METHOD 2. GRISAILLE UNDERPAINT
1. Draw freehand with charcoal - or trace the image with graphite and transfer.
2. Prevent smudging of the drawing by applying a Fixative
3. Oil out with the 'Viscous Emulsion".
4. Under paint: Use black and white and grays only.
5. Let dry at least 24 hours or until tacky dry and the paint does not smear if rubbed.
6. Oil out with the 'Viscous Emulsion".
7. Over paint: Use all colors desired.
8. Let dry at least 24 hours or until tacky dry and the paint does not smear if rubbed.
9. Oil out with the 'Viscous Emulsion".
10. Finish: Use all colors desired.
11. Oil out with the 'Viscous Emulsion" before applying additional corrections or layers

METHOD 3. MUTED COLOR UNDERPAINT
FOR THE UNDERPAINT:
Use the muted 'primary colors': dull Red, dull Blue, dull Yellow, plus, Burnt Umber, Black, White.
FOR THE OVERPAINT:
Use the 'bright' primary colors: bright Red, bright Yellow, bright Blue, plus, Burnt Sienna, Black, White.
1. Draw freehand with charcoal - or trace the image with graphite and transfer.
2. Prevent smudging of the drawing by applying a Fixative.
3. Oil out with the 'Viscous Emulsion".
4. Under paint: Use the muted colors only.
5. Let dry at least 24 hours or until tacky dry and the paint does not smear if rubbed.
6. Oil out with the 'Viscous Emulsion"..

7. Over paint: Use all colors desired - muted and bright.
8. Let dry at least 24 hours or until tacky dry and the paint does not smear if rubbed.
9. Oil out with the 'Viscous Emulsion". Always paint INTO the wet 'emulsion 'oil out'.
10. Finish: Use all colors desired - muted and bright.
11. Oil out with the 'Viscous Emulsion" before applying additional corrections or layers.

METHOD 4. UNDERPAINT WITH BURNT UMBER

Some say burnt umber should not be used in lower areas of a painting because it absorbs too much oil. This is bad advice, as the Old Masters frequently used umber in lower areas because it dries very fast. Think of the umber as a sponge. Even a sponge will absorb great amounts of water, until it reaches its absorption capacity. Then, it absorbs no more. If you paint on a non-absorbent ground, and if all your paints are well bound, you have no fear of the umber absorbing oil from its neighboring paints.

Burnt Umber is the fastest drying color. Rubens, Rembrandt and others used this method because it lets you 'draw' and 'paint' at the same time to lay in the design of the painting. I do recommend adding either a blue or a warm red to the umber because, UMBER is a lifeless color. After the thin Umber dried, it was followed with a Grisaille and it was allowed to dry. It was then followed by using full color. Always 'oil out' with the Emulsion, in between the layers, unless you want a dry brush effect.

1. Draw freehand with charcoal - or trace the image with graphite and transfer and 'fix'..
2. Prevent smudging of the drawing by applying a Fixative
3. Oil out with the 'Viscous Emulsion".
4. Paint with Burnt Umber mixture: Create dark by applying thicker paint. Create light by 'rubbing' thinner paint on or use a rag to 'wipe back' areas to expose the surface. Keep the darkest areas translucent.
5. Let dry at least 24 hours or until tacky dry and the paint does not smear if rubbed.
6. Oil out with the 'Viscous Emulsion".
7. Over paint: Use all colors desired.
8. Let dry at least 24 hours or until tacky dry and the paint does not smear if rubbed.
9. Oil out with the 'Viscous Emulsion". Always paint INTO the wet 'emulsion 'oil out'.
10. Finish: Use all colors desired.
11. Oil out with the 'Viscous Emulsion" before applying additional corrections or layers.

METHOD FIVE: SCRATCH INTO WET OIL PAINT.

Use any color you desire and with a wide brush, paint the entire surface with oil paint. Then use a scratch tool and scratch your DRAWING into the wet paint. Use a brush to blend out any lines you do not want. Scratch again and blend out again and repeat this until you have the outline drawing you desire. Let this dry. Now OIL OUT and apply colors onto the surface.

This method can be expanded by first [painting a layer of any color onto the surface and allowing it to dry. Then applying a layer of oil paint color on top then scratching into the wet oil paint. By changing the first color from bright yellow to red or to blue, unique linear effects can be created.

METHOD SIX: EL GRECO'S METHOD
El Greco painted fast and with simple means. He first painted his canvas a rich brick red. He let this dry. Then after the OIL Out he drew the design with a dark oil paint made of blue and umber. Then into the wet dark color he applied grays and white to get a 3-D effect. He let this dry. He applied an OIL OUT then applied his bright colors on top. Francisco Goya sometimes painted the canvas surface a BRIGHT VERMILLION RED. Then, he followed El Greco's method. Goya, like Rembrandt, made effective use of applying his paint with a palette knife that he then blended a bit with a stiff brush.

METHOD SEVEN: VAN GOGH'S METHOD
Vincent Van Gogh would OIL OUT the surface so his paint would easily slide on the canvas. He used a bright blue to make an outline. Into this wet bright blue he applied thick oil paint in many colors. Van Gogh would sometimes paint a painting in just a few hours. This method is used today by many artists who aim for fresh DIRECT PAINTING effects. An inspection of Van Gogh's original paintings show he sometimes made corrections after the painting had dried.

*****

'UMBER OIL' and 'HALF-WHITE' FOR UNDERPAINTING

Franz Hals' virtuosity of oil paint application is unexcelled by any other painter with possibly his only equal being Rubens. The beauty of color, and paint textures in Hals' work is amazing. In Hals' own words, he began his painting in a "DEAD COLOR". This means he used muted colors in his UNDER PAINTNG, as a foundation for the colorful OVER PAINTING. This term used by Hals, "dead coloring', is also called by other names such as a ' monotone', or 'grisaille'.

Use of 'dead coloring' was an expanded development over the method used by the Flemish painters such as the Van Eyck brothers. The early Flemish masters made an elaborate ink outline drawing on a pure white gesso priming. Their oil colors were applied thinly on the drawing, creating jewel-like colors due to the 'inner light' from the gesso. The method was slow, restricted, laborious, and most paintings were relatively small. Hals' method was developed by the 16th century Italians such as Tintoretto and Titan who did away with the intricate under drawing.

Titian recognized the importance of using a white under painting to give his colors that jewel-like appearance. Thus was born use of the 'dead coloring' 'grisaille' method. This method allowed the painter to apply pure white paint at any stage and layer of the painting, not just in the bottom gesso priming. Titian's method allowed him to paint massively large paintings with great speed. The drawing of the design composition was made with oil paint, muted "dead colored' value tones, and was part of the painting process.

One important requirement for PERMANENCE in oil painting of layers is that the bottom layers must be fast drying while top layers must be slower drying. DO NOT paint fast drying top layers on top of semi-dry, slow drying bottom layers.

This brings up the subject of UMBER OIL. I did not invent this. In Frederic Taubes' book of mid 20th century, he gives instructions on this concept. It is easy to make but requires a bit of caution.

PROCEDURE: Add a bit less than a level teaspoon, of dry umber powder [burnt or raw umber] to a quart of sun oil. Shake. It is ready to use immediately. The oil will turn very dark - as seen in concentration - but when thinly applied, it is transparent but ' muted'. This muted tone is not a disadvantage in creating the 'dead coloring' stage. Use this umber oil to create AGUADO for an under-painting 'oil out', and to make a muted CSO - for under painting. Its advantage is that it will accelerate the drying of the paint.

HALF-WHITE FOR UNDERPAINTING: Before using slow drying white paint in the under painting, mix some burnt umber to it. I call this a HALF- WHITE, but it does not use 50/50 of umber and white. Just a 5% of umber to the amount of the white will greatly increase the drying.

EXAMPLE OF PAINTING WITH AGUADO

PLEASE NOTE: In this example I am making references to photos on my website.
SUPPORT: 12 INCH x 12 INCH, 1/2 inch birch plywood. FIRST: Seal the support with two coats of Traditional Rabbit skin glue size [this is called SIZEING]. THEN: mix traditional Rabbit skin glue with Calcium Carbonate to make gesso. Apply two thin coats of gesso. THEN: Apply one thin coat of glue Size to seal the ABSORBENT gesso, to render it NON-ABSORBENT. It is VERY important to seal and isolate the gesso so it will NOT remove oil from the paint through absorption.
Some teachers say to leave the gesso partially absorbent so the oil paint can 'stick' to the gesso. THIS IS FALSE INFORMATION. There is NO NEED to create a MECHANICAL LOCK for oil paint. If your eyes could for a moment see at the microscopic level, you would see the gesso is full of cavities. A layer of glue does not fill those cavities as liquids conform to the shape of their surface.

UNDERDRAW : VELAZQUEZ would not have drawn with a pencil. He drew with the dark paint. I drew the image with pencil. I did not fix it. I mixed a little VENETIAN RED TUBE PAINT with the AGUADO, to give it a warm color on the gesso. I brushed the AGUADO mixture on the surface with a wide brush. I used a rag to wipe it thinly evenly. Excess was removed. This took seconds. INTO THIS wet paint film, I continued the next step.

UNDERPAINT: I believe in leaving BLACK to the finish stage. One gets all the darks one needs by mixing BURNT UMBER and ULTRAMARINE BLUE in equal amounts. AS with the CSO method, one mixes 50/50 of the CSO with the tube paint. THIS creates a viscous sticky paint. A BRISTLE BRUSH is needed to under paint as it easily moves the viscous paint. The viscous paint blends extraordinarily easy, yet the CSO mixture keeps all brush marks sharp if not blended. I used this dark paint to define the image and some shadows.

I mixed what I call a HALF-WHITE. This is a mixture of Titanium Dioxide WHITE TUBE OIL PAINT with enough BURNT UMBER to about a level 3 or 4 on a VALUE scale [PURE WHITE is 1 and PURE BLACK is 10]. This HALF-WHITE keeps the white value in check and eliminates the washed out CHALKY white effect common to beginning painters. WITH THIS half white I painted into the wet paint and created what is known by many names: DEAD COLOR/ MONOTONE/ GRISAILLE. VAN EYCK would have made a detailed pencil drawing and would have carefully INKED it. I draw with loose gestures.

USING VELAZQUEZ' technique. I used the brush end to scratch a DOVE into the wet oil paint. A paint layer will completely cover up the lines, until hundreds of years later-as the oil paint becomes more translucent, then the lines will peek through the thin paint.

I used two brushes.
One a 1/4 inch ROUND BRISTLE and the other a thin fine sable. The lines of the feather were scratched into the wet paint. Light colored paint applied with the thin sable brush are visible. The under-painting stage is easily done. It is smooth, fast, unhindered. Very little blending is required because the bristle brush easily blends the viscous CSO PAINT. THIXOTROPY is a wonderful quality. You can see the fine wet LIGHT COLORED paint lines are painted ON TOP OF the wet DARK PAINT LAYERS. They blend as one wishes. LINES and brush marks are at your command. You can leave them sharp or blend them smooth...easily.

THIS WAS THE END OF THE FIRST DAYS WORK.
THIS BEGAN AT 11AM and FINISHED ONE HOUR LATER. THE NEXT DAY - 20 HOURS LATER / AT 8 AM- I BEGAN TO OVER PAINT IN FULL COLOR.

The paint from the previous day was dry. This fantastic quality is one of the benefits of the SUPERIOR OIL of the OLD MASTERS. I use no additives to my oil. It helps to paint with UMBER and ULTRAMARINE BLUE in the lower stages as these colors are fast drying colors. Mixing the umber oil paint with the white helps to dry the white paint- white is known to be a slow drying color.

EACH OF THE TUBE COLORS was mixed with CSO. The surface was brushed with AGUADO as the OIL OUT and wiped evenly. THE OIL OUT APPLICATION IS EASY .

IN THE SPACE OF one and a half hours, I finished the COLOR STAGE. The other details show the scratch lines that defined the dove, which are covered. The lines of the branches are left visible on purpose to be seen by the student.

THE FINISH STAGE COMES NEXT It is the hardest yet most rewarding part. I decide what changes the painting needs by living with the painting, and seeing it every day under normal family conditions, hearing the comments of others and, more important seeing ALL THE BAD THINGS I DO NOT LIKE in the painting. Also, in my sleep, I solution the difficulties of the painting. I am never in a hurry to FINISH the painting. This stage is where the glazes, the fine details, the corrections are slowly made. It is seemingly never ending.

During this stage, I recommend switching to the VISCOUS EMULSION as the OIL OUT MEDIUM. The AGUADO is 98% TRANSPARENT. THE VISCOUS EMULSION is 100% TRANSPARENT.

*****

AGUADO FAQ AND ANSWERS
THE AGUADO MIXTURE IS REALLY NOTHING MORE THAN A THINNED CSO ... CONTAINING ONLY THE SUPERIOR OIL AND A SMALL AMOUNT OF CHALK ...THEREFORE, IT IS FULLY COMPATIBLE WITH THE EMULSIONS. THEY BOTH CAN BE USED IN THE SAME PAINTING

THE AGUADO MIXTURE IS 98% TRANSPARENT THE EMULSIONS ARE 100% TRANSPARENT.
USE THE EMULSIONS AS THE OIL OUT. ON VERY FINE DETAILED WORK AND ON THE FINAL FINISH LAYERS USE THE VISCOUS EMULSION AS THE OIL OUT AND ADD THE VE TO THICK PAINT TO PREVENT WRINKLING. WARNING: ADDING AGUADO TO THICK IMPASTO MAY CAUSE WRINKLING. EMULSION CAN THIN THE PAINT. AGUADO CANNOT BE USED TO THIN PAINT EMULSIONS ALLOW MICRO-FINE DETAILS AGUADO DOES NOT ALLOW MICRO-FINE DETAILS.

IF ONE IS VERY CAREFUL, ONE CAN TOUCH THE TIP OF THE BRUSH INTO A JAR OF AGUADO, AND WITH ONE DROP OF AGUADO, THIN THE THICK CSO OIL PAINT BY MOVING THE BRUSH IN CIRCLES. NORMALLY, THE THINNING OF CSO OIL PAINT IS DONE ON THE GRINDING TABLE ONLY. THE PROBLEM IF YOU PICK UP TOO MUCH AGUADO ON THE BRUSH, YOU WILL CREATE OVERLY THINNED OIL PAINT THAT WILL DRIP. DO NOT DIP THE TIP OF THE BRUSH INTO THE EMULSIONS. AN EMULSION MUST ONLY BE MIXED WITH OIL PAINT WITH A PALETTTE KNIFE AND GROUND WELL WITH IT.

*****

PAINTING PROCEDURE EXAMPLE 'THE LION AND THE BIRD'

This is another example of how I painted a painting. The under paintings here in this painting are in OIL. One can under paint with Acrylics or with CSO-EGG TEMPERA or with CSO CASEIN TEMPERA or with MILK OIL PAINT, and over paint with oils. Do not apply any temperas or acrylics on top of oil paint.

DAY ONE
1/2 inch birch plywood. The wood was sealed with two coats of clear Rabbit Skin Glue. Then two thin coats of Traditional gesso were followed by one coat of clear Rabbit Skin Glue to isolate the gesso. NO UNDERDRAWING. Oil out with AGUADO. Tube paint mixed with CSO 50/50. The image was painted in one color, Venetian Red. . Scratch marks to define vague areas serve as an invisible drawing that will be covered.

DAY TWO, NEXT DAY
The paint was dry. You are ready for the next layer when a vigorous oil out application of the AGUADO with a bristle brush and wiping off of excess AGUADO will not smear the under paint layer from yesterday. I do not use BLACK in any under layers. I use PURE BLACK only in the FINISH STAGE. I make a DARK color by mixing equal amounts of BURNT UMBER and ULTRAMARINE BLUE tube paint. IT is mixed 50/50 with CSO. This gives the tube paint a luster and hardness in drying and the CSO gives it the requisite VISCOSITY to allow THIXOTROPIC applications of WET paint on top of WET PAINT.

The dark paint is thin and with a bristle brush application on the AGUADO oil out it glides effortlessly on the surface. NOTE: I now have the THREE important tones. The pale gray from the toned gesso (as Rubens did], the mid tone of the Venetian Red, and the DARK tone. The Light gray values of the Grisaille are important to give a Three-D effect.

INTO this wet surface I began to paint in some local color, the tan of the lion, the blue of the back ground, and some GRISAILLE in the bird and areas of the lion. I do not use PURE WHITE because it dries too slow. I make a 'half-white" which is a mix of Burnt Umber and White. I use Titanium Dioxide.
The umber accelerates the drying of the white and any raised impasto. The lowered value of the half-white keeps the VALUES in check, and increases color variety. THIS was allowed to dry over night

DAY THREE : NEXT DAY The paint was dry and I applied the AGUADO OIL OUT. ALL colors except were mixed with CSO. The painting progressed with some details and improvement of textures, etc.
DAY FOUR : NEXT DAY The next day the paint was dry. Oil out with AGUADO. All colors are mixed with CSO. PURE BLACK WAS USED FOR THE FIRST TIME. The painting is 90% finished. As time permits, the next steps will be to continue the color development.

DAY FIVE: I did no work on the painting.

DAY SIX: The surface sheen had diminished , so I applied an AGUADO coat on the entire surface, making it as thin as possible. This final ultra-thin AGUADO clear coat also dried to a diminished sheen. To increase the sheen, I applied an ultra-thin coat of the VISCOUS EMULSION as a final permanent layer.

COMMENTS

The FINAL ultra-thin ' oil out' with the VISCOUS EMULSION on the dry finished painting is a PERMANENT LAYER of the painting. DO NOT CONFUSE it with removable resin varnishes of dammar that become yellow and last only 40-60 years and require removal and replacement. THE VISCOUS EMULSION oil out film is part of the actual painting. It is permanent. It dries to a crystal clear NON-YELLOWING FILM.

PREPARING THE SUPPORT

HOW TO PREPARE WOOD PANELS AND RAW CANVAS WITH OLD MASTER HIDE GLUE SIZING and ...GESSO

1. Buy only top quality, good weight, TIGHT weave Cotton or Linen canvas. Hold it up to the light. If you see the weave is loose, buy one that has a tight weave. If using wood, use only high quality hardwood plywood. Note that OAK has small dimples in the grain. These must be filled in by scraping gesso into them.

2. Mix and stir well, 1 volume ounce [same as liquid ounce] of dry Rabbit Skin Glue granules in 10 fluid ounces of water. Allow to stand in a capped jar overnight. The glue forms a rubbery solid packed gel. CAUTION: One major manufacturer gives instructions to mix one volume ounce of dry glue granules with 23 fluid ounces of water. I tested their ratio mixture and it failed to seal the support.

3. Next day, remove the jar's cap and place the COLD jar of gelled glue in a pot of COLD water or in a double boiler. Do not let any water get into the jar of glue.

4. Light the stove to a moderate high flame. In 8 minutes the water will be boiling. The solid glue gel will quickly become fluid. Stir the glue for an additional 3 minutes more or less until it is fluid and HOT. Touch the glue. It should not BOIL. It should be HOT, not warm, not cold nor cool. Place some in your hand and rub it around. You will notice it will be very STICKY and VISCOUS.

5. FOR RAW CANVAS – lightly stretch taunt and tack the raw canvas firmly to its stretchers. Use a wide brush and apply a LIBERAL coat --on the canvas. Make sure it completely soaks and penetrates the canvas all the way through to the other side. Apply a SINGLE coat to the back to insure the threads are fully saturated with glue. Use the palm of your hand to smooth the glue to make sure the front coat of glue is thin but fully covering the canvas. Keeping the canvas vertical helps the glue to flow downwards, to avoid puddles.

7. Place the wet canvas in a well- ventilated and dry warm area, and allow it to dry hard. It takes less than an hour. Then reheat the glue as before. Apply a second liberal coat and let this dry well and hard. You will notice the second coat will be more shiny than the canvas with only one coat.

8. FOR BARE WOOD, apply two liberal coats of the hot glue, allowing the first coat to dry hard.

9. AFTER THE BARE WOOD IS SEALED [SIZED] WITH GLUE,
You can do a number of different things at this time.
[A] If you will begin by painting with any type of TEMPERA as an under painting for oil paint, you must apply a coat or two or more of thin gesso made of chalk with the glue. DO NOT seal this glue gesso so the tempera can adhere.
[B] If you will begin painting with oil paints, you can apply one coat or more coats of glue gesso. Then, you must then seal the glue gesso with a thin coat of hot glue before oil painting.
[C] You can choose to apply a coat of oil paint on top of the bare sized wood- instead of a glue gesso, and wait for it to dry before beginning the oil painting. Some masters painted on the sized canvas without having applied an oil paint primer. There are many reasons for using an oil primer of any color or color mixtures, be it white, light or dark and as a single coat or a double coat of oil paint.

IMPORTANT TECHNICAL POINTS ON WHEN TO SEAL THE GESSO
1. BEGIN by sealing the support with glue and applying a glue gesso.
Do not seal the gesso with glue if the goal is to solely paint with an Egg tempera or a Casein tempera paint. The gesso MUST remain absorbent for the TEMPERA PAINT to adhere.

2, If you are using EGG OR CASEIN TEMPERA PAINT as the under painting for eventual OIL PAINT over painting, do not seal the gesso with glue. Allow the gesso to remain absorbent so the TEMPERA will adhere. Once the TEMPERA PAINTING is dried DO NOT SEAL the tempera painting with a SEALANT such as a VARNISH. Instead, IMPREGNATE the tempera paint with sun oil to allow the Tempera to breathe and CURE over time.

THIS CONCLUDES THE ABRIDGED EDITION
"OIL PAINTING LESSONS WITH REMBRANDT AND 'CALCITE SUN OIL':
Artists Health and Safety Without Hazardous Solvents, Resins, Varnishes and Driers "
Copyright by Louis R. Velasquez , December 2012

PART THREE
OIL PAINTING LESSONS
For BEGINNERS WITHOUT A TEACHER

This book was written specifically for you, the BEGINNER. The beginner who has no teacher to guide them must work extra hard and never give up. When I was age 13, I began to teach myself to oil paint by reading books and magazines. I am confident you can do it also. All you need s some determination and some patience. If you are an artist you already have both of those fine qualities.

I include a video I produced to help you understand and to guide you as if I was standing next to you. The video is in real time and it demonstrates the procedures as I narrate. You can watch this video free on YOUTUBE .

To watch the video on YOUTUBE
go to their website at www.youtube.com
Then type in these words
CSO VELASQUEZ - BEGINNERS BOOK- OIL PAINTING
Please watch the video all the way through before beginning to oil paint.
The video will prepare you for the exciting world of oil painting.

There are three main lessons in the video.
HOW TO OIL PAINT
HOW TO DRAW
HOW TO DESIGN A PAINTING (AND HOW TO TRACE)

The video also that discuss other issues related to oil painting.
They will give you a well-rounded approach to being an artist.

Before beginning to oil paint
Please obtain the materials that are listed on the MATERIALS LIST.

MATERIALS LIST

2 bristle brushes . You need a size 4, and a size 1
Buy the ones that have a round ferrule and of natural hair. The ferrule is the metal part that holds the hairs to the wooden handle. They are called "rounds". Don't buy those called "flats" or other shapes. Do not buy expensive brushes.

2 soft hair brushes. You need a size 2 and a size 0
Again, do not buy expensive brushes. Buy those with round ferrules, and natural hairs. Try to buy these with springy hairs? that mans that when you bend the hairs down, they spring back up. If you must , you can buy synthetic hair brushes since they are lower in cost.

1 flat haired brush , 2 or 3 inches wide. Very low cost from a hardware store.

OIL PAINT IN TUBES
EIGHT colors of tube oil paints. Later you can buy more, but now you do not need them. Buy medium sized tubes. Buy lower cost student paints. Professional level oil paints are very expensive. The ones you need are listed below:

Titanium dioxide white : This white paint is the only one to buy. Do not buy any other white paint. Others are lead or lead mixtures and are poisonous .
White oil paint is used most, so buy a large tube.

Burnt Sienna: This is a bright brown.
Mars Black : This is a warm brownish black.
Yellow Ochre: This is a dull yellow

Venetian Red : This is a dull red
Ultramarine Blue : This is a bright blue

Bright Red : Buy the red of your choice. Do not buy the Cadmiums Or Bariums. They are hazardous colors. Read the labels on the tubes and buy a bright red that you like as long as it is non hazardous and completely safe.

Bright Yellow : Buy the yellow of your choice. Do not buy the Cadmiums Or Bariums. They are hazardous colors. Read the labels on the tubes and buy a non hazardous bright red that you like.

A NOTE ABOUT SAFE OIL PAINTS

Make it a point to always wash your hands after oil painting. If you bought safe colors, you will be safe. Please read the labels on the tubes and do not buy any oil paints that are listed as hazardous. Ask the store manager for help.

One small bottle of "alkali reined stand linseed oil" .
This oil is very thick and is as thick as honey. You will see it shown in the video.

One small bottle of "alkali reined linseed oil".
This oil is very thin, almost as thin as water. You will see it shown in the video.

3 medium sized canvas panels. Buy any size between 9 inches X 12 inches ....or up to 16 inches x 20 inches. These are made for students and are made at a factory. Cotton canvas is glued to hard cardboard and they are not expensive.

An Easel: If you cannot afford an easel, you can use a straight back chair to hold the canvas panel as you paint. The video shows you a low cost easel.

A Grinding Tablet : Buy a low cost glazed floor tile. Make sure it is glazed. A size about 12inches by 12 inches or up to 24 inches by 24 inches.

One palette knife: I recommend you buy one with a straight blade. Some are made with a crooked neck, but these are hard to grind with.

Vine Charcoal : all you need are a few sticks. They are about 3 to 5 inches long and very narrow and they break easy because they are delicate.

One fine tipped permanent marker in black
(optional : liquid India ink that is waterproof and permanent. Also a thin long hair brush. Watch how they are used in the video)

Paper towels: Paper towels are safer than rags, and cleaner also. They are disposed of at the end of each day. Also a small trash can to place used towels.

Liquid non-fat milk: buy one pint and keep it refrigerated when not in use. This milk is also called " skim milk" or " fat free" milk. DO NOT Buy whole milk or low fat milk. DO NOT BUY milk sold in a can or carton that requires no refrigeration. These have additives that stop the milk from drying.

Dry powdered non-fat milk: Do not buy powdered whole milk or low fat powdered milk . DO NOT BUY milk sold in a can or carton that requires no refrigeration. These have additives that stop the milk from drying.

One small glass jar: You need one [about six ounce] clear glass jar with a tight fitting cap.

Masking tape or Scotch Tape: One small roll of 1/2 inch wide tape

VIDEO LESSON NUMBER ONE
HOW TO OIL PAINT

Please view the video first.

Some of the procedures are very simple and are not shown in the video.

After you viewed the video, you can easily follow these instructions.

STEP ONE: SEAL THE CANVAS BOARD
[This step is not demonstrated in the video]

You must first seal the canvas board so it is 100% non- absorbent.

Place the canvas board in a vertical position. This prevents puddles of the milk.

Place a newspaper under the canvas board to soak up excess milk.

Pour some liquid non-fat milk in a bowl.

Use a wide flat 3inch low cost brush and begin applying the milk at the top in horizontal strokes. Use a lot of milk. It's ok if it drips down.

Keep applying the milk in horizontal strokes until the entire canvas board is covered.

Let it dry. Depending on weather it might takes an hour or more.

If the day is sunny, place it outside in the shade not in direct sun.

If the day is wet and rainy, place it in a dry warm room with a fan for ventilation.

Once it is dry, you are ready for the next step.

STEP TWO: DRAW OR TRACE THE IMAGE ON THE CANVAS BOARD

Find a photo of someone you like.

A family member, a celebrity, or even a pet.

If you have a valuable photo, make a photo copy to use, so the valuable photo is not ruined. Magazines are full of photos of famous persons.

If the photos are small, you must make an enlargement.

MAKE SURE, the head is at least eight to ten inches high.

IF YOU CAN'T DRAW WELL, THEN TRACE
In the video, review the section on HOW TO DESIGN A PAINTING .
There is a demonstration with instructions on how to trace a photograph onto a canvas board. After it is traced, then use ink to outline it.
Use **either** permanent fine tipped markers
or liquid India ink as demonstrated in the video.

If you DO draw well, then follow my demonstration. Begin with vine charcoal and then after the excess dust is removed, you can ink the outlines.
Use either the liquid India ink that is waterproof and permanent. Or use fine tipped permanent markers.

Now that you have the drawing on the canvas board, you must prepare the paints.

STEP THREE : MAKE THE MILK GEL
Use the grinding tablet.
Follow the instructions as seen in the video.
Making the "MILK GEL" is simple. Make sure it is not loose and runny.
It must be in a "STAND UP" condition.

STEP FOUR: MAKING MILK OIL PAINT
We will learn how to mix the MILK GEL and the OIL PAINT together ,
so we can make MILK OIL PAINT
We will learn how to paint a MONOTONE painting.
The word "Mono" refers to one color, but we are using two colors that are very dull, plus black and white.

Follow the video demonstration.
Place the oil paints on the GRINDING TABLET.

Use only these four colors:
BLACK
WHITE
YELLOW OCHRE
VENETIAN RED

Now, place an equal amount of 'milk gel' next to each color.
Use your palette knife to mix them together well … then GRIND.
There is a difference between mixing and grinding.
When you GRIND, you must apply pressure on the palette knife.
Follow the demonstration in the video.

STEP FIVE:
THIN AND THICKEN THE MILK OILPAINT

Once you mixed the MILK GEL and the OIL PAINT together, you now have MILK OIL PAINT.

Make tests on thinning and thickening the oil paint as you see in the video.

IMPORTANT: Remember, you cannot thin or thicken the oil paint, until you first mix the milk gel together to create MILK OIL PAINT.

STEP SIX: PAINTING THE MONOTONE
WE BEGIN TO PAINT WITH THE UNDER PAINT LAYER

Many great painters of the past and today use a method of painting a dull colored monotone layer. This allows them to slowly think and slowly plan the painting.

They begin with a drawing of some kind. Then they begin the first layer of oil paint in dull colors, or with one color only. They add black for the SHADOWS and white for the LIGHTS …the one color, or the dull colors, is the MID TONE VALUES . Beginning with a drawing and a monotone makes designing the painting easier.

If the one color is GRAY, then the under paint layer is called a GRISAILLE, "GRIS" is the Latin word for "gray".
There are other names for the under paint layer.

Some artists call it the " dead color" because it has no bright colors.
Others call it the "monotone" because it is made of lights, darks and medium tones.

In the 16th century, the under paint layer was called "verdaccio" because it had a greenish color. In Latin languages, the word "verde" means " green".

Regardless of which dull colors or color you use, (and you can experiment with all of them) , they allow the artist to concentrate on a few important concerns.

It is easier to design your painting when using a dark, a light and a medium tone. You will also see how easy it is to create a three dimensional appearance of realism with just three tones.

Painting a monotone lets us focus on the drawing. Drawing is made easier if you do not need to concentrate with color.

We can also focus on Textures. Here you sometimes paint with thick paint and other times you scrub the paint on thinly. A variety of Textures in a painting adds interest.

The great Renaissance painters of Italy called this division of labor,
DISEGNO y COLORE ... which translates as, DESIGN and COLOR.

MILK OIL PAINT IS DIFFERENT THAN TRADITIONAL OIL PAINT
It is important to know the difference between these two oil paints.
Milk Oil Paint is made by mixing milk with oil paint.
Traditional Oil Paint has no milk in it.

IMPORTANT TO REMEMBER:
YOU CAN PAINT ... Traditional oil paint on top of Milk Oil Paint.
YOU CANNOT PAINT ... Milk Oil Paint on top of Traditional Oil Paint.

As long as you are painting with MILK OIL PAINT, you can over paint and add new layers of Milk Oil Paint as many times as you want. This allows you to add details and make corrections.

However, the moment you begin to over paint with Traditional Oil Paint, you cannot use Milk oil Paint again on the same painting.

MILK OIL PAINT dries very fast.
Thin washes dry in five minutes and thick impasto dries in approximately one hour. As soon as it dries, you can add new layers of Milk Oil Paint. Or, if you think you are ready, you can go to the next step of applying TRADITIONAL OIL PAINT on top of the finished MILK OIL PAINT monotone.

STEP NUMBER SEVEN
THE CLEAN UP OF THE GRINDING TABLET
The video shows how easy it is to remove the dried MILK OIL PAINT from the grinding tablet. You must clean it before you can go onto the next steps because we need a clean surface to work on.

STEP NUMBER EIGHT:
THE OVER PAINT LAYER
WE WILL USE TRADITIONAL OIL PAINTS
IN OVER PAINTING THE BEAUTY OF BRIGHT COLORS

TRADITIONAL OIL PAINT dries very slow.
Sometimes it takes 3 days or more for thin paint layers to dry.
Some colors dry faster than others. The color white dries very slow.

The first methods of oil painting in Europe in the 14th century made use of very thin paint. This allowed the bright white surface of the support (canvas or wood panel) to brighten up the thin bright colors. They did not use a monotone. They made a very detailed drawing in ink and then colored it in with thin oil paint. This method allowed them to create paintings of great realism.

Later in the 1500's, the classic method of oil painting by the Old Masters was to use a monotone, and to paint the shadows very thinly. This allowed the white of the canvas to show through so it made the dark colors livelier. They also painted the light areas very thickly. This made the paint areas pop forward as if in three dimensions.

In the last step, as seen in the video, we did exactly that. We painted a monotone. We made a drawing and we painted with thin washes of dark paint and then we added thick paint in the lights. Thick paint is called IMPASTO. Thin paint is called GLAZES. The word for medium paint layers is called SCUMBLING because sometimes we drag the medium thick paint over other layers.

STEP NUMBER NINE:
MAKING THE EMULSION

Before we can begin the COLOR OVER PAINT LAYER with TRADITIONAL OIL PAINT, we must make the EMULSION.

An Emulsion is a miracle of nature.
An emulsion is the mixing of an oil based liquid WITH a water based liquid.
The video demonstrates how to do it.
Place three spoons of the thick stand linseed oil in a jar.
Make sure ALL of the thick oil comes off each spoonful. This is very important.
Then add two spoons of the liquid milk.
Add a couple of penny coins to help in the mixing.
Cap the jar and shake vigorously until the two liquids are well mixed.
The emulsion will be a white opaque color.

STEP NUMBER TEN:
SET UP THE COLOR PALETTE
We will use the same grinding tablet for this.
Place as many of the oil paint colors you want on the surface .
Only place about a half inch of each color.
Use a little at a time so you do not waste your oil paint.
It is easy to remix more if you need more.
Place two to three drops on the tablet next to each color.
DO NOT ADD MORE than just a few drops of the emulsion.
Use the palette knife to mix ...then grind ...the emulsion with each color.

WE WILL NOT THIN THE OIL PAINT
The emulsion is used only for conditioning the oil paint.
The emulsion s not a painting medium for thinning the oil paint
We will not be thinning the oil paint as we paint.
We will paint with a " conditioned oil paint".
I will explain why later in the instructions.

IMPORTANT:
WE WILL NOT BE USING ANY MORE *MILK OIL PAINT* FROM THIS POINT FORWARD.
FOR ALL FUTURE CORRECTIONS WE MUST USE ONLY THE *TRADITIONAL OIL PAINTS* CONDITIONED WITH THE EMULSION.

STEP NUMBER ELEVEN:
APPLYING THE "OIL OUT"
The word "Oil out" stands for a very important procedure in oil painting.
It means: "Oil rubbed in and oil wiped out"
This instruction is goal oriented and informative.
It means that we must wipe off all excess oil from the surface.
The "oil out" is a lubricant so the oil paint will flow easily on the surface as you paint.

IMPORTANT
DO NOT use the Emulsion for the " oil out".
DO NOT use the THICK OIL for the " oil out".
Use only the THIN OIL for the "oil out".

STEP NUMBER TWELVE:
APPLY TRADITIONAL OIL PAINT

Learn to RUB the Oil paint with a stiff bristle brush if you want a thin layer.
In France they call this rubbing " frotagge" . In Spain they call it "frotar".
In English we can say "RUB".

Learn to lightly apply oil paint with a bristle brush if you want a thick layer.
Learn to blend the paint with the bristle brush.
Use the SOFT HAIR brush to add details.

As you paint, keep a paper towel in the other hand, so you can clean your brush tips of unwanted colors from time to time.

To remove unwanted oil paint from the surface, wipe it off with a dry paper towel. You will notice that the drawing and the monotone will not be disturbed by the wiping. Then, you can start over with different colors if you wish to.
There is no need to apply another " oil out" as the surface continues to be damp.

STEP NUMBER THIRTEEN:
USE OF BLACK OIL PAINT

Please ignore all those books and art teachers who advise you not to use the color black. All the greatest masters used the color black very effectively.
Rembandt, DaVinci, Michelanglo, all used black paint.

Oil painters must use the color BLACK to get depth in their painting.
I created a saying, " Black is the depth of the night and white is the sparkle of the stars".

If you CAREFULLY use pure black and pure white...your paintings will have great color and lighting depth. This will make them stand out powerfully.

In my painting experience and in my studies of Rembrandt's original paintings, I see he used Black last. I tell students to use PURE BLACK as the very last color as the painting is being finished. The same, for pure white. These two pure colors, are used as ACCENTS. They provide the final touches.

STEP NUMBER FOURTEEN
TRADITIONAL OIL PAINT

Because the traditional oil paint dries so slowly, you must take care at the end of the painting day, not to smudge the surface.

You can continue to paint the next day, but be careful .
Since the paint surface is wet, you do not have to apply an " oil out".
If you let the painting dry, then the next time you want to apply more traditional oil paint, then you must apply a new " oil out ", before painting.

IMPORTANT: Remember, once you began to oil paint with the TRADITIONAL OIL PAINTS … you cannot use MILK OIL PAINT.

STEP NUMBER FIFTEEN:
STYLES IN PAINTING

In the video, I painted in a loose sketch Impressionistic style.
I love the freedom of this style. Some artists prefer painting in a very detailed realistic style. And, others love to paint in broad non-objective applications of color. You, the artist must make your own choices to experiment and paint in your very own personal way.

You have heard the statement, " beauty is in the eye of the beholder".
I disagree with that and I believe this," beauty is in the eye of the Artist".
Every artist can do one thing better than any other artist,
and that is to, " express their personal feelings and opinions!"

STEP NUMBER SIXTEEN:
THINNING THE OIL PAINT

If you have ever painted with WATERCOLORS , you know you must thin the paint with water. It's the only way sometimes to be able to apply the paint because watercolor painting never uses IMPASTO . It only uses thin washes of colors.

OIL PAINTING is uniquely different. When we oil paint, we DO NOT LIQUIFY the oil paint. We use it in a " CONDITIONED" thickness. So, do not buy one of little cups that some oil painters use. You will not be dipping your brush into any PAINTING MEDIUMS or liquids.

Learn to apply more or less pressure on your brush to get the right amount of paint on the painting.

Learn to wipe your brush hairs off from time to time, with a dry paper towel.

STEP NUMBER SEVENTEEN: VARNISHING A PAINTING

It is not necessary to apply varnish to an oil painting.
Many artists do not want their oil paintings to be varnished.

VIDEO LESSON NUMBER TWO
HOW TO DRAW

Drawing is a skill you gain by practice .
The more you do it, the better you become.
It involves the coordination of your eye, your brain, and your hand.
Pretty soon it becomes second nature and you don't even think about the various steps.

Not everybody learns how to draw with great skill. For these artists, please see the portion in the video on DESIGNING A PAINTING. There you will watch a demonstration on HOW TO TRACE a photograph. It is very simple to do.

VIDEO LESSON NUMBER THREE
HOW TO DESIGN A PAINTING

An important part of every painting is the DESIGN.
There are many Art books you can buy that help explain DESIGN.
In my own opinion designing a picture s based on pure INTUITION.
DESIGN is how things are arranged. We design things every day in everything we do. We design, when we comb our hair, or when we choose what clothes to wear. Not everybody dresses the same. That would be boring. What we love dress DIFFERENTLY than others. We want to be recognized for our ORIGINALITY and CREATIVITY.

Designing a painting involves similar concepts.
Everybody values ORIGINALITY and CREATIVITY.
So when you design your painting, use your personal feelings, your personal opinions, and your INTUITION. This will show others you are ORIGINAL and CREATIVE.

The video makes a comment about two types of SPACES.
These are POSITIVE SPACE and NEGATIVE SPACE.
train your eyes to LOOK at the SHAPES of the NEGATIVE SPACES.

Everything that is a thing ... is a POSITIVE SPACE.
Everything that is not a thing ...
 like the background air, or areas, is NEGATIVE SPACE.
Both types of spaces are equally important .
With practice you will understand the relationship of these two spaces.

VIDEO LESSON NUMBER FOUR
MISCELLANEOUS INFORMATION, ABOUT BEING AN ARTIST
These instructions will help you to be a better artist.

FREDERIC TAUBES [1900-1981]
A GREAT AMERICAN ARTIST AND ART EUCATOR
I earned to oil paint by reading books and magazines.
I especially read the books by the great American Artist, Frederic Taubes.
Unfortunately, his methods use solvents, resins varnishes and driers.
I used all of these as a young man and as an adult because I did not know any better. In fact, every artist was taught to use the same hazardous materials in every art school and college. No one really paid much attention to the health hazards involved.
Frederic Taubes' books are important to read, but it is safer not to use any hazardous or dangerous materials.

THE GREAT MASTERS OF PAINTING

If you study the lives and paintings of the Great Masters you will gain great knowledge that will open up your creativity and originality .

Today with the Internet, we can study the paintings of every great master artist.

MNEMONICS
FOR HELPING REMEMBER FACTS

The word " Mnemonic" is pronounced " Nemonic".
The "M" is silent and is not pronounced.

When you do study DESIGN, you will learn there are
7 ELEMENTS OF DESIGN
and
7 PRINCIPLES OF DESIGN

I use a mnemonic to be able to remember them all.
A mnemonic is a simple sentence. I will teach you mine. You can create your own that might be better for you .

For the 7 ELEMENTS : Simple Simon Loves T.V. Cheap Food
Take the first letter of each word. It will stand for one of the Elements.
S: shapes
S: spaces (negative and positive)
L: lines
T: textures
V: values (this mans lights and darks)
C: colors
F: form (this refers to 3D forms)

For the 7 PRINCIPLES: Every Big Ugly Monkey Chews Ripe Peanuts
E: emphasis. This means you give something importance
B: balance
U: unity
M: movement. This means you arrange thins so your eye follows
C: contrast
R: rhythm
P: pattern

Designing a painting uses a lot of common sense and personal intuition.

VIDEOS FOR PROFESSIONAL AND ADVANCED ARTISTS

I have produced other videos for professional artists which you may find helpful. Go to **www.youtube.com** Type in the title of the video you wish to see. As time passes I will produce new free videos to guide Artists with safe painting materials.

Typing the words **CSO VELASQUEZ** will locate all my videos on Youtube.

CSO VELASQUEZ- AIR PUMP LINSEED OIL PART 1
CSO VELASQUEZ- AIR PUMP LINSEED OIL PART 2
CSO VELASQUEZ- DAVID HOCKNEY- Secret Knowledge
PART 1 - VAN EYCK SECRET MEDIUM - CSO VELASQUEZ
PART 2 - VAN EYCK SECRET MEDIUM - CSO VELASQUEZ
PART 3 - VAN EYCK SECRET MEDIUM- CSO VELASQUEZ

THIS CONCLUDES THE VIDEO LESSONS.
Please continue to read the following topics.

THE ART OF BEING AN ARTIST

I recommend every Beginner read the following pages of PART THREE.
I will try to explain what, or why, are the reasons for being an "Artist". This book is mainly a guide for "making " a painting. It involves the materials and how they are used in order for them to be long lasting and archival. Artists put so much effort into making their work, they want the finished art to be around for many years, so it may be appreciated.

CRAFTSMANSHIP is a term that describes the " making" of objects for human use. Objects such as a chair or table are important and serve a function. For thousands of years, humans made functional objects by hand. This hand-made quality is the keystone to "craftsmanship" .

Today, because of the Industrial Revolution of electricity and machinery, businesses began the mass production of functional objects. Yet, still today, hand-made objects are valued and appreciated for their hand made beauty.

Paintings too, like a chair or table, are hand crafted functional objects.
But something SPECIAL, exists in paintings. This quality of something very special is recognized in paintings, music, poetry and other areas is
What we call 'ART'.
I recall learning that " ART" is the result of " INSPIRED CRAFTSMANSHIP".

***Please note:** In order to be fair, the ancient word " craftsmanship" has always excluded the word "woman", and it should include it. Women artists have always been as gifted as men artists. I have heard the term " craftpersonship" used . Perhaps it should be used always.*

INSPIRED CRAFTWORK !
THE REASONS FOR MAKING PAINTINGS
Art is created by humans because of a need to express their personal ideas about the world they live in, and the need to express their personal sense of beauty. Here below are several topics that I , as an artist, have always thought about and tried to better understand. They are the REASONS for making paintings.

AESTHETICS [pronounced Esthetics](THE CONCEPT OF BEAUTY)
On the cover of this book is a collection of small paintings of my daughter Sandra. They are placed next to each other in a frame. Each painting measures 7 inches by 5 inches. Each painting is in the style of a different historical era. They represent European based styles from the 15th century through the 20th century.

I painted these to demonstrate how an artist might choose a different style to paint the picture of the young girl. Every person who looks at this series of paintings has a favorite. No one agrees as to which one is best. In fact, it is IMPOSSIBLE to say which one is best, because we all have different opinions about what " Beauty" is.

Throughout history, persons have attempted to define "Beauty". Some persons, who believe they are "experts", have made rules, expecting others to follow them. Creative artists have always ignored these rules. Creative artists make their own rules about what is beautiful or not. Creative artists follow their instincts and intuition.

In paintings, we can see Aesthetics in the style of the paintings.
My book will not give an opinion on what style of painting is best.
We are fortunate to live in the modern era, where we have access to libraries, museums, and the Internet. We live in the "information age" and we can use the resources to our advantage to create interesting artworks.

THE TECHNICAL PART OF PAINTINGS
My book is about the TECHNICAL part of paintings.
This means ... it is about the materials we use, and the manner we use them.
However, as you learn the lessons in this book and video.
I will ask you to follow my instructions as best you can. This means, I need you to follow the STYLE that I use in teaching the lesson. You do not need to copy the style exactly.

Once you learn the materials we use and how we apply them, you can create your own paintings in your own styles. You will love the creativity of exploring the ideas learned in this book and videos, as you develop new styles as you paint your own pictures.

The small paintings of my daughter on the cover, show a historical development of painting in Europe. It is very important that you understand that the European Oil Painting history is a very small part of the Art history of the world.

European oil painting dates from the 1300's through the present. This is a period of 700 years. Art from Africa is over 100, 000 years, and Art from the American continents is over 17,000 years old. Australia's Aboriginal Art is very ancient. Some cave paintings in Europe are 50,000 years old, but they are not oil paintings.

If you study the Art of the entire World, you will expand your consciousness.
You can use the art from all parts and all eras of the World in creating your own personal NEW visions of the world.

BEAUTY IS IN THE EYE OF THE ...?
It has been said: " Beauty is in the eye of the beholder."
This means the person viewing the art can decide on whether or not the artwork is " beautiful" , "relevant" , " meaningful" , or " important".

I strongly differ with that view because the "beholder" is passing judgment on the creative efforts of another person's individual aesthetic , or, cultural views.
I believe it is best not to pass judgment.
Instead, the "beholder" could ask questions about the artwork. By doing so, the beholder's personal biases are set aside, and one can learn something new.

I prefer to say: " Beauty is in the heart and mind of the artist." It is the artist, in fact, who is doing all the creative work. If we ask questions, instead of passing biased judgments, we can learn new things.

MISSION STATEMENTS WRITTEN BY ARTISTS
Prior to the modern era of technology, few master artists ever spoke about their views on aesthetics. Only one letter written by Rembrandt exists, in which he tries to explain what his goal was in painting one particular painting. Rembrandt lived in the 1600's. Vincent Van Gogh lived in the 1800's and wrote hundreds of letters about what he was trying to accomplish with his paintings.

Today, artists are expected to write a "mission statement", which is usually a brief paragraph explaining their objectives in painting. Since artists are always evolving, the mission statement changes accordingly.

TECHNICAL MATTERS OF IMPORTANCE

THE OIL WE WILL USE IN OUR LESSONS
For these Lessons in the book and Video, beginners will use a low cost linseed oil that can be used immediately. The oil is available in every art supply store.

If one chooses, they can prepare the SUPERIOR OIL of the Old Masters.
This oil has to be processed at home. When using the AIR PUMP, it takes 25 days to produce the oil.

One can also choose to use the AIR PUMP on a small bottle of Alkali Refined Linseed Oil. This takes only 15 days to produce a faster drying linseed oil.
DO NOT use the Air Pump on the thick Stand Linseed Oil.
Use it only on the THIN linseed oil.

A BRIEF HISTORY OF ARTIST'S OIL
Artists have used different kinds oils for oil painting. The oils artists most commonly used are Linseed oil, walnut oil, and poppy seed oil. We will use only linseed oil because it has been the main oil used by the master painters.

Linseed oil and some other vegetable oils are classified as "DRYING OILS ".
They dry hard by exposure to the air. Many other vegetable oils are called "non-drying "oils. One is olive oil and it never dries. Butter is a non- drying fat obtained from milk.

Linseed oil has been used since antiquity, but our modern use of linseed oil for oil painting began in the 1100's. Still, it was not popular because it dried very, very slowly. This slow drying oil, frustrated artists and persons who wanted to buy paintings. So, instead of using oil paints, artists painted with **tempera paints** because they dry within minutes. The most popular **Tempera** was made from eggs. It is called Egg Tempera paint. Another popular **Tempera** was Milk Tempera which is called Casein.

In 2011 I created a new Oil Paint. It is called "MILK OIL PAINT".
It is fully explained in the video.

In the 1300s, artists learned a few important things about linseed oil.
They learned that if the linseed oil was exposed to constant air and constant heat, it would begin to thicken like honey. This thickened linseed oil became a faster drying oil for oil painting. Soon the Tempera paints became obsolete, and all major artists were painting with oil paints. Egg tempera painting was revived in the 1800's and today many fine artists use it.

In the 1800's Manufacturers learned how to mass produce linseed oil. They process it with caustic chemicals. It is the oil used by most artists today.
It is called Alkali Refined Linseed Oil.

THE 21ST CENTURY
The EXTRAORDINARY 'AIR PUMP OIL'

Today we can use our electrical technology to create oil that dries even faster than the oil used by the great Old Masters. We can use a low cost aquarium air pump to pump air constantly through the oil. It takes between ten and fifteen days for the oil to be ready for use.

This electrical technology lets us create a fine oil that dries very fast. This allows us to eliminate all toxic and hazardous metal driers that were once added to oil paint in order to make it dry faster. Now, we can eliminate the hazardous materials and we can paint more safely.

TEACHERS AND BEGINNERS AND AIR PUMP OIL
Teachers and Beginners without a teacher, may wish to use the new AIR PUMP OIL. A video series I produced is free to watch on the Internet.
Please go to the website www.youtube.com
Then type these words in the search box
CSO VELASQUEZ AIR PUMP OIL
Please pay special attention to the details.
You may also go to my website : www.calcitesunoil.com
There you will see photographs that teach you how to set up the " air pump".

IMPORTANT POINTS ON THE AIR PUMP OIL
The weather is very important for processing your " AIR PUMP OIL" .
If it is done outside, the weather must be DRY with low HUMIDITY.
If it is done inside , the room must be DRY with low HUMIDITY.

If the weather is HOT and MUGGY outside, like it sometimes is in Florida, the air pump will pump MOISTURE from the air, into the oil. This then will Produce a Very slow drying oil. If the air outside is muggy and humid, use the air pump inside in a dry warm room.

If the weather is DAMP and RAINY outside, like it is in Oregon or Washington, the air pump will blow moisture from the air into the oil and the oil will be slow drying. If the air outside is wet and humid, use the air pump inside in a dry warm room.

MATTERS OF CREATIVITY
THE OLD MASTERS ' DRAWINGS
The Old Masters used drawings as a way to PLAN a painting.
If a painting was ordered, the painting was first designed.
This would let the artist and the customer know what
the final painting would look like.

You can think of the drawing as a BLUEPRINT for the painting.
It was much like how an architect will draw blueprints for designing a house.
Once the blue print plans were finished, any competent builder could follow the blue print, and could build the house.

The Old Masters were painters who had to earn a living. They were able to draw a design and finish the painting by themselves, but sometimes they had too many customers. Then they would just draw the design. Once the drawing was perfectly designed, they hired competent assistants to finish the painting from the finished drawing. If they decided to, they could have the assistant make lots of copies of the same painting.

Sometimes, the Master artist was not pleased with the painting made by the assistants. The Master would then make corrections by adding and changing parts of the painting. The Master would then ... sign his name on the painting.
In previous centuries, this was an accepted tradition.

Today, this is not the normal procedure for artists.
Yet, some modern artists are following exactly that procedure . Salvador Dali is an example of a modern Master who has hired assistants to help finish his paintings.

HOW AND WHY ARTISTS MAKE DRAWINGS
Artists draw in various ways ... for specific reasons.

SOME COPY NATURE
Artists sometimes copy something they can see in front of them. This
COPY drawing has an important purpose. It is how an artist learns what something really looks like. If every motorist tried to draw a stop sign, they would learn exactly what it looks like.

SOME DO NOT COPY NATURE
Artists sometimes do not want to copy something exactly as it looks.
They wish to change how it looks as they DESIGN a painting. They might draw the neck of a person longer, or the face might be made thinner. They might draw the feet really large the way a cartoonist might draw.

SOME TRACE PHOTOGRAPHS
Some artists do not draw well, but they have very creative ideas.
So, they TRACE photographs. Grandma Moses was a famous artist who died at the age of 101. She did not begin to paint until she was 80 years old. She did not draw well, so, she would cut photographs out of magazines. Then she would arrange them on the canvas. Then she would tape them down and would use a TRANSFER PAPER to TRACE the photos onto the canvas.

SOME ARTISTS PROJECT PHOTOGRAPHS
Today some , but not all, modern artists use projectors in a dark room. They project photographs onto the canvas and they trace the images. This is not a modern idea. In the 1400's , artists found out how to use mirrors and glass lenses to make crude projections. They would trace the images and by this method they made paintings that look like photographs...400 years before photography was invented.

MY PERSONAL EXPERIENCE WITH TRACING

I do not enjoy tracing. I once painted a picture of a snow goose. I took a photograph of a dead goose that had been treated by a taxidermist. It looked very life like. I bought a projector and traced every line of that goose onto the support. It was so boring, that I never traced another photo.

MY PERSONAL WAY OF DRAWING

I love the emotional and physical passion of drawing ! I love swinging my hand and fingers as I see the lines unfold an image as I CREATE something new.

When I draw I follow a certain thought. I say to myself , " vague design -outline define." This means that I depend on myself to be very loose as I begin. I draw with light thin lines in the beginning. The more sketchy it is the more important it is to my CREATIVE IMAGINATION. I begin to see objects and images in the numerous sketchy lines and shadows.

Once I am finished with the sketchy drawing, I then slow down and I carefully draw outlines right over the sketchy lines. All this time, I keep my mind open to new images that I can see in the drawing. I change things as my heart desires.

INTUITION is a very important component of drawing and painting. You must learn to trust yourself, meaning your ideas, thoughts, and feelings.

A MODERN REVELATION FOR ARTISTS
DAVID HOCKNEY AND SECRETS OF THE OLD MASTERS

The Old Masters from Northern Europe , in the 1400's painted some of the best preserved oil paintings in history. Their oil paintings have a "jewel like " appearance because of the great beauty of their sparkling colors. Their paintings are full of extraordinarily fine naturalistic details. Many portraits they painted, look exactly like photographs.

In the late 20th century, the famous artist, David Hockney, published a book titled "Secret Knowledge". I recommend that every art student read his valuable and important book. , Mr. Hockney proved conclusively that many of Europe's most famous Old Master artists PROJECTED and TRACED the images. By tracing, they were able to paint pictures that look like photographs. He demonstrated how by using mirrors and glass lenses they could PROJECT the images onto the canvas or wood panel.

Mr. Hockney also shows that many great Masters did not trace.
Many Old Masters, like many Modern Masters today, can paint and draw very realistically without projecting and tracing images. Neither Michelangelo nor Rubens traced, and their paintings look realistic, but they do not look like photographs.

Many art students draw poorly, but they are very creative. These students can learn how to trace and can then create fine paintings that are very beautiful.

THE MODERN DIRECT PAINTING METHOD OF VINCENT VAN GOGH

The video does not demonstrate the DIRECT PAINTING METHOD.
Before beginning to paint a picture some artists draw the outline before they paint. Others do not draw before they paint. They prefer to draw and paint at the same time, with the paint.

Vincent Van Gogh would set up his easel in front of the SUBJECT . He preferred painting directly on the white canvas. He would use bright blue oil paint and with a small brush, he would draw an OUTLINE of the subject .

By outlining the subject he was actually DESIGNING the COMPOSITION of the painting. The subject could have been a LANDSCAPE ... or a PORTRAIT .. or a STILL LIFE .

Once he made the bright blue outline, he then would FILL IN the spaces and areas with his oil paints while the blue outline was still wet. This method allowed Van Gogh to complete a painting very rapidly.

THE DIRECT PAINTING METHOD

The video does not demonstrate the DIRECT PAINTING METHOD.
To paint with this direct method you simply LEAVE OUT THE MONOTONE.

You can still begin with MILK OIL PAINT if you wish, because it dries so fast it offers an advantage. Then complete the painting with the TRADITIONAL OIL PAINT.
You can paint the entire painting with just MILK OIL PAINT
OR- you can paint the entire painting with TRADITIONAL OIL PAINT
OR- you can begin with MILK OIL PAINT underneath, and finish with TRADITIONAL OIL PAINT on top.

IMPORTANT: ONCE YOU begin with the TRADITIONAL OIL PAINTS, you CANNOT USE MILK OIL PAINT
This method of painting is done in one layer. It does not use a monotone.
After the painting dries, a correction layer can be applied.
Begin by obtaining the photograph of the subject you will paint

INSTRUCTIONS for the
DIRECT METHOD OF OIL PAINTING
[also called 'Alla Prima']

STEP ONE : PREPARATION
Seal the support you will paint on so it is non-absorbent
-Follow the instructions in PART THREE
Draw and ink the portrait on the support. Freehand or trace
-Follow the instructions in PART THREE
Prepare the emulsion
-Follow the instructions in PART THREE
Condition the paint with the emulsion, on the grinding table
-Follow the instructions in PART THREE

For this method you can buy extra colors
Read the labels and do not buy hazardous colors. Ask the store manager for assistance. Read the labels!
   Bright Primary colors : Red Yellow Blue
   Bright Secondary colors : Purple, Green, Orange
   Bright brown : Sienna brown
   Black : Mars black
   White : Titanium Dioxide white (use only this white)

STEP TWO : PAINT WITH ANY AND ALL COLORS
You can make a bright color dull, by mixing a bit of brown sienna
Add a bit of black to darken a color
Add a bit of white to lighten a color
Begin to apply paint thinly.
You can add thicker paint as you go
    Paint the medium toned colors first [it helps]
    Paint the darks
    Paint the lights
    Blend as you paint
Mix colors to create exciting unexpected colors
Scrape off the paint of any areas you do not like

STEP THREE: CORRECT THE COLORS
Add a bit of black to darken a color
Add a bit of white to lighten a color
Paint the paint thicker or thinner
Blend as you paint
Scrape off the paint of any areas you do not like

STEP FOUR: MAKE CORRECTIONS
After the painting dries, corrections can be applied .
Before applying the corrections, apply an "Oil out ".

THE ADVANTAGES
OF THE DIRECT PAINTING METHOD
1. The completed painting has a fresh sketchy quality
2. The painting is quickly finished , sometimes in just a few hours
3. The creative responses of the artist are immediately painted

The Direct Painting method is **NOT** primarily concerned with painting in a photo-realistic style.
The Direct Painting method is more concerned with FORM EXPRESSION .
When the artist is not concerned with painting photographically, the artist can have more freedom of expressing the 7 FORMAL ELEMENTS .

HOW TO MAKE A DIFFERENT EMULSION
BY USING EGG INSTEAD OF MILK
This added information is included because it might be an exciting lesson for beginners and students to learn. It is not demonstrated on the video, but is demonstrated on my DVD titled, " OIL PAINTING WITH CALCITE SUN OIL".

The video and book instructions teach you how to make an Emulsion of milk and oil. An artist can also choose to make an emulsion of egg white and oil. It takes more time and effort. It is a good project to learn. Then, in future oil painting, you can choose either emulsion to 'CONDITION' the tube oil paint colors as the video demonstrates.

INSTRUCTIONS

REQUIRED: TWO EGGS, A BOWEL , A SPOON and a GLASS JAR

Break both eggs carefully. Carefully separate the white from the yolk. Discard the yolk. WE WILL NOT USE THE YOLK. If any yolk gets into the bowl, carefully remove it. Place the egg whites in a bowl. Use a metal spoon. Do not use an electric blender nor a plastic spoon. Beat the egg white until it froths . Periodically use the spoon to remove the froth and place the froth in a clean jar. Continue to beat the egg white in the bowl. Periodically remove the froth as before. Continue this until all the egg white has been frothed and removed. Let the froth stand still for about 30 minutes so it will distill. Periodically break through the froth to allow air. When finished, the pale yellow liquid is called GLAIR.

MIX THE GLAIR AND THE THICK OIL

Use a teaspoon. Place two spoons of the glair in a small jar. Place three spoons of the thickened linseed oil into the same jar. Take your time. Make sure all the sticky oil gets off the spoon each time. Add a couple of pennies or small stones into the jar. Cap the jar tight. Shake this well, vigorously . Count from 50 to 100 to insure the mixture is correctly made.

The completed emulsion will be a very opaque white color. The egg emulsion will last only a few days before it begins to decompose. Place the capped jar in a cool place with the lid tightly on. Once you see a tan or brownish color, or detect a bad odor, discard the entire jar and contents. Some artists keep it in the refrigerator but it will gain water though condensation.

YOU MUST HAVE A GRINDING TABLE

This is a low cost, glazed floor tile. Do not get a pure white nor a solid black because they are hard to see the colors well. Any mid tone color is ok. The size can be about 12 inches by 12 inches, or preferably larger.

CONDITIONING THE OIL PAINT
Squeeze out a small daub of each oil paint color onto the grinding table.
If you see a lot of oil come out when you squeeze the paint from the tube, then, you must put the paint daub on a paper towel. This will blot out that excess oil. It only takes about 15 seconds. Once done, use the palette knife to transfer the paint to the grinding table

Now, Place two drops of the emulsion next to each daub of paint.
Use a palette knife to mix the two together. You need to GRIND the two together. The difference between MIXING and GRINDING is in the pressure you apply. Mixing requires no pressure but grinding does.
First, just mix the two together. Now, you must grind the two together very well using pressure. It only takes seconds.

We mix the emulsion with the tube oil paint for several reasons.
1. It accelerates the drying of the paint
2. It makes the paint more glossy with rich color depth
3. It increases the flow for easier application and blending
4. It stops the paint from dripping

THE LANGUAGE OF PAINTING
Is FORM and CONTENT

The word FORM, in painting means two things.
One meaning is 3D FORM
An example is this. The Form of a water pitcher is a three dimensional object.
Another meaning is the DESIGN FORM: One can say "the Form of a seashell is very intricate and very complicated with all its colors, and textures."

FORM
The word **FORM** in discussing and creating paintings, refers to
the FORMAL aspects of DESIGN.
Design is a word that can be described as ARRANGEMENT, or STRUCTURE and also COMPOSITION or FOUNDATION.
Generally they refer to the organization of the painting. How things are arranged or placed on the canvas.

FORM, as a way to organize things in the painting , uses several different words. Humans made these words up so they could intelligently say what they thought of these things when they talked with others about them.

FORM, refers to the FORMAL considerations of a painting .
These are 7 ELEMENTS OF DESIGN and 7 PRINCIPLES OF DESIGN.

INTUITIVE DESIGN [FORMAL DESIGN]
One can Design by INTUITION alone without ever learning the words created by academics. As proof, I showed them many famous and precious examples of African paintings, some being thousands of years old, made by persons who had no art schools or art colleges nor even a written language.

CONTENT

"**CONTENT**" can be just as complicated to understand as the word "FORM".
Content in a painting has to do with what the painting is about.

What does a painting "mean"?
Paintings are silent and normally do not have signs. Today in most museums persons can rent an AUDIO TOUR to explain what the paintings mean. Without that, a person looking at a painting is left on their own to interpret for themselves , what the painting MEANS, or is all about.

CONTENT is different from the SUBJECT in the painting.
A painting of a boy and a dog is the subject.
A picture of a boy and a dog, where the boy was walking
away and the dog was tied to a chain and the dog begins to cry.
This is the content, this is its meaning.

Pictures of simply colors and lines shows it is hard to know what the subject is.
The pictures make sense when it is explained that they are close up views of things seen through a microscope.
These highly magnified close ups of natural objects can be a piece of wood, another a butterfly wing, or a sidewalk.

These lessons demonstrate that the CONTENT of a painting could be anything that gave it a certain meaning. Many times a painting has a different meaning to different people.

WRITING ABOUT CONTENT AND FORM

SOME ARTISTS DO WRITE ABOUT THEIR WORK
Artists create paintings, and their paintings represent their personal ideas and their meanings. Some artists write about what that MEANING is by writing about what they are trying to "SAY" through their paintings.
This is helpful, because if they don't write down why they made the painting and what they were thinking about, some "Art expert", will come along and will write down their own opinion about what the artist was trying to say.

SOMEARTISTS DO NOT WRITE ABOUT THEIR WORK
Few of the greatest painters wrote down what they were trying to express in their paintings. Most were just trying to earn a living by painting pictures for money. To them it was a job, like any other job people have.

Today in many art classes, teachers will discuss the MEANING OF CONTENT in student paintings. This is because people enjoy discussing thoughts and hearing opinions. This communication joins people together for intellectual discussions.

It is important to remember that all comments about the meaning of artworks, unless expressed by the artist, are PURELY SUBJECTIVE , meaning, they are simply opinions that cannot be proven or disproven.

THIS CONCLUDES THE LESSONS FOR BEGINNERS
BEGINNERS ARE ENCOURAGED TO READ OTHER PARTS OF THE BOOK AS TIME PASSES TO BETTER UNDERSTAND THE ART OF OIL PAINTING

PART FOUR
MISCELLANEOUS

This section contains various topics of interest to both beginners and teachers.

SAFETY IN OIL PAINTING

An article by ALESSANDRA KELLY is not included here because of copyright restrictions. This EXCEPTIONAL essay by a very fine Artist/ Professor can be read at her website. See her website for much more great information: http://www.alessandrakelley.com/Hazards.html

FIRE PREVENTION SAFETY WITH LINSEED OIL

In the over 50 years of using linseed oil I had heard the often repeated WARNING that rags soaked in linseed oil will SELF COMBUST—they will catch fire by themselves. FINALLY one day on YOUTUBE I saw an experiment that proved the statement. THEREFORE: When using rags or paper towels when oil painting, place the used rags and towels in a bucket of water. Then when it is time, dispose of them safely.

TOXIC PIGMENTS IMPORTANT NOTICE ON SAFETY: My claim of SAFETY and PERMANENCE is limited to the "Calcite Sun Oil" ingredients and the Emulsions described in this book. I repeat that use of any fine powders requires use of an adequate dust mask to prevent inhalation. I assume no responsibility for the choices of the dry pigments or of the tube oil paints made by artists. Many pigments and oil paints are toxic, carcinogenic and hazardous to human health. I refer readers to Monona Rossol's book in the bibliography.

AESTHETICS AND ORIGINALITY

My teaching experience with hundreds of students encourages me to share my perspective regarding the concepts of creativity, originality and the aesthetic evaluations of artworks.

For many years I have bought and studied numerous books and articles on the subject of Oil Painting. Some inexpensive and others very expensive academic studies, but none of them contain the technical knowledge of my new discoveries described in my book. This book would have saved me countless hours of lost time, frustration, and use of ineffective methods, as I struggled to figure out the answers to many of the problems presented by oil painting. I am happy to teach others this knowledge insuring safety, permanence, and a better understanding of the oil paint medium that will aid their development.

Knowing how to use the materials and methods of oil painting is of paramount importance, but it is only half the challenge artist's face. As an art educator, I have experienced first hand the mind of the student, with its innocent ignorance caused by incomplete information, and its creative, intuitive, brilliant intelligence born in every human being. This section will address the need for the artist to be guided without any restrictions, in order to understand the important part that personal expression, creativity, originality and assessment play in making artworks. Aesthetics, the philosophy of the concept of 'beauty', is important to understand as is the use of content and what that content is created to say to the viewer.

1. EXPRESS YOURSELF. Paint the things you have experienced. Express your feelings and ideas about them and use images that will say what you want the viewer to hear. Be simple or be profound.

2. TRUST YOUR INTUITION. You have a uniquely individual, 'personal aesthetic sensibility'. It is reflected in your artwork, by the way you see, feel and understand this world, and in how you INTUITIVELY apply the Formal Elements and Principles of Design. The Elements are: Shape, Space, Line, Texture, Value, Color, Form. The Principles are: Emphasis, Balance, Unity, Movement, Contrast, Rhythm, Pattern. It's a fact, 25, 000 years ago, prehistoric cavemen and women painted some of the world's great artworks, and they were only guided by their INTUITIVE "personal aesthetic sensibility".

3. ORIGINALITY. Name any great artist and their work looks like that of no one else.
The master artists that were 'realists', did not paint their world as they saw it, even if their art looks very 'real'.They distorted visual reality by changing, deleting, and emphasizing, in order to create their designed artwork. Sometimes the Fine Arts are called the 'Plastic Arts'. You can envision what we can do to a soft piece of plastic. We can twist it, stretch it, form it... change it.
My favorite question of my art students was, "What color is a rose?".
At first they would say, "red", but they soon learned to say, "any color you want it to be!"

4. EVALUATION. Modern Art gave us freedom. Freedom from rules, manifestos, dogmas, restrictions.
Today we can paint in any style or mixtures of styles we can imagine. An important component of creative art is that it be 'new' and original, and experimental, and you can do this in a realistic 'objective' style or

a 'non-objective' style or mix the two. There will always be a ' connoisseur' who will try to tell you that Jackson Pollock is a greater artist than Andrew Wyeth, or vice versa, but that opinion is only important to him/her, and no one else. It is impossible to measure subjective criteria for evaluation. Each historical epoch, each generation, and each culture creates their own values in deciding quality in art. There are no rules in creative art, and you can never make a 'mistake' when making creative art.

REMEMBER " Beauty is in the eye of the ARTIST, ... NOT ... in the eye of the beholder"

FREEDOM OF EXPRESSION
FREEDOM FROM RULES

Artists value one thing above all others: FREEDOM OF EXPRESSION and FREEDOM FROM RULES.
I agree – nothing, not even technical matters should prevent artists from doing whatever it is they want to do. One of my favorite artists is Jackson Pollock, but I don't wish to paint like him, nor to use his choice of materials which are acrylic house paints splattered with a stick on a canvas on the floor.

The CSO/EMULSIONS oil painting materials and application procedures require artists to follow instructions of mixing and application - with minimal deviation. My testing, experimentation and noting the results guide me in giving instructions. Artists who deviate, will have different results, such as dripping paint, and poor adhesion, cracking etc.

Over the years, I have asked artists new to CSO/Emulsions, to follow my instructions as I have written them. Not to restrict their creativity, but to understand how CSO works. THEN to experiment for themselves and alter and introduce new knowledge that best suits them.

The CSO/EMULSIONS method is superior to the SOLVENT-VARNISH-RESIN method of oil painting. My book explains why. Even with the solvent method, one must follow technical rules or---defective results are sure to follow. One of the principal RULES in the solvent method is to paint FAT ON LEAN. If you violate that rule, the paint will crack. The CSO method does not need to follow the fat on lean rule because the CSO method uses NO SOLVENTS or Resins, or Varnishes.

There are some creative artists, contemporary and ancient.....who never sign their work and criticize those who do as being egotistical, because to them, nothing is permanent and fame is not important. Some ancient cultures spend months in creating an artwork in metal, in the sand or in sculpture, only to destroy it after it is finished. The MAKING of the art is the important experience, they believe, not the selling or saving of it.

I do believe artists should sign and date their art and to sell or trade it and to discuss it and to save and share it as an expression of a human artist. Imagine if Da Vinci destroyed his Mona Lisa. To me, ART is a window and a Mirror: ART is a window that allows me to view art from across the centuries and see humans as they were back then. I see their clothes, buildings and activities and see the FORM decisions of the creative artists who made the art. ART is a mirror because we humans create art that is a response to our experiences of our current lives. We look in the mirror and see ourselves and our friends, clothes, buildings and try to decide OUR own FORM decisions on representing what we are experiencing.

MY ARTISTIC SELF-EXPRESSION

A CREATIVE ARTIST IS FACINATED AND EXCITED ABOUT LIFE.
AN ARTIST EXPLORES THE ENDLESS ASPECTS ABOUT LIFE AND SEEKS TO UNDERSTAND THEM. THEIR FACINATION IS THE FORCE THAT INSPIRES THEM TO EXPLORE AND MOVES THEM TO CREATE THEIR EXPRESSIONS AND IMPRESSIONS IN A VARIETY OF MEDIA, BE IT VISUAL, AUDIO, LITERARY OR PHYSICAL ACTIVITIES.

IT DOES NOT MATTER WHAT SUBJECTS YOU PAINT, NOR IN WHICH STYLE.
WHAT MATTERS IS 'HOW' YOU AS AN INDIVIDUAL PERSON, SEES AND EXPERIENCES THE WORLD AS YOU LIVE IT. THE VALUE OF ANY CREATIVE PAINTING IS BASED ON THE PERSONAL EXPRESSIONS OF EACH VISUAL ARTIST WHO IS EXPLORING THE INFINITE VARIATIONS OF COLORS, LIGHTS, SPACE ARRANGEMENTS AND PAINT APPLICATION.

When I paint, draw, dream or think.
There are FOUR AREAS I concentrate on: SUBJECT – DESIGN- COLOR- APPLICATION
First the SUBJECT: What is the subject or idea I want to portray?
Second, the DESIGN: How am I going to arrange the subject on the surface of the canvas?
Third, the COLOR: Color and Light are one and the same in that it is LIGHT that lets us see colors. Colors in the early morning are different than those at mid-day or evening. As an artist I need to choose my colors and lighting for this painting.
Fourth, the APPLICATION: How the paint is applied will enhance the aesthetic responses of the viewer. Some Old Masters painted very thinly. Others painted very thickly. Others mixed up the consistency and how the paint was applied.
EACH PAINTING is an exploration of these four areas of concentration.

Procedurally, some Old Masters said an artist painter should " divided the labor" when making a painting. This meant that if you first draw and paint in grays, the ideas and design are worked out without having to think about "color" or, the 'application issues'. Others like Van Gogh just painted direct alla prima.

AUTHOR'S BIOGRAPHY
Louis Richard Velasquez

"Le gusta hacer cosas con las manos, y las hace bien."- Joaquina Cordero de Velasquez c.1950
[Words I heard my grandmother, Joaquina Diaz-Cardenas de Velasquez say to my mother when I was a child]

I was born on October 25, 1943 in Porterville, California, in the United States of America.
My parents, Jose Fortunato Diaz-Cordero Velasquez , and Maria Magdalena Reyes- Cardenas Escudero , immigrated from Mexico in the 1920's, and worked in agriculture. When not in school, my two brothers and I were farm workers, harvesting crops with our parents. Dropping out of college, I joined the U.S. Army in 1964, serving my three years in Germany as a Military Policeman and a Paratrooper. Returning to California, I settled In San Diego, and spent the next twenty-two years as a law enforcement officer. Retiring in 1989, I eventually returned to college and received my B.A. Degree in Art in 1999. I received my teaching credential in 2000, and began a career as an art teacher in the public school system, until I retired in 2005. I am happily married to my wife Lilia Castaneda- Salazar Velasquez, and I have two daughters, Sandra and Elena.

I have painted in oils since about age twelve. I am proud of the 6' X 12' oil painting I completed in 1961 at age 17. Since 1965, it has been on continuous exhibition in the Porterville Historical Museum, in Porterville, California. While a police officer, I created a cartoon character, "Johnny Recruit, an Introduction to Law Enforcement for Children", to teach children of the valuable services provided by police officers. I also created a cartoon character named "Buddy Burro, America's Happiest Donkey". This cartoon character promotes racial equality and justice. See www.buddyburro.com.

Since 1964, I have traveled several times to most European countries, to study the masterpieces of the Old Masters of oil painting. My favorite masters are Rembrandt, Rubens and Velazquez, though I hold all of the others in high esteem. I have never stopped painting, except for a five year period from 2000 to 2005, when my new career as a teacher completely took all my time, dedication and energy.

Since my youth, I have always searched for - and always researched - a subject of the greatest importance for an artist: The question of the make up of the grinding medium used by the Old Masters to make the paint and their medium to thin it , and the application methods they used to insure achieving the desired results, both leading to efficiency and permanence. Over the years, safety had become an important issue.

After 2000 I began an intensive search and conducted many experiments, that augmented my previous decades long search into the methods and materials used by the Old Masters. The result was the formulation of the 'Calcite Sun Oil/ Emulsions method of Oil Painting'. I am not related to the Spanish master Velazquez, but I admit it is a coincidence in my development of "Calcite Sun Oil", based on the scientific studies of his magnificent paintings.

MY EDUCATION AS A PAINTER

I began to oil paint in 1957 as a 13 year old. I learned by reading the books and magazine articles of the famous American artist and educator, **Frederic Taubes**. For the next 40 years I traveled all over Europe and the USA, studying the original paintings of the greatest Masters, and from 1964 to 1968 I lived in Germany. During those years I read everything I could find on the subject of the technical aspects of Oil Painting. I studied new and old books and ancient manuscripts translated into English. This was the era before the marvelous information search engines of the internet.

As a youth and adult, I used the same materials everyone else was using: Hazardous materials that were bought at the Art store. I slept with an open can of turpentine filled with brushes, next to my bed. I suffered much from sinus problems and I never read the small print warning on the bottles.

In 1981 Frederic Taubes died and the 'Taubes' brand of **copal resin mediums** I had used for years, went off the market. I began to use a mixture of dammar resin varnish, linseed oil and turpentine without knowing the chemical disadvantages of such a fragile and impermanent medium. Sadly, the same mixture is still being taught to art students in colleges and universities today. Professors who should know better - of the health hazard these materials pose to students as well as of the impermanence of the medium mixture- simply do not. They were never taught, any options ... and they never sought out any answers. The work I have completed will revolutionize oil painting although it will take many years to change the established mind set.

In 2000 I began my work and published the first version in 2004. In 2008 I published a revised edition. In March 2012, I rushed an incomplete edition to publication because my declining health might prevent its publication. Now, in December 2012, I have taken my time to revise this manuscript into a better organized more coherent book.

I am confident readers will learn many things of lasting value to help them master the oil paint medium with safety and permanence, and to learn of the use of fast drying tempera paints for under painting for oils. The safety of the artists, as well as the safety of the paintings they will make are an important goal of this book.

HISTORY OF THE
'CALCITE SUN OIL /EMULSIONS' METHOD OF OIL PAINTING

2000: After 40 years of oil painting with Solvents, resins, varnishes, driers and alkali refined linseed oil I began this work which resulted in the creation of the Calcite Sun Oil / Emulsions method of oil painting [CSO] and other developments for Fine Art painting.

2000: My identification of the superior UNREFINED FLAX OIL used by the Old Masters. This very important development is named *'The Rebirth of the Old Masters' Superior Oil'*. This extraordinary oil is the foundation of the 'Calcite Sun Oil' method of Oil Painting and without it, the CSO method could not exist.

2000-2009: Sustained research with development of several new cleansing methods of SAFELY removing the mucilage from the UNREFINED FLAX OIL, with my identification of Psyllium Husk as an important ingredient for mucilage removal.

2000: Developed the ratio formula of ' Calcite Sun Oil', a modern grinding oil, based on published reports of scientific examination of microscopic sized paint samples by important scholars of Rembrandt's and Velazquez' paintings. This was followed by development of three additional mixture variations.

2000: Creation of two Emulsions used in conjunction with CSO; the 'Viscous emulsion' and the ' Non viscous emulsion'. Including my discovery of the crucial application method of the two emulsions and their uses in oil painting, which I believe to be part of the lost Van Eyck secret medium/method. The two emulsions used with CSO allow the artist of today to achieve the paint quality and permanence of the Old Masters with complete Control, Safety and Permanence.

2004: Published the first edition of my book containing the CSO/EMULSIONS method of oil painting. The first book ever to be published with ratio mixtures of calcium carbonate powder and flax/linseed oil, as an oil painting binder.

2004: Application for a provisional patent with the US Patent Office for CSO, with approval in 2006.

2005: Publication of the CALCITE SUN OIL website.

2008: Published the revised edition of my 2004 book, sold globally through online bookstores.

2009: Developed the 'CSO-FIXATIVE' method of fixing a charcoal drawing without aerosol sprays

2009: Developed the ' CSO-AGUADO' medium, the first expansion of the original CSO/EMULSIONS method of oil painting, allowing artists to work on large sized paintings with speed and efficiency. Scientific evidence indicates Rubens used a similar mixture.

2009: Developed the 'CSO-EGG TEMPERA' medium. The first expansion in over 600 years, of Cennino Cennini's 15th century Egg Tempera method. This new fast drying medium allows impasto applications, designed for under painting of oil paints as well as for Egg Tempera purists.

2010: Developed "CSO-EGG GESSO". A cold gesso of archival ancient artists materials of egg glair, vinegar and chalk. This broke the 600 year old tradition of using the egg yolk in Egg Tempera painting.

2010: Published the book: 'CSO-EGG TEMPERA', and the two DVD's titled: 'OIL PAINTING WITH CALCITE SUN OIL', and, 'CSO-EGG TEMPERA PAINTING'.

2010: Developed 'CSO-CASEIN TEMPERA', a NEW formula of the ancient and simple Casein medium.

2010: Posted my research on RUBENS' THIXOTROPIC METHOD and his use of CHALK, EMULSIONS, and PINE TREE TAR RESIN. **Warning:** The Rubens research study uses hazardous materials and is not for children or artists wishing to eliminate all hazardous materials.

2010: Development of a SAFE NEW thixotropic OIL OUT medium, named 'ESPESO' resulting from the Rubens study.

2011: Creation of a new oil paint called, 'MILK OIL PAINT' designed for beginning artists and school Art classes with new mixtures and new application procedures. See the DVD: 'OIL PAINTING WITH MILK: Safety for New Painters and School Art Classes', Also creation of the new DVD: 'THE NEW MILK OIL PAINT AND THE VAN EYCK SECRET MEDIUM' designed for advanced and professional painters.

2012- Publication of the book " SOLVENT FREE OIL PAINTING". This is a collection of all my studies to date in one volume.

December 2012: The publication of this new book which is a REVISED EDITION of the previous book. Books are important in that they are the repository of information, but limited in their ability to instruct. The best method of learning oil painting is having a live teacher, but if a teacher is not available a DVD is a good substitute. I recommend artists view my DVDS before reading the book.

BIBLIOGRAPHY

1. Bomford, David . et al. Art In The Making: Rembrandt, National Gallery, 1988, London, England.   ISBN 0-947645-49-7

2. Brandt, William T.. A practical Treatise on Animal and Vegetable Fats and Oils: Comprising both fixed and volatile oils… (1888) ASIN B000884334 (1896) ASIN B000862QZS, H.C. Baird, Philadelphia.

3. Brown, Jonathan and Garrido - Perez, Carmen. Velazquez: The Technique of Genius , Yale University Press, 1998, New Haven and London.

4. Church, Arthur Herbert. The chemistry of paints and painting, Google books, reprint of original Seely and Co. Limited 1890, Essex Street, Strand, Great Britain

5. Dorner, Max. The Materials of the Artist, And their use in painting, with notes on the techniques of the Old Masters, Harcourt Brace Jovanovich, 1962, USA.

6. Fels, Donald C. Lost Secrets of Flemish Painting : Including the First Complete English Translation of the De Mayerne Manuscript, B.M. Sloane 2052', Alchemist Inc., 2001, Hillsville, VA, USA.

7. Garrido - Perez, Carmen. Velasquez : Tecnica y Evolucion , Museo Del Prado, 1992 , Madrid, Espana.

8. Hermans, Erma, ed.. Looking Through Paintings: The Study of Painting Techniques and Materials in Support of Art Historical Research , Archetype Publications, 1998, Belgium,.

9. Laurie, A.P.. The Painter's Methods and Materials, Dover Publications, 1967, New York, N.Y. USA.

10. Massey, Robert. Formulas for Painters, Watson Guptill, 1967 -79, New York, USA.

11. Nicholas, Knut. The Restoration of Paintings. Konemann, 1999, Cologne, Germany

12. Rossol, Monona. The Artist's Complete Health and Safety Guide, Allworth Press, 2001, N.Y, USA

13. Taubes, Frederic. The Mastery of Oil Painting , The Studio Publications, Inc. , 1953, New York and London.

14. Taubes, Frederic. Studio Secrets, Watson Guptill Publications, Inc., 4th Ed. 1946, New York, USA.

15. Thompson, Daniel V.. The Materials and Techniques of Medieval Painting, Dover Publications, Inc., 1956, New York, USA.

16. Van De Wetering, Ernst. Rembrandt, The Painter at Work , Amsterdam University Press, 1997 , The Netherlands.

17. Wehlte, Kurt, The Materials and Techniques of Painting, Kremer Pigments, Inc., 1967-75, New York, USA.

DISCLAIMER

This disclaimer cites that large quantities of calcium carbonate mixed with Oil paint has been firmly established - by the scientific studies made at the Prado Museum, in Madrid, Spain - to have been added to the paintings of 17th century master, Diego Velazquez. The full account of the studies can be found in the book published by the Prado, Museum in 1992, authored by Ms. Carmen Garrido-Perez and titled, Velazquez: Tecnica Y Evolucion. Velazquez' paintings are claimed by experts to be in excellent condition, except for those that have been mistreated or mishandled through the course of the last 340-380 years of their existence. Studies into Rembrandt's paint has also been proven to contain calcium carbonate, and this fact has been published by Professor Dr. Ernst Van De Wetering, a leading expert on the work of Rembrandt, and in the publication by London's National Gallery (see the bibliography).

Neither the author nor his agents accept any responsibility for any paintings made by others using the mixtures and/or materials, or application methods that do not meet the expectations of permanence, nor of an inability to achieve the results or handling qualities, as expressed in this book. As clearly stated in the book , the craft of painting requires a certain amount of eye-hand coordination, and a highly developed manual skill to manipulate painting tools in order to achieve the results described in this book, as well as studious attention to ratio mixtures of ingredients and correct procedures of application.

I consider the study of the use of Calcium Carbonate in the use of oil painting as an exciting study that needs additional investigation and experimentation. There are many unanswered questions, but they will be solved over time. The paintings of Rembrandt and Velazquez give us solid reason to trust in their use of Calcium Carbonate in their oil paint. My methods and use of materials, detailed in this book , are an attempt to recreate their results. Unconvinced persons should refrain from using the information in this book, and the materials and mixtures herein presented, or use them at their own risk. My methods and use of basic materials expressed in this book are not intended to convince anyone, nor to represent that they are the best way, nor the only way, one can use or mix the basic materials of oil painting.

IMPORTANT NOTICE ON SAFETY: My claim of SAFETY and PERMANENCE is limited to the "Calcite Sun Oil" ingredients and the Emulsions described in this book. I repeat that use of any fine powders requires use of an adequate dust mask to prevent inhalation. I assume no responsibility for the choices of the dry pigments or of the tube oil paints made by artists. Many pigments and oil paints are toxic, carcinogenic and hazardous to human health. I refer readers to Monona Rossol's book in the bibliography.

END OF BOOK
December 19, 2013

www.ingramcontent.com/pod-product-compliance
Lightning Source LLC
Chambersburg PA
CBHW080243180526
45167CB00006B/2390